# How Student Journalists
# Report Campus Unrest

# How Student Journalists Report Campus Unrest

Kaylene Armstrong

LEXINGTON BOOKS
Lanham • Boulder • New York • London

Published by Lexington Books
An imprint of The Rowman & Littlefield Publishing Group, Inc.
4501 Forbes Boulevard, Suite 200, Lanham, Maryland 20706
www.rowman.com

Unit A, Whitacre Mews, 26-34 Stannary Street, London SE11 4AB

British Library Cataloguing in Publication Information Available

**Library of Congress Cataloging-in-Publication Data Available**

Library of Congress Control Number: 2017957928

ISBN 978-1-4985-4115-2 (cloth : alk. paper)
ISBN 978-1-4985-4116-9 (electronic)

∞™ The paper used in this publication meets the minimum requirements of American National Standard for Information Sciences Permanence of Paper for Printed Library Materials, ANSI/NISO Z39.48-1992.

Printed in the United States of America

To the other Dr. Armstrong. What pun we have as a paradox.

# Contents

# Introduction

When newspaper historian Frederic Hudson published his history of journalism in 1873, he briefly noted the existence of college newspapers, devoting just three pages of his 789-page tome to a discussion of student media. He included these few paragraphs in his chapter on the transient press. Of the student press, he noted that "some of the contributions are marked with ability and a show of genius," yet "it is not expected, from the nature of things, that they are to be permanent institutions."[1]

Hudson was equally disdainful of college journalism education, noting that the University of Virginia and Yale were both planning courses in journalism. "The true college for newspaper students," he insisted, would be found at professional newspapers where James Gordon Bennett's *New York Herald* or Horace Greeley's *New York Tribune* "would turn out more real genuine journalists in one year than the Harvards, the Yales, and the Dartmouths could produce in a generation."[2] Still, he conceded, college newspapers "are a means of educating young men to the profession of journalism" and may one day produce "distinguished and influential journalists."[3]

Hudson would likely be surprised at how some of his predictions about student newspapers turned out. As he correctly surmised, many influential journalists have since began their careers on their college newspapers; for instance, television news anchor Walter Cronkite wrote for *The Daily Texan* during his time at the University of Texas at Austin.[4] Among others, Tom Wolfe, one of the "new journalism" writers who combined writing nonfiction stories with fiction techniques, who was the sports editor at Washington and Lee University[5]; Bob Novak, who was a newspaper columnist, a commentator on CNN, and most notably known for his work on the Valerie Plame CIA scandal, wrote sports for *The Daily Illini* at University of Illinois[6]; William F. Buckley Jr., founder of *National Review* and known for his opinion writing, was chairman of the *Yale Daily News* where he wrote editorials[7]; and broadcast journalist Dan Rather was the editor-in-chief of *The Houstonian* at Sam Houston State University.[8]

But Hudson's prediction that the student press would not survive was one that did not come true. Indeed, a student newspaper, whether published on paper or online, continues to survive at almost every college and university in the United States.

The student press, in general, continues as perhaps the oldest genre of newspaper still in existence. Hudson points to the *Gazette* as the oldest student newspaper where Dartmouth student Daniel Webster (Class of 1801) published work (more about that in chapter 1). Indeed, the college student newspaper has been a more enduring fixture on the landscape of newspapers than many professional newspapers. The professional newspapers that define the various historical eras that Hudson identified—such as party press and penny press—have come and gone. The financial demands of publishing a newspaper have been so daunting throughout much of the history of U.S. newspapers that it is no wonder many large, professional general-interest newspapers have been forced out of existence. Today, even some of the oldest and supposedly most stable of newspapers, such as *The New York Times* (founded in 1851) and *Boston Globe* (1872), at times teeter on the brink of insolvency with multi-million-dollar budgets and huge deficits. In the current economic climate, professional papers of all sizes continue to close or cut back. Yet the college student newspaper, despite changes in format and publication schedules, has continued to appear, oftentimes published on a shoestring with a handful of volunteer reporters and editors.

Being a student journalist has always come with challenges. This book will focus on some of the challenges these students have surmounted to produce the best newspaper possible. Student reporters and editors—who told the stories of others when they worked on their student newspapers—now tell their own stories, some for the first time. The backdrop for this examination of college newspapers is student unrest. During such times, the student press is put to the test in many ways that its professional counterparts are not. These student journalists must juggle their newspaper responsibilities with school, family, and other obligations. They often face intense pressure from the administration, alumni, and community to write stories a certain way or entirely ignore some stories. Each set of student editors and reporters must define the role they hope to fill and then work hard to actually accomplish it. That may require deciding if advocacy or objectivity is the ultimate goal.

After a brief look at how student newspapers began, this book examines the primary challenges student journalists have faced. It does not intend to recount the story of every student newspaper that ever covered campus unrest nor every challenge. Indeed, such a formidable task would be impossible.

Instead, it focuses on how the students reported on particular protests that are representative of the issues that were behind most of the unrest through the 1960s—racial issues, free speech rights, the Vietnam War—and then the racial issues that continued in 2015 and beyond.

The first protest considered here occurred in 1962. The editors of *The Mississippian* at Ole Miss found themselves in a situation many other student newspapers at the time did not: they were given free rein to report on integration in any way they chose. They describe what they experienced the night a deadly riot broke out on campus as well as the difficulties they faced in the months that followed.

Stressful experiences such as campus unrest also require student journalists to figure out the role their newspapers will fill and then try to meet the challenge of filling that role. *The Daily Californian* staffers did that in 1964 when they tackled reporting on the Berkeley Free Speech Movement, trying—as their editor said—to fill the role of the campus conscience. In 1968, student journalists at Howard and Columbia found themselves writing about student protesters taking over the administration buildings on their respective campuses. Yet each newspaper staff viewed its responsibility differently. The Howard *Hilltop* staffers, with some who participated in the protest, saw their role as that of advocates for change whereas the *Spectator* editors at Columbia, who turned down an offer to help lead the protest, focused on reporting as objectively as possible.

In May 1970, student newspapers faced a harsher challenge than ever before. National Guardsmen had fired on protesters at Kent State in Ohio and four students were dead. The reaction was felt nationwide. It was as if a volcano that had been building pressure for years had finally erupted, spewing out violence that touched hundreds of universities across the country.[9] More than 500 universities and colleges closed their doors in the wake of the shootings, some for a day or two, others for the remainder of the term.[10] About 100 campuses reported damage from the violence.[11] "Protests were so common," maintains one author, "that wire services began reporting campuses that did not have demonstrations."[12] Reporting what was happening in Kent became difficult for many student newspapers because they were grappling with their own protests that followed in its wake. The staff of the *Kent Stater* faced a sad reality; they would never get to report on what happened because the campus was immediately closed for the remainder of the term and publication of the newspaper ceased. The *Kent Stater* editor as well as editors from other college newspapers around the country tell their stories of what is perhaps the most momentous time in the history of higher education in the 1900s.

Have the challenges changed? In many ways, student newspapers continue to face the same challenges as they did prior to 1970. Fast forward to 2015 and a protest at the University of Missouri in Columbia. Here *The Maneater* staff members struggled with similar challenges student journalists faced about fifty years earlier in trying to get the news out accurately while also trying to be successful college students.

The story of how these student newspapers covered those protests will be told through the people who lived it, who felt the bullets whizzing by, who opted to participate in the protests or chose only to cover it, who spent long hours late into the night to get the latest news out, who now realize they were privileged to have played a part in creating "the first rough draft of history."[13]

## NOTES

1. Frederic Hudson, *Journalism in the United States, from 1690 to 1872* (New York: Harper & Brothers, 1873), 711–712.

2. Ibid., 713.

3. Ibid., 712.

4. Don Carlton, "Cronkite's Texas: A Q&A with Walter Cronkite," Dec. 4 2009, accessed May 2016, https://news.utexas.edu/2009/12/04/cronkites-texas-a-qa-with-walter-cronkite.

5. "About Tom Wolfe," accessed April 26, 2013 http://www.tomwolfe.com/bio.htm.

6. "Illini Media Hall of Fame–2007," accessed April 26, 2013, http://alumni.illinimedia.com/famers/view/35.

7. Thomas Kaplan and Paul Needham, "William F. Buckley '50 died at 82," *Yale Daily News,* February 28, 2008, accessed April 26, 2013, http://yaledailynews.com/blog/2008/02/28/william-f-buckley-50-dies-at-82/.

8. Amanda Morgan, "Dan Rather Returning to Sam Houston State University: Former CBS Anchor to Join Gibson in President's Speaker Series," *The Houstonian* (Huntsville, TX), September 27, 2011, accessed April 26, 2013, http://www.houstonianonline.com/news/dan-rather
-returning-to-sam-houston-state-university-1.2638829#.UXrrD6LCaSo.

9. R. E. Peterson and J. A. Bilorusky,*May 1970: The Campus Aftermath of Cambodia and Kent State* (Berkley, CA: The Carnegie Commission on Higher Education, 1971), p. 18.

10. Ibid., 17.

11. Ibid., 18.

12. Terry H. Anderson, *The Movement and the Sixties* (New York: Oxford University Press, 1995), 350.

13. Andrew Romano, "The First Rough Draft of History," *The Daily Beast,* accessed May 22, 2013, at http://www.thedailybeast.com/newsweek/2012/12/23/an-oral-history-of-newsweek-magazine.html.

*Chapter One*

# In the Beginning

## DEVELOPMENT OF STUDENT NEWSPAPERS IN THE 1800S

When the *Literary Focus* began its one-year run in June 1827, it apologized to readers that it was a month late in coming. "Circumstances beyond our control have, however, defeated until now, the accomplishment of our design,"[1] the editors explained. Though they did not detail those circumstances, it is likely that the students at Miami University in Oxford, Ohio, had taken on a project that required more work and expertise than they had anticipated. Just months before, the university's two rival literary societies, the Erodelphian and the Union, had pooled their resources and bought a printing press in Cincinnati. They carted it over thirty-five miles of primitive roads in southern Ohio, set it up in the college building and began what would later be heralded as the oldest university newspaper in the United States.

Today's *Miami Student*, which began publication under that title in 1867,[2] traces a broken path back to the *Focus* when it makes the "oldest university newspaper" claim on its nameplate.[3] It is one of more than 100 college publications that can also trace their roots into the 1800s, depending on how they choose to draw the lineage lines. Most of those begin somewhere in the 1870s or 1880s, a handful earlier than that. By 1890, they were all part of the throng of more than 12,000 publications being printed in the United States,[4] a figure that did not include the unnumbered newspapers and magazines that came and went in those same years without being counted.

Why did students begin these enterprises? What did these ventures entail? When did they begin and what did they look like? What roles did the student newspapers play? This chapter explores answers to these questions in two ways. First, an examination of more than two dozen student publications begun in the 1800s at various universities around the country considers the

1

first three questions. Then, through a study of one college newspaper, this chapter concludes with a discussion about the developing role of the student newspaper in the first sixty years of the twentieth century, leading up to the tumultuous 1960s that are the focus of the majority of this book.

Research shows student publications began for several reasons: to provide information about the world, to fill needs of the students, to represent the college or university to the rest of the country, and to act as an agent for change. Research also gives an insight into the first student newspapers, what they looked like and what they wrote about, all to further understand how those newspapers tried to accomplish what they set out to do. Newspapers selected for this study were those available digitally, either from the college or university library of the campus where it originated or from other resources accessible online. The *Kansas State Collegian*, with roots in the 1800s, provides the basis for examining the role of the student newspaper in the twentieth century. Kansas State was the first college or university in the country to have a degree in printing when it began to offer industrial journalism classes in 1911.[5] The student newspaper was a natural laboratory for students to apply those skills in a practical way as they filled the various roles a student newspaper plays on campuses across the country: bulletin board, cheerleader, campus historian, public relations agent, campus gossip, advocate, entertainer, critic, and, of course, a source for news and analysis—at campus, community, state, and even international levels.

## WHY START A STUDENT NEWSPAPER?

In many ways, student newspapers blended with all the other publications of the nineteenth century because they also faced a similar history of a struggle for survival, many lasting only a year or two. By the 1870s, however, the student publications were viewed as something different. Rowell's *American Newspaper Directory*, which listed every serial publication (newspapers, magazines, and journals) that the directory editors could find information about, also included the category of college publications in 1879. The book, mostly designed for potential advertisers, listed information about individual publications by state and city, and then in the back collected names of the publications by genre. Here, educational publications were listed together. While some of those were journals for educators or about education in general, most were student-produced. In 1879, that included fifty-five newspapers, magazines, and literary journals that were listed as being published by students at a college or university. In the 1882 edition, the number more than doubled.

Why were students drawn to publish newspapers? It was certainly not a cheap venture or even likely to be a very profitable one. Besides, there were other local publications in almost every town where students could have submitted their work. What did they hope to gain by starting their own? In the early 1800s, college students were not aspiring to be journalists. They were not seeking opportunities to pad a portfolio. College-educated individuals were not even welcome in journalism until the 1860s.[6] And, until the late 1880s and 1890s, newspaper reporting was not even a steady job, certainly not a vocation to work toward.[7]

One might say that the reasons for students starting a newspaper are as varied as the publications themselves. Yet, the age-old desire to see one's work in print, to have it read by others, to play the role of ambassador for one's college, or to be the voice for change were the aphrodisiacs that lured them in and kept them trying over and over again to make a campus newspaper successful. By the second half of the 1800s, the students were no longer trying to convince the world that their voice had a valued place in bringing the world to campus and taking their campus to the world. Instead, they were promising to be a better quality voice than their predecessors, a mantra that still rings in the ears of student journalists today.

Students were also tenacious about their efforts to keep the student newspapers alive. As mentioned in the introduction, historian Fredric Hudson predicted their demise.[8] He likely would be surprised to see that almost every college and university campus in the United States still has a student newspaper even if it is just in a digital format.

The editors of the *Literary Focus* offered no explanation about why they had begun this enterprise of printing a student publication in 1827, perhaps assuming that the college community already knew their aims. "We hope it will meet the expectations of our friends, and give that satisfaction, for which it has been our endeavour [sic] to qualify it," they proffered, not on the front page but on page 13. The issue was just sixteen pages, each page no larger than half a sheet of modern copy paper. After thanking their generous audience, the editors promised to do all they could to deserve the public's respect and then ended this short editorial commentary with a quote from the last number of *The Rambler*, a publication written and edited by English essayist Dr. Samuel Johnson: "We envy not the honours [sic] which wit and learning bestow, in any other cause, if we can be numbered amongst those, who gave ardour [sic] to virtue, and confidence to truth."[9]

Editors of the successor to the *Focus, The Literary Register,* pointed to the value of a weekly community newspaper as the primary reason to start a second publication after the *Focus* failed. In a rapidly changing world, they wrote, "It is of vast importance, then, that we and our children should be regularly informed of all the steps by which this great change is to be produced." Newspapers can bring literary and scientific advances to the masses, not just the educated few, and can bring the entire world into one's home.

"The loss to a growing family which has not this means of weekly information must also be immense,"[10] they intoned.

That desire to bring the world to campus was apparent throughout many of the student newspapers of the 1800s. When they could get their hands on it, students added national and foreign items to the mix of news they provided. On February 4, 1878, *Yale News* included reports about world events with "Special Cable Dispatches" that had arrived that day. Short items from London, Glasgow, Liverpool, Paris, Berlin, Rome, and Turkey appeared on the front page.[11]

The *Harvard Register* editors were unabashed in their desires: they wanted to see their work in print before a large audience. "Every one knows the singular sensations that are excited by seeing his own lucubrations in print for the first time, even in the corner of a newspaper," the editors wrote in the opening issue in 1827. "What, then, must be *our* feelings, on beholding our meditations ushered into the world in this portentous and alarming form, staring us in our very face from the interior of a decently sized book, with fine paper, fair, broad pages, and printed covers, and all to be read by more than—*a hundred!*"[12]

Some newspapers saw themselves as ambassadors for the college or university. The *University Chronicle* and *The Oracle*, competing publications at the University of Michigan, appeared for the first time on the same day, March 2, 1867. In their opening editions, they each pointed to eastern colleges as they made their cases for students supporting the student newspapers on their Ann Arbor campus. The *Chronicle* asked for the student body's help in producing a paper that would prove to the Eastern colleges that looked down on those in the West that the University of Michigan was a quality institution. "One of the best methods of asserting our claims is through the medium of a paper issued and sustained by the students," the editors wrote.[13] *The Oracle* pointed to several Eastern college publications when it explained what benefits a student newspaper brings to a campus: "They [student newspapers] tend by an interchange of views, and a free expression of sentiment, to promote good fellowship among the members. They excite an honorable emulation in literary pursuits; and give much information on subjects of interest connected with the institutions where they are published. They lift the curtain, and reveal a glimpse of the real existence of the student."[14]

Some college and university students pushed their way into the publishing world to fill what they saw as unmet needs on campus. Students at Vassar College had long asked permission to have a student publication when faculty finally approved a quarterly literary magazine in 1872. "We have felt injured and misused because this consent has been so long withheld," the editors of *The Vassar Miscellany* wrote in the first edition. "We have had, heretofore, no means of expressing our opinions, and much that we have often considered unfairness in our instructors has been, probably, ignorance of our real wants."[15]

Even a college with other student publications could have needs that yet another student-produced newspaper on campus could try to address. In 1873, *The Magenta*, forerunner to *The Crimson* at Harvard University, said it was not trying to compete with *The Advocate*, a literary publication that began in 1866 and continues today; it was just trying to offer more. "We shall be content with the humbler task of satisfying the curiosity of our readers about what is going on in Cambridge and at other colleges, and of giving them an opportunity to express their ideas upon practical questions. It ought to be added perhaps, that, while we make no pretension to wit, we hope not to be dull. There will be several poems and lighter sketches to prevent any impression of heaviness."[16] When the university changed its school color from magenta to crimson in 1875, the newspaper changed its name as well but offered no hints that the mission or purpose of the paper would be altered by the name change.

Student newspapers also played a role that administrators did not necessarily like—activist for change. Editors of *The Lehigh Burr* saw that as one of their key responsibilities. Lehigh University in Bethlehem, Pennsylvania, had long been without a publication beyond a once yearly statistical accounting of the year, the editors wrote in the first issue of the monthly *Burr* in 1881. They saw their possible mission as four fold: "information, amusement, reform and editorial bread and butter." However, because the "collegiate public" was above needing information from a student newspaper and "the Editors, of course, live on air," the newspaper would concentrate on just reform and amusement. In regard to reform, they wrote, "we simply present matters as they appear to students' eyes, in the most forcible language at our command, and without any claim to infallibility." The idea of working for reform is embodied in the name they chose for the publication. A burr, which is a seed that can grow, in some cases, into a mighty tree, is a prickly thing that requires careful handling. "In short, it may not be sat upon with impunity," the editors warned anyone who might have had designs on squashing their efforts.[17]

Some student newspapers came into being because, quite simply, it was time. *The Tech* reported in its first issue on November 16, 1881, that only one other publication, the *Spectrum*, preceded it at Massachusetts Institute of Technology. It was time for another paper, *The Tech* editors said, and the plans were big: "It will be its aim to promote the interest of the students of the Institute and maintain a friendly spirit among them, breaking down the ancient barriers of class and department. . . . It will open an avenue for the expression of public opinion, and will aim, in every possible way, to help all in the development of their young manhood and young womanhood." It also saw itself as one of the ways the rest of the country would become acquainted with what MIT had to offer. [18]

Almost every new volume of any student newspaper brought a panel of new editors with new ideas, a different focus, and a new naivety. Many expressed their concerns that they were really untrained journalists and begged the indulgence of their readers as they learned their way around the art of putting out a newspaper. When *The Lafayette College Journal* became just *The Lafayette* as it began its tenth year, the editors said change in the monthly's name came with many improvements besides a new cover and font; it also brought new responsibilities for editors who were "anxious to make the contents of the paper correspond with its improved typographical appearance, and yet fearing the inability to do this. Our effort shall be to edit a monthly that shall represent the interests of the students and alumni alike, and be altogether worthy of their support and perusal." [19]

## NEWSPAPER DESIGN IN THE 1800S

To really understand student newspapers of the 1800s, one must also understand that the newspaper had not yet evolved into the kind of publications that are considered newspapers today. From the present view of a newspaper, the college papers of the nineteenth century would not be considered newspapers at all. Whereas most newspapers today come as fairly standard broadsheets (as small as 11 x 22 inches) or tabloids (about 11 x 17 inches), newspapers in the nineteenth century came in a variety of sizes, from the octavo (about 6 x 9 inches) monthly *Berkeleyan* at the University of California in Berkeley to the massive 26- x 40-inch monthly *University Mirror* at the University of Lewisburgh in Pennsylvania (now Bucknell University), and everything in between. About three-fourths of the college newspapers were roughly the size of a modern sheet of copy paper. [20]

Inconsistency was a hallmark of almost all the student newspapers throughout the 1800s. Individual publications varied their publishing schedules and even their numbering systems. A perusal of *Yale News* editions shows students began the publication with volume 1 as one would expect, but when new editors took over a year and a half later, they started again with volume 1, reasoning that the new version of the paper would be so different from the old paper that starting at volume 1 again was warranted. [21] *The Miami Student* began its second volume with the new school year in 1867 with the promise to appear every fourth Tuesday of the month. In February, the schedule changed to the second Wednesday. The April issue came out on the fourth Tuesday and the May issue on the fifth Saturday. The next school year, the students started publishing on the third Wednesday of each month. Other newspapers began their volumes in mid-year. For example, *The Argo* at Williams College in Massachusetts changed volumes in April, took a break for part of the summer, and resumed the same volume in the fall.

The page numbering system also varied between publications. Many used the style of consecutive page numbering similar to that of some journals today. *The Columbia Spectator* is a good example of this. The first issue of volume eight that was published on February 25, 1881, began with page number one and ended with page 16. The second issue began with page 17 and ended with page 32, and so on for each succeeding issue. The ninth and final issue of the volume wound up with page 136 on June 21, 1881. Other publications like the *University Chronicle, The Miami Student*, and the *Yale News* started each issue with page number one.

## THE COST OF DOING BUSINESS

Unlike many student newspapers today that are available free on campuses because of some campus support, colleges and universities in the 1800s did not offer financial support to student publications, not even in the form of fees collected from the student body. Every student newspaper had to support itself through subscriptions that averaged about $1 a year throughout the century. One of the cheapest publications, The *Institute Journal* at the Henderson Masonic Male and Female Institute in Tennessee charged a quarter in 1882. Perhaps the most expensive, the *Hamilton Literary Monthly* at Hamilton College in Clinton, New York, sold for $3 a year in 1879.[22] Individual copies of most publications were often about 10–15 cents.[23] The *Yale News* debuted as a daily in 1878 and charged 5 cents a copy. A week later it dropped to 3 cents and then began its third week at 2 cents. The editors said they had found the productions costs were less than expected, hence the lower rate.[24] *The Daily Cardinal* at the University of Wisconsin sold for 3 cents a copy when it rolled off the presses in 1892.[25]

For many college student publications, money was a constant problem, and few student newspapers lasted beyond a few years at most colleges. The *Literary Focus* and *The Literary Register* each survived one year at Miami University. After the first full year of operation, *The Harvard Daily Herald* found itself $700 in debt, which helped convince the editors that a merger with the more established weekly *Crimson* was a better option than quitting, so that is what they did in 1883.[26]

## FILLING THE PAGES—CONTENT

The contents of the nineteenth-century student newspaper would hardly be considered newspaper-like by today's standards, either. Most of the monthly, semi-monthly and weekly newspapers contained a lot of literary pieces (essays, poems, short fiction) and only a few of the more newsy items. The literary works almost always were presented first. Essays on various contemporary issues were likely considered news because of the timeliness of the topics. Short (often one sentence long) news items appeared at the back of the paper. That news could be anything from announcements of campus events to plain, old-fashioned gossip or jokes and humorous stories.

The *New York Tribune* rankled the *Yale News* when it characterized the new campus paper as being "filled with the college news of a sensational character." Reporting on the *Tribune's* comment, the *News* threatened to sue the *Tribune* if any such libel occurred again.[27] The *Tribune*, however, was accurate in its assessment; much of the campus daily's fare was nothing more than campus gossip. For instance, in that same issue, the "Yale Log" column made fun of the teaching style of an unnamed professor (students probably knew who it was, though, because of the nickname they privately used for him): "'The little tooter' is skipping the objectionable passages in Horace. A sure way to make the fellows read'em, little one!" And then the paper tattled on a tired student: "Tarbawse fell asleep in chapel yesterday; was awakened at 5 in the afternoon by the Key's Sexton. This is the second offense."[28]

*Yale News* was not the only paper to pass off gossip for news. *The Lehigh Burr* in 1881 presented a mixture of short campus announcements, advice and gossip in a column titled "Kernels." *The Oracle* at the University of Michigan ran more than three columns of items titled "Gossip" in its first issue in 1867. Tongue in cheek, the editors suggested that because funding for a memorial chapel had failed, the campus should just dispense with chapel exercises entirely. They speculated about the upcoming junior exhibition, noted the recent selection of azure blue and maize as the school colors (still used today) and encouraged the practice of each class selecting a hat style to distinguish the class. The class of 1868 was ridiculed for wearing an "Oxford hat" or "mortar board," which is similar to those worn at high school and college graduations all over the country today.[29] Several papers, such as *The Argo* at Williams College in Williamstown, Massachusetts, included a "Personals" column that updated the college on the whereabouts of former students and the accomplishments of current students.

The kinds of articles the newspapers published changed as the century progressed. *The Literary Register*, edited by professors of Miami University (including William Holmes McGuffey of *McGuffey Reader* fame) from June through August 1828, began to include more than the literary pieces that the *Focus* used exclusively. In the first issue, the *Register* editors included extracts from letters, one from Pennsylvania about witnessing the aurora borealis. They apologized for having little news because they had not received much from other newspapers.[30] Like all the newspapers of the time, they extracted items from other newspapers from around the country and across the globe, if they could get copies of them.

Exchanging news among student newspapers was a common practice throughout the 1800s, just as it had been among all kinds of U.S. newspapers since the first newspaper published in 1690. Indeed, modern-day wire services rely heavily on the contributions of member newspapers for news stories they send throughout the world to subscribers. Though the student newspaper in the 1800s might use some items from the larger professional papers, like the *New York Mirror*, they usually ran reports of events at other college campuses that were gleaned from other college newspapers. In many ways, the exchanges acted like a news syndicate such as the Associated Press would become for professional papers later in the 1800s. The first issue of the *Purdue Exponent* in December 1889 included a playful invitation for other student newspapers to join in trading news: "To her brother exchange editors she would say in the words of the Yankee pedler [sic], 'Let's swap.'"[31] Student editors were grateful for the cooperation of other colleges in making the exchanges successful. *Tech* editors thanked *The Tuftonian* at Tufts University for being "the first college paper to acknowledge the existence of *The Tech*" at MIT in 1881.[32]

Although the news exchanges gave fledgling student newspapers more copy to fill the pages, it also presented a picture of what college life was like elsewhere. An account of the Yale College graduation gave Miami University students a glimpse of how another institution handled such ceremonies.[33] Sometimes the exchanges brought news of advantages other institutions offered students. In 1867, the *University Chronicle* at the University of Michigan reported a new gymnasium was opening at Dartmouth College and wondered when the students in Ann Arbor would have one as well.[34] In 1881, *The Columbia Spectator* at Columbia University often ran an entire page of short items from other university and college newspapers. Many editors were not afraid to criticize other student newspapers. The *Purdue Exponent*, often positive about the reporting at other publications, was critical of a poem published in another publication, noting that without such poor quality writing, "the literary character of that paper would not now be undergoing such a severe strain."[35]

The student newspapers also wrote about various issues of the day, some campus-related and some that people throughout the country were discussing. *The Columbia Spectator* chimed in about the minimum grades students should receive in order to move to the next class standing. The result was the formation of a campus committee to formulate a plan throughout the university for a uniform percent that students must earn each year in order to pass.[36] In Michigan, the report on a lecture by a renowned suffragist, referred to only as Miss Dickinson (probably Anna Elizabeth Dickinson, a popular lyceum speaker at the time), sparked a discussion about how other newspapers had covered Miss Dickinson's speeches and had ridiculed her personally. Criticize the message, not the messenger, the editors wrote in their call for more chivalrous behavior.[37]

Any discussion of student newspapers must include humor. Though some universities had humor magazines (like *The Harvard Lampoon,* started in 1876), many of the student publications included humorous columns or small items. The *Yale News* "Risibilia" column sometimes included jokes: "It is said a piece of lemon bound upon a corn will cure it in a few days. That's lemon aid, n'est ce pas [is it not]?" The "Yale Log" column also included tidbits around campus that were also often funny—and sometimes a little bawdy: "'Vulva' of the medical school has sent in a petition to the legislature to have his name changed."[38]

Sports stories began to show up in student publications in the 1860s and were becoming more prominent in the early 1880s with a lot of interest in the sporting activities at other colleges. A short note in 1867 reported that the baseball and cricket clubs at the University of Michigan were adopting uniforms "when playing match games and on similar occasions of importance."[39] The sophomores at Miami University in Ohio challenged the juniors to "a match game of base ball" to relieve the monotony of college life in June 1867. (The sophomores won.)[40] *Yale News* noted in January 1878 that Princeton had ended its rugby season and was preparing for baseball with only two returning players.[41] *The Tech* at MIT included a "Sporting Notes" column in the second issue of its paper in 1881. The report included results of the Athletic Club's games of fencing, "hitch and kick" (similar to the modern broad jump), "running high" (high jump), a half-mile run, and a potato race (collecting potatoes placed several yards apart and running with the full basket across the finish line).[42] *The Argo* at Williams College in Williamstown, Massachusetts, spent almost an entire column reporting on the schedule of the upcoming class-championship series of baseball with members of the various classes on campus competing against other classes to claim the campus honor. It also included results of two baseball games.[43] A few weeks later, it reported the results of the 1882 Seventh Annual Intercollegiate Athletic Association track and field meet (with a bicycle race and tug-of-war included as events) where Harvard retained the championship cup, with Columbia second and Yale third.[44] *The Michigan Argonaut* at the University of Michigan noted in November 1882 that while rugby was defunct at Dartmouth, "the eleven of Harvard and Columbia" had squared off, and Harvard had scored two goals and four touch-downs to Columbia's ten safety touchdowns. "The defeat of the eleven at Harvard is what makes the *Dartmouth* so despondent."[45] A report on a rugby game between departments on campus filled almost a full column of the same issue.[46]

The student newspapers carried ads when they could get them, but they did not look like today's newspaper ads. Instead, they ran like classified ads do today, usually the same column width as the editorial copy. They filled pages at the back of the paper and used various sized fonts, often quite ornate, with occasional drawings added. Some, like the *Purdue Exponent* in 1889 and *The Tech* at MIT beginning in 1883, sported a cover, with at least one page of the ads before and after the pages of copy, a bookend style typical of many professional publications.[47] The *University Chronicle* at the University of Michigan ran almost three full pages of ads in its first issue in 1867. Published every two weeks, the paper also listed its ad rates on the front page of that first issue. The smallest ad, one square of ten lines for one month, cost 50 cents. An entire column cost $4 for one month and went up to $12 for four months. Five local businesses bought full-column space in the first issue.[48]

## WHICH IS OLDEST? THAT DEPENDS . . .

The question about which student newspaper is the oldest is a thorny one. As noted before, it can depend on how the individual student publication chooses to trace its lineage. At Miami University, *The Miami Student* places its beginning with the *Literary Focus* in 1827. However, the students at Miami University were not the first undergraduates to venture into the world of the printed word. The *Dartmouth* student newspaper at Dartmouth College in Hanover, New Hampshire, claims to be the oldest *student* newspaper. They make that claim based on the fact that Daniel Webster and other Dartmouth students wrote for the local community newspaper, the *Dartmouth Gazette,* beginning in 1799.[49] The *Gazette* was started by Moses Davis and continued to operate in the town for at least twenty years, covering local and college news.[50] As was the case for almost all newspapers of the day, the *Gazette* was a money-making enterprise. It happened to employ students and cater to the college community but was not sponsored by the college. Other newspapers came and went in Hanover before the students edited a publication called *The Magnet* beginning in 1835. A literary periodical with the name the *Dartmouth* began publishing in 1839. The student newspaper at the college continues under that name today and claims the original *Dartmouth Gazette* of 1799 as its beginning point.[51]

The *Literary Focus*, which was entirely published by students who owned the press, was also not the first publication on a college campus that featured student writing. *The Literary Register* at Harvard University beat the *Focus* by a few months when it began publishing in March 1827. It also lasted one year. The earliest student periodical at Harvard was a semi-monthly literary journal titled *Harvard Lyceum*, which appeared 1810–1811 and was produced by the senior class. Another literary publication, *Harvardiana*, lasted four years, 1834–1838.[52] Other Harvard publications included the literary *Harvard Advocate* founded in 1866, *The Harvard Echo,* a daily founded in

1878,[53] and *The Harvard Daily Herald,* begun in 1882. The *Harvard Crimson,* Harvard's current daily student newspaper, traces its beginning to *The Magenta,* published every two weeks beginning on January 24, 1873. The name changed to *The Crimson* on May 21, 1875, after Harvard changed its school color to crimson. It became a weekly publication in 1882, merged with the *Daily Herald* in 1883 and then began daily publication. It claims to be the oldest *continuously* published college daily, publishing even during the World Wars in the twentieth century.[54]

   *Yale Daily News* claims the title as the oldest college daily,[55] beginning daily production five years ahead of *The Crimson* on January 28, 1878. It was called *Yale News* and published daily, Monday through Saturday and then just Monday through Friday. During some periods, such as the World Wars, its publication scheduled was curtailed, thus validating Harvard's *continuous* claim. Like Harvard, *Yale News* was not the first student publication on campus. Among its predecessors were *Yale Courant* in 1865 and *Yale Record* in 1872.[56]

## THE ROLE OF THE STUDENT NEWSPAPER: *KANSAS STATE COLLEGIAN* THROUGH 1960

Even in the digital age, newspapers continue to play an important role in society.[57] Student newspapers also have filled important roles on college and university campuses though those roles are often defined differently each year or even each semester as a new cadre of editors and reporters takes over and hopes to make their mark. It is beneficial, then, to consider how the role of the student newspapers has changed since their beginning in the 1800s. Here, we will consider the *Kansas State Collegian* and its role through the first sixty years of the twentieth century.

   The *Collegian* is not as old as the Yale newspaper, but it did begin life in the 1800s—1896 to be exact—as *The Students' Herald.* It eventually became the *Kansas State Collegian,* a name it continues to bear today. It serves Kansas State University, located in Manhattan, Kansas, in the northeast part of the state. The university began in 1858 as Bluemont Central College with fifty-three students. Five years later, it became the first fully operating land-grant college in the country, and the name changed to Kansas State Agricultural College. By 1900, it had an enrollment of more than 1,300 students. In 1931, the name was changed to Kansas State College of Agricultural and Applied Science, and in 1959 the word "College" became "University."[58] Today it is generally known as K-State, boasting more than 23,000 students.[59]

   The student newspaper was not the first newspaper published on the campus. It was preceded by *The Industrialist* in 1875. Courses in printing had been offered at the campus beginning in 1873, so the publication of a newspaper two years later was a natural. The weekly *Industrialist* was produced by the faculty and staff of the college as the official campus newspaper. Students were allowed to submit items to the paper, and student editors were elected in 1891. After five years with this arrangement, students worked to get their own publication going, and *The Students' Herald* was born in 1896. *The Industrialist,* later named *The Kansas Industrialist,* lasted until 1955 when it was changed to *The Trumpet,* a bi-monthly magazine format and later a quarterly newspaper that published until 1964.[60]

As did other student newspapers mentioned earlier, *The Students' Herald* in its first issue explained its purpose, which was "to speak as the voice of the students on all occasions. Where there is need of improvement, we want to be found. Where there is work to be done, we want our hand to be at the wheel. Where the student's interests are involved, we will exert every effort to secure justice."

The editors listed three objectives: "First, the improvement of the students from every point of view; second, the advancement of the college literary societies; third, the advancement of the institution in every way possible. Aside from our particular objects we will advance public interest wherever possible." They also cautioned that a good newspaper is like a banquet full of variety, so readers should not "condemn the entire spread because pickles and onions are included."[61]

In January 1900, in its fifth year of publication, the editors acknowledged the work of the students who preceded them and noted that they were continuing with the founding goals: "furnishing an organ for the student thot [sic], of developing the literary genius of students and doing all in its power to advance the good and welfare of our Alma Mater." They then encouraged students to continue the practice of sharing their thoughts and passing along news tips.[62]

In April 1913, students abruptly changed the name of the paper to *The Kansas Aggie,* referencing the school's founding as an agriculture college. Despite the name change, they continued the numbering system and published the first issue as No. 49 of Volume 18. The new name would better represent the school, the editors wrote, without any explanation about why they did not wait until the new school year began in the fall. It is likely, however, that the leadership of the newspaper was at odds with each other. A story announced that the new name came with a new constitution that allowed all subscribers to vote for the key editor and business manager positions. The story also announced elections the next week to fill some of those positions on the paper.[63] A year later, also mid-year, students changed the name again, this time to a moniker that has stuck for more than 100 years: *Kansas State Collegian.*

As the twentieth century began, the Kansas State student newspaper continued to look and feel much like the student newspapers that had appeared in the previous 100 years. Stories began in the upper left-hand corner of the page, running down the first column, and then continuing up to the top of the second column, and so forth. The stories at the top of the page had multideck headlines, some with four or more decks. The *Aggie*, for instance, used a five-column format. On the front page, the stories that began in columns one, three, and five each had four-deck headlines of varying size type, whereas the stories that began in columns two and four had two-deck headlines of boldface type only slightly larger than the body typeface. Often just a bold-faced line indicated a new story further down in the column.

By 1917, the *Collegian* used a seven-column format, with three-deck headlines at the top of columns 1, 3, 5, and 7. Some of the decks sported as many as five lines of type that formed an inverted pyramid. News items were short, often no more than a few paragraphs in length. The front page, which seldom featured photos, might have twenty-five to thirty of these short items. No apparent thought was given to hierarchy. Though the most important news might appear in that upper left-hand column of page 1, the remainder of the page felt as if it had been typeset and placed in the order that the stories were received, as if the typesetter started with the top of a pile of papers and worked down through pile. Even one-sentence ads for products at local stores might be included on the front page, used as fillers on the bottom of the columns.

For many years, the top sports story of the day filled the last column on the right. Any battle with the University of Kansas Jayhawks made a splash on the front page, sometimes plastered across the top and always emphasizing the rivals the two schools had become. As the years went by, the front page hierarchy began to emerge. The most important stories took positions at the top of the page, though rarely with headlines that covered more than a column at a time. If a story was longer than one column, it continued at the top of the next column, sans headline. In the 1940s, with an eight-column grid, it was not unusual to see more than twenty stories on the front page and few photos. The newspaper used photographs early in the century, but they were usually just posed portraits of individuals or groups. By the fall of 1938, action football photos began to appear.

By 1960, the newspaper was taking on a more modular, modern look as a five-column tabloid. Cartoons "Peanuts" and "Little Man on Campus" appeared on the editorial page. The issues it covered were pertinent for the day. Civil rights and lunch counter sit-ins to protest segregation were topics at other college newspapers and certainly in the *Collegian*.

The newspaper used a variety of nameplate styles through the years, including one that used a period at the end of the name. The period was dropped in the fall of 1916. Many newspapers in the 1800s followed the practice of adding the period to the nameplate, including all of the newspapers listed earlier in this chapter. *The Students' Herald* used the period the first day it appeared January 8, 1896. *The Kansas Aggie* included it when it first appeared in 1913 as did the *Kansas State Collegian* in 1914. Research turned up no explanation for using the period this way, which *The New York Times* did until 1967. However, a font expert said it is probably a holdover from Victorian-era British publishing that was rigid about a period being added at the end of lines.[64]

From the beginning, just like all student newspapers, students had to buy copies of the twice-weekly *Collegian* paper or take out a subscription. Student activity fees started supporting the *Collegian* financially in 1934.[65] In 1949, the student council proposed raising the fee to $1.50 per semester, which would help the newspaper become a daily.[66] That's just what it did later that year. At that time, the newspaper began to use United Press wire services to help fill the daily pages. It also started running stories from other college newspapers that it acquired through Associated Collegiate Press, a story sharing service among college newspapers.

## FILLING THE ROLES

The college press has continued to develop and change and eventually has taken on many different roles as it functioned to meet the needs of the students. The *Collegian* provides an excellent example of how some of the various roles of student newspapers manifest itself through the first sixty years of the twentieth century. A perusal of the *Collegian* from its earliest days until 1960 shows how the newspaper performed such disparate functions as community bulletin board and campus gossip, cheerleader, campus historian, public relations agent, advocate, entertainer, critic, and, of course, source for news and analysis about the campus, the community, the state, country, and even the world.

In many ways, until the 1930s, the *Collegian* had the feel of a modern neighborhood bulletin board where people post notices about upcoming events and items for sale. The front page would be a hodgepodge of items, some just a sentence long, others a few paragraphs. The *Aggie* often featured boxed notices, looking much like an advertisement, at the bottom of page 1 with information about plays, ball games, and lectures on campus. Though most of a single inside page was devoted to sports during most of the time in the first three decades, the other inside pages of the *Collegian* were often filled with one or two sentence notices about sorority/fraternity events and even engagement and wedding announcements. In its role as the campus gossip, the newspaper also featured snippets about individual students that might include reports of their illnesses, travels, and visitors. Similar notices like these appeared in small professional newspapers until well into the 1980s.

As the campus cheerleader, the newspaper was obviously a champion of the students. Editors seemed intent on finding things to praise about the student body, often using language that reflected the cheerleader role. Students who did well in any competition might be mentioned in a story, but winning brought the top headlines. The newspaper also promoted school spirit and chastised students when it appeared the zeal was waning in supporting the various teams that represented the school in sporting events.

Some universities and colleges have employees who are charged with keeping a history of the campus. Many campuses today, however, would have to have someone delve into a number of sources to write a complete history of their campus, and their first stop would be the student newspaper. While this certainly would not be considered a complete or totally accurate, reliable source, it does function as a record of some of the happenings on the campus, though certainly with a student perspective. Though most departments at Kansas State had stories written about some of the things that happened there, events occurring in the journalism department usually were more likely to be covered in the newspaper.

As noted earlier, many student newspapers began in the 1800s because students wanted to promote their campuses to the rest of the world. In keeping with that goal, the student newspapers usually did not contain criticism about university administrators or campus policies as it would reflect poorly on the reputation of the university. The *Collegian* was no different in its function as a public relations agent. Indeed, it was not until the late 1930s that the newspaper started to more closely consider such matters and occasionally publish something critical of the administration. One of the first times the newspaper ran a story above the nameplate was to criticize, yet it was focused on the state legislature that had cut funding for the college. The piece, which was more editorial than news, explained that teachers were leaving because the salaries were so low.[67]

Many times, the newspaper became an advocate for various causes. For example, in 1914, with the beginnings of what would later become known as World War I pushing many people in Belgium and France into starvation, the *Collegian* offered strong editorial support for a fundraising effort. For six weeks, the twice-weekly paper ran updates in every issue on the effort to raise money to buy a train-car load of wheat that could be ground into flour on campus, packaged in sacks bearing the school's name, and sent to Europe. At times, the stories begged students and faculty to dig deeper to contribute to the cause; some stories named contributors and the amounts they donated. A few years later, an almost unheard-of seven-deck headline announced that students had surpassed an $8,000 war fundraising goal by $2,000, attributing the generosity in part to the newspaper's appeals.[68]

Like all student newspapers, the *Collegian* had a lot to say about issues specific to the campus. For instance, since the earliest days, the smoking ban on campus was a returning topic in the pages of the newspaper. At times, the newspaper took a position that supported easing the ban because it was "out of tune" with modern society.[69] Smoking was allowed on the campus in 1944 (not inside buildings, however), but was under fire in 1948 when a lengthy front page story criticized students and faculty who disobeyed the rules and smoked near buildings and in doorways.[70] The newspaper also wrote about issues that were common to all college campuses through the years (many still written about today): problems with parking,[71] cafeteria offerings,[72] and registration woes.[73]

Entertainment was also a role the newspaper filled. Sometimes that included running stories about the entertainment industry and movie stars. It was common in the 1930s to have movie stars serve as judges in the campus beauty pageants. Movie stars Don Ameche, who in his later years starred in the 1985 science fiction film "Cocoon," and swashbuckling heartthrob Errol Flynn both served as judges on campus in 1939. Student journalists also provided the entertainment through columns with such titles as "Horning In," "Twitterings," sports commentary in "Bleacher Babble," fashion in "Chic Chatter," and record reviews in "Platter Patter," all found among the writing in 1939.

No matter how much criticism can be heaped on student newspapers' failure to offer a complete accounting of all campus events, the *Collegian* did chronicle a great deal of what happened on the Manhattan campus and some of the community and world as well. It noted the adding of the "S" on Mount Prospect in May 1930, the various name changes of the university, the enrollment of the first Black student in 1929, flu and polio epidemics that sent dozens of students to the campus hospital at various times. During World War II, the pages were often filled with news of former K-State students now in the military, updates on rationing, and other concerns at home. The proposed field house in February and March 1949 made the newspaper's front page every issue (twice a week) for five weeks. The legislature had promised to fund the project but did not pass the appropriation when expected. Student reporter Bob Chisholm stayed on the story until it was finally approved. When fraternities blockaded campus entrances, sometimes through brute force, for about half a day on February 25, 1960, the issue was also front-page news for several days. The newspaper supported the administration's desire to punish the students but then took the students' side when the administration announced punishment before going through proper channels first. And it also took on the role of public relations agent, warning students that behavior such as the blockade tarnished the image of the entire school.[74]

Through the years the newspaper also reported some of the happenings in the city around the university, often referring to the business district nearest the campus as Aggieville. In 1929, for example, only a month after the Valentine's Day Massacre in Chicago left seven mobsters dead in a rival gang shootout over control of illegal liquor business, law men in Manhattan, Kansas, chased four suspects who were also running liquor. Officers shot into the tires and gas tank of the car before finally stopping the men. The student newspaper praised the officers: "The gang wars of Chicago haven't a thing on Aggieville when it comes to liquor chases and gunfire."[75] After the newspaper went daily in 1949 and started using the United Press news service, the paper published a lot more national and international news instead of mostly focusing on local stories or issues at other campuses around the country that they gleaned through exchanges.

The students were not afraid to tackle controversial issues, even in the early part of the century. For example, an editorial in 1929 discussed the furor being raised in Missouri over a survey of students there on the topic of sex. The *Collegian* editorial noted that in Kansas, where married students were regularly asked to participate in surveys, no such problem seemed to exist because administrators were not afraid to let students at Kansas State learn about sex.[76] In 1940, shortly after more than a thousand male students at the university had to register for the draft, the editors pointed out concerns with the system and noted that people should not think those opposed to the process of conscription are any less loyal to the country than those who willingly signed up.[77]

The *Kansas State Collegian* is a good example of a typical college student newspaper that has continued to survive into the twenty-first century. Like many other student publications, its history stretches into the nineteenth century, making it possible to claim a heritage more than 115 years deep. During the World Wars, when some student newspapers either ceased publication or cut back dramatically, the *Collegian* continued to publish twice a week. It was one of the times it shined at one of the roles student newspapers have taken on through the years: advocate for a cause. In one case as noted, it was raising money to help starving people in Europe.

The newspaper also at times filled some of the other roles a student newspaper might have: community bulletin board and campus gossip, cheerleader, campus historian, public relations agent, entertainer, critic, and source for news. However, this was not an evolution from one role to the next. Indeed, at any given time throughout the first sixty years of the twentieth century it might fill any one or all of these roles. When the newspaper became a daily in 1949 and started using wire stories from outside the Manhattan community, the newspaper's primary focus seemed to shift toward providing more traditional news stories, written in a style that readers would recognize today as traditional journalism. The paper seemed more professional and less amateur, not only in its look but in its content. Gossip and campus-centric humor appeared less often. Student journalists seemed to tackle more serious campus stories and issues.

From the beginnings in the 1800s, student newspapers dealt with many of the same concerns as their "professional" counterparts: They were often financially unstable; they sometimes struggled to find enough news to fill their pages; they used the exchanges with other newspapers to provide news. They also had many of the features of the newspapers run for profit, though by today's standards one would say they lacked a lot of features now recognized as newspaper standards, such as illustrations/photos and interesting layouts. Until later in the 1800s, most did not use headlines to separate stories, which began in the left-hand column of the first page and ran from one column to the next until the end of the paper. Instead of headlines, an indentation of type, extra spacing or a centered dash would be used to indicate a new item. When headlines began to appear, they were simple label heads such as "Exchanges," "Personals," "Commencement" and the like. Bylines were not the standard in the 1800s, and most tagline names at the end of an article were pseudonyms or only initials. Stories often referred to students by just their last name, assuming everyone on the campus knew who that was. If editors were listed somewhere in the publication, it was usually just their first two initials and last name.

Like their professional counterparts, student newspapers have continued to evolve since they first appeared in the nineteenth century, and despite Hudson's gloomy prediction in 1873, they have continued to survive into the twenty-first century. From the first edition of each newspaper, the students were often idealistic about the purpose their publications would fulfill: to meet a need on campus, to bring the world to the students, to serve as ambassadors for the college, to bring prestige to the campus, to stroke the egos of students who wanted to see their words in print, to champion reform. Underlying every effort at every campus, though usually not expressed in print, was the unifying goal expressed in the first issue of *The Pennsylvanian* at the University of Pennsylvania in 1885 when editors pleaded for subscribers to support the paper "which is now, essentially and thoroughly, the college paper."[78] Throughout the past two centuries, student editors regularly encouraged fellow students to contribute articles to the newspaper and consider the newspaper their own. Indeed it is that unifying acceptance of a student publication as *the* college paper that has propelled so many student newspapers through more than 100 years of existence. That same spirit continues to keep student newspapers alive today at colleges and universities across the country.

## NOTES

1. *Literary Focus* (Oxford, OH), June 1827: 13.

2. Walter Havighurst, *The Miami Years 1809-1984* (New York: G. P. Putnam's Sons, 1984).

3. *The Miami Student,* accessed July 23, 2012, http://www.miamistudent.net/.

4. Frank Luther Mott, *American Journalism: A History of Newspapers in the United States Through 260 Years: 1690–1950, Revised Edition* (New York: The MacMillan Company, 1950), 411.

5. "Kansas State University: A Brief Chronology," accessed July 23, 2012, http://www.lib.k-state.edu/depts/spec/flyers/ksu-history.html.

6. Michael Schudson, *Discovering the News: A Social History of American Newspapers* (New York: Basic Books, 1978), 68.

7. Ibid., 70.

8. Fredric Hudson, *Journalism in the United States from 1690—1872* (New York: Harper & Bros., 1873), 711–12.

9. *Literary Focus* (Oxford, OH), June 1827: 13.

10. *Literary Register* (Oxford, OH), June 2, 1828: 1.

11. "Special Cable Dispatches for Yale News," *Yale News* (New Haven, CT) February 4, 1878: 1.

12. *Harvard Register* (Cambridge, MA), March 1827: 1.

13. *University Chronicle* (Ann Arbor, MI), March 2, 1867: 1.

14. *The Oracle* (Ann Arbor, MI), March 2, 1867: 1.

15. *The Vassar Miscellany* (Poughkeepsie, NY), April 1872: 53.

16. "The Magenta," *The Magenta* (Cambridge, MA), January 24, 1873: 2.

17. *The Lehigh Burr* (Bethlehem, PA), October 1881: 1–2.

18. "Greeting," *The Tech* (Boston, MA), November 16, 1881: 1.

19. *The LaFayette* (Easton, PA), October 1884: 1.

20. *American Newspaper Directory* (New York: Geo. P. Rowell & Co., 1882).

21. The *Yale News* (New Haven, CT), January 9, 1879: 1.

22. Ibid.

23. Most newspapers listed the subscription and single copy prices on their masthead or in the first column on the left of the front page.

24. *Yale News* (New Haven, CT), January 30, 1878: 2.

25. Allison Hantschel, *It Doesn't End with Us: The Story of the Daily Cardinal* (Westminster, MD: Heritage Books, 2007), 4.

26. Greg Lawless, ed., *The Harvard Crimson Anthology: 100 Years at Harvard* (Boston: Houghton Mifflin Co., 1980), 15

27. *Yale News* (New Haven, CT), February 4, 1878: 1.

28. Ibid., 3.

29. *The Oracle* (Ann Arbor, MI), March 2, 1867: 3.

30. *The Literary Register* (Oxford, OH), June 2, 1828: 14.

31. *Purdue Exponent* (West LaFayette, IN), December 15, 1889: 17.

32. "Locals," *The Tech* (Boston, MA), November 30, 1881: 21.

33. "Yale College Commencement," *The Miami Student* (Oxford, OH), June 7, 1867: 3.

34. *University Chronicle* (Ann Arbor, MI), April 11, 1867: 5.

35. "Exchanges," The *Purdue Exponent* (West LaFayette, IN), April 15, 1890: 197.

36. *The Columbia Spectator* (New York, NY), March 11, 1881: 18.

37. *University Chronicle* (Ann Arbor, MI), March 7, 1868: 3.

38. "Yale Log," *Yale News* (New Haven, CT), January 29, 1878: 2.

39. *The Oracle* (Ann Arbor, MI), March 2, 1867: 5.

40. "Sophomores vs. Juniors," *The Miami Student* (Oxford, OH), June 19, 1867: 4.

41. "Other Colleges," *Yale News* (New Haven, CT), January 30, 1878: 2.

42. "Sporting Notes," *The Tech* (Boston, MA), November 30, 1881: 21.

43. "Base Ball," *The Argo* (Williamstown, MA), May 20, 1882: 23–24.

44. "Intercollegiate Athletics," *The Argo* (Williamstown, MA), June 3, 1882: 40.

45. "College World: Clippings and comments," *The Michigan Argonaut* (Ann Arbor, MI), November 4, 1882: 93.

46. Ibid., 84.

47. Schudson, *Discovering the News,* 14.

48. *University Chronicle* (Ann Arbor, MI), March 2, 1867: 7–8.

49. Baxter Perry Smith, *The History of Dartmouth College* (Boston: Houghton, Osgood and Company, 1878), 163–166.

50. The Rauner Special Collections Library has bound copies of Vol. 1 No. 1 (August 27, 1799) through Vol. 20 No. 26 (1820).

51. Smith, *History of Dartmouth College.*

52. See Harvard/Radcliffe Online Historical Reference Shelf, Student Publications, http://hul.harvard.edu/ huarc/refshelf/StudPub.htm.

53. *American Newspaper Directory,* 163.

54. Lawless, *Harvard Crimson Anthology,* 15–20.

55. "About Us," *Yale Daily News,* accessed September 7, 2010, http://www.yaledailynews.com/aboutus/.

56. *American Newspaper Directory,* 36.

57. Tom Rosenstiel, Amy Mitchell, Kristen Purcell and Lee Rainie, "The Role of Newspapers," September 26, 2011. Pew Research Center. Accessed May 16, 2017, http://www.pewinternet.org/2011/09/26/part-3-the-role-of-newspapers/.

58. "Kansas State University: A Brief Chronology," accessed December 11, 2012, http://www.lib. k-state.edu/depts/spec/flyers/ksu-history.html.

59. "About K-State," accessed December 11, 2012, http://www.k-state.edu/about/.

60. "K-State Keepsakes: EXTRA! EXTRA! Campus Newspapers," June 27, 2007, accessed December 14, 2012, Ksulib.typepad.com/talking/2007/06/k-state-keeps-1.html.

61. "Salutatory," *Students' Herald,* (Manhattan, KS), January 8, 1896: 2.

62. "The Students' Herald" editorial, *Students' Herald* (Manhattan, KS), January 11, 1900: 127.

63. "The Why of 'The Kansas Aggie,'" *Kansas Aggie* (Manhattan, KS), April 2, 1913: 1.

64. Warren Bingham, email interview by author, January 26, 2012.

65. "K-State's Student Paper First Appeared in 1896," *Kansas State Collegian* (Manhattan, KS), October 6, 1942: 1.

66. "Student Council Votes to Recommend Raise in Fees for Daily Paper," *Kansas State Collegian* (Manhattan, KS) , March 4, 1949: 1.

67. "Holes Are Left in K-State Faculty as Underpaid Profs Move On . . . " *Kansas State Collegian* (Manhattan, KS), September 11, 1939.

68. "Fund above $10,000 Mark," *Kansas State Collegian* (Manhattan, KS), November 6, 1917: 1.

69. "Editorial," *Kansas State Collegian* (Manhattan, KS), December 11, 1928: 2.

70. Darrell Cowell, "Students, Faculty Violate Campus Smoking Rule by Smoking on Steps and Building Entrances," *Kansas State Collegian* (Manhattan, KS), September 28, 1948: 1.

71. Morris Kostetter, "Student Parking Being Investigated, Students and Faculty Make Suggestions," *Kansas State Collegian* (Manhattan, KS), February 27, 1950: 1.

72. "Irate K-Staters Request General Investigation of College Cafeterias, Several Students Threaten to Picket Cafeteria for Remedial Action," *Kansas State Collegian* (Manhattan, KS), December 3, 1948): 1; "Cafeteria Offers to Settle Dispute," *Kansas State Collegian* (Manhattan, KS), December 7, 1948: 1.

73. "Lines and More Lines—Enrollment is Rough," *Kansas State Collegian* (Manhattan, KS), February 4, 1949: 1.

74. Don Veraska, "What is K-State Administration's Next Move Against Blockaders?" *Kansas State Collegian* (Manhattan, KS), February 29, 1960: 1.

75. "Law Stages Shootout Act in Aggieville," *Kansas State Collegian* (Manhattan, KS), March 12, 1929: 1.

76. "Sex and Schools," *Kansas State Collegian* (Manhattan, KS), March 15, 1929: 2.

77. "Conscription Serves to Protect Our Ideals," *Kansas State Collegian* (Manhattan, KS), October 25, 1940: 2.

78. *The Pennsylvanian* (Philadelphia, PA), December 15, 1885: 1.

*Chapter Two*

# Nobody Told Us What to Write

The First Amendment of the U.S. Constitution has guaranteed press freedom for more than 200 years, but every year, at least one college student newspaper suffers censorship, usually from campus administrators or disgruntled student government leaders. The censoring today occurs in five primary ways:

1. Prior restraint: not allowing publication in the first place.
2. Prior review: requiring student journalists to allow officials to review and approve copy before publication
3. Denial of funding: withholding funding in response to student newspaper content.
4. Newspaper theft: removing newspaper stacks without permission to keep others from reading it.
5. Firing the adviser: censoring indirectly by removing the adviser as a retaliation for content.[1]

All of these means of censorship are meant to do one thing, according to Frank LoMonte, executive director of the Student Press Law Center: control the student press. "By far the greatest danger to the ability of students and educators to discuss issues of public concern on college campuses is image-obsessed administrators, who increasingly regard transparency and accountability as annoyances to be minimized."[2] The situation has gotten so serious that many states have considered enacting legislation to protect the student press. By March 2017, five states had passed laws while many others continue to work on such laws.[3]

Censorship of student media is not unique to the twenty-first century. Student newspapers have been subjected to it since they began. Before the

1960s, censorship seemed routine on college campuses, and advisers and students could do little to stop it.[4] In 1962, the editors of *The Mississippian* at Ole Miss knew the practice was common at many other student publications, but it didn't happen to them. Though the students faced pressure from many sources, the administration continued to let them publish whatever they wanted. They counted themselves lucky.[5]

## COVERING INTEGRATION AT OLE MISS—1962

Everyone at Ole Miss knew integration was likely to occur on the 4,500-student campus when school began in the fall of 1962. The first issue of the daily student newspaper for the fall term featured a story about it on the front page. The chancellor had no comment for *The Mississippian* about James Meredith's fight to become the first black student at the University of Mississippi, but students were talking about it. Some raised concerns that their own education could be interrupted. Others told of receiving anonymous calls about burning effigies and crosses. Few people actually turned out to a rally to burn Meredith in effigy, and the burning never occurred.[6]

As the courts continued to affirm Meredith's petition to attend Ole Miss beginning that fall, *The Mississippian* editor Sidna Brower had a simple plan: cover events surrounding integration as they occurred. "I never thought there would be a riot and two people killed," she recalled of the deadly night of September 30, 1962.[7]

It was one of the first times during the tumultuous decade of the 1960s that federal or local officers of some kind would be called to a college campus to deal with protests. As with almost all the major protests of the era, numerous books and articles have detailed the events that led up to the riot and then the riot itself.[8] Quotes and even entire pieces from the student newspaper have appeared in many of those publications, but no one has really considered the newspaper's role in helping to create the historical record of what is perhaps the most important event in Ole Miss history.

At least one book's author interviewed several students for his work, including *The Mississippian* editor/reporter Jan Humber, who covered the riot and some of the events that preceded it for the student newspaper.[9] Humber said the author told her that her reporting of the events had been among the most accurate of all the press stories,[10] a fact that still makes her proud today.

Both Humber and Brower are critical of the coverage of the events by the professional press, particularly the Jackson, Mississippi, metro papers where they say many stories misconstrued facts or just plain got them wrong. Rather than support the student press in its efforts to cover integration, the Jackson newspapers, and one columnist in particular, criticized the student reporters and editors.

At the same time, the campus administration, which at many colleges and universities is often at odds with the student newspaper, was supportive of *The Mississippian*. Though the newspaper was published on campus and had some faculty oversight, campus officials took a hands-off approach. Student editors and reporters were allowed to publish any story they liked without fear of reprisal or prior censorship, something that many of their counterparts across the country have battled throughout the history of student newspapers and indeed continue to face today. Basically, Brower and Humber said they found that "nobody told us what to write," so they forged ahead to report the integration issue as it unfolded on their campus.

Though the editors felt completely free to report as they wished, their work was not completely free of influence from outside forces. They faced challenges that all journalists encounter in their work, challenges that can define how the job is done. These included such things as problems with access to information, time and space constraints, and technology limitations. The students also had to contend with pressures from many sides such as well-meaning faculty members, the White Citizen's Council (a white supremacist organization that was active throughout Mississippi at the time), and their fellow students who wanted the newspaper to take a stand against integration.

This chapter examines the challenges the student staff faced and looks at how *The Mississippian* covered the integration issue as the staff worked to do the best job possible. This chapter also recounts the stories of the editors, Sidna Brower and Jan Humber, who wrote the articles and made the decisions. It tells not only the challenges they faced, but the threats of violence leveled against them, the harassment they suffered from the statehouse to the sorority house, and the impact it had on the rest of their lives.

Still, the student editors considered themselves to be working on one of the freest newspapers in Mississippi at the time. The claim held a lot of truth. Professor James W. Silver, who had a front row seat for the integration issue at Ole Miss, wrote that the typical newspaper in Mississippi at the time was part of the "vigilant guard" that protected what he termed "the closed society" of Mississippi that refused social change though much of the country was beginning to embrace civil rights and desegregation. With a few exceptions such as the *Delta Democrat* in Greenville, a couple of other dailies and a few weeklies, the newspapers of the state steadfastly supported maintaining the values of the South—white supremacy and segregation of the races— even if that meant "manipulating information with little regard for accuracy or integrity."[11]

Silver, who wrote a journal article and a book in the early 1960s that described "the closed society" of Mississippi at that time, found parallels between the pre-Civil War 1850s and the 1950s—both were times when the state fought against social change. "The all-pervading doctrine then and now has been white supremacy—whether achieved through slavery or segregation—rationalized by a professed adherence to state rights and bolstered by religious fundamentalism." The key requirement is that any person or organization that does not conform must be "silenced with a vengeance. . . . Violence and the threat of violence have reinforced the presumption of unanimity. . . . Today [1960s] the totalitarian society of Mississippi imposes on all its people an obedience to an official orthodoxy almost identical with the pro-slavery philosophy."[12]

It was in this atmosphere that student journalists at Ole Miss were publishing a newspaper. Though Brower, a senior, was the new editor at *The Mississippian* for the 1962–1963 school year, she was no stranger to the student newspaper or the integration issue. She had been the managing editor the previous year and had followed Meredith's quest, which was first reported on the front page of *The Mississippian* in January 1962.[13] She was also well versed in newspaper work, having spent the summer working in two bureaus for the Memphis *Commercial Appeal.* When she returned to campus in September, she was ready to report about Ole Miss. Within a few weeks, Brower's name and her editorial calling for peace would be read by people all over the United States and would be the impetus for her nomination for a Pulitzer Prize. By Christmas, the student Senate would vote to reprimand her for that same editorial and others that followed.

## THE MISSISSIPPIAN

*The Mississippian,* the third attempt at a student newspaper on the Ole Miss campus, first appeared in 1911.[14] The folio line in fall 1962 listed the volume as 52. In September 1961, student editor James "Jimmy" Robertson took on the task of turning the weekly newspaper into the state's first student daily, publishing four days a week when school was in regular session. Originally the newspaper was published Monday through Thursday, but by the fourth week of the more rigorous daily schedule, that changed to Tuesday through Friday. A story announcing the new schedule gave no reason for the change,[15] and Robertson no longer remembers why. However, it is likely that students found preparing a Monday morning edition on Sunday night was a more arduous task than they had anticipated because it cut into their weekend activities, especially because so many students left the campus on the weekends.[16] Despite the production schedule change to a four-day-a-week daily, the newspaper kept its original name until the spring of 1968 when it officially became *The Daily Mississippian.*[17]

In the early 1960s, the newspaper offices and journalism department were housed in Brady Hall, a building first constructed as an infirmary in the early 1900s and named for school nurse Minnie Brady. It was torn down in 1977 to make way for Coulter Hall, which now houses the chemistry department. [18] Brady Hall was located near the University Avenue entrance to campus, and it was a comfortable place where a close group of students hung out all the time, even if they did not have a class. They often would relax in a unique porch swing located on the front of the building. [19] Faculty and students alike enjoyed the swing, which was seldom unoccupied. [20]

"There was camaraderie there," Humber said of her time at Brady Hall. "It was kind of us against the world." Some of the people she worked with became her good friends and remain so today. After graduation, she married the editor from 1961–1962, Jimmy Robertson. "I fell in love with his editorials, which were not typical Mississippi editorials at any newspaper in the state at that particular time, before I ever even met him," she said. [21]

Both Robertson and Brower ran campaigns to get elected by the student body to serve as editor of the newspaper during their respective senior years—Robertson for 1961–1962 and Brower for 1962–1963. The practice of electing the editor continued until 1990 when a committee was established to select the editor. The first editor selected under this new committee method was an African-American, Lee Eric Smith. [22] In the 1960s, though, in order to run for the position of editor, a student had to have completed a certain number of journalism credits, which Robertson, a history major, had done even though he was not majoring in journalism. "When Jimmy Robertson ran, he was not a journalism student," recalled Brower, who majored in journalism. "And a lot of the journalism students refused to work for him. I agreed to work because I got a little money [as an editor]. I felt like it was an opportunity to get a little experience, so I was his managing editor," which was an appointment the editor made. [23] While Brower was campaigning for the editor's position the next spring, Jan Humber filled in as managing editor, and Brower would later ask her to resume that post again that fall. [24]

The tabloid-sized newspaper, measuring 11 ¼ x 16 ¾ inches in a five-column format, was published on a used, two-unit Fairchild Color King press located in the journalism building. Besides being the only college daily in the state, *The Mississippian* was the first daily newspaper to be printed on an offset press. [25] Students wrote the stories, but a paid staff of people would typeset the text, paste up the paper, and run the press to print the newspaper. The press was a major problem because it was so unreliable. "[Administrators] weren't sure a daily [student newspaper] would work and did not want to sink much money into it," Robertson said of the "worn out press" that printed the newspaper. "I recall that we got the paper 'on the street' before midnight on the date shown on the masthead every scheduled publication date except three. On those three, and many others, the damn press broke down, and getting it back in operation was a helluva chore. I was down there many a night, primarily sweating it out whether we would get the paper out at all. This was a daily factor that dominated all else."[26] Still, Robertson said, "I thought it was a pretty damn good looking paper."[27]

Brower remembers that student fees helped fund a small portion of the newspaper, but advertising was expected to pay for the majority of the cost. That was not always easy, though, and after the first year, the newspaper's status as a daily was in jeopardy. "I was told that I needed to get the newspaper in the black or we would have to go back to being a weekly," Brower said. "I guess I have James Meredith to thank for making that possible because we did meet that goal."[28]

Throughout the first term of the 1962–1963 school year, the newspaper was almost always four pages, with a few eight-page issues and only one larger than that, a sixteen-page edition on the first day of publication for the term, September 18, 1962. However, beginning in mid-March, 1963, the newspaper was always at least eight pages, with a sixteen-page edition at the end of the year on May 14, 1963. Because newspapers print on both sides of the sheet, only an even number of pages is possible. The smallest newspaper is four pages, with the front and back of the typical two-page roll of paper printed before folding it in half. The size of a tabloid newspaper is increased in increments of four pages. Broadsheet size newspapers need only have even numbered pages if the press is able to accommodate a single-page roll of paper (called a dinky) that is printed on the two sides and inserted inside the folded pages. *The Mississippian* never ran more than sixteen pages because that was the maximum number the press could accommodate.[29]

The copy-to-ad ratio varied greatly throughout the year. For instance, the four-page paper that appeared on November 15, 1962, was about 37 percent advertising and 63 percent editorial copy; whereas the eight-page edition that was published April 5, 1963, had only about 21 percent advertising and 79 percent editorial space. If the student newspaper only had to cover its expenses and not make a profit, as Brower indicated, then having a smaller ad-to-copy ratio would be acceptable. She no longer remembers the space requirements to pay the expenses, which was a job she left up to the business manager anyway.[30] However, things must have been going well enough by March 1963 to support the larger, eight-page papers every day.

As Brower noted, her first concern as editor was making sure the newspaper had the copy it needed each day, which meant figuring out how to report as much of the campus news as possible because at the beginning of the year the newspaper could not afford a wire service. (The newspaper began using stories from United Press International, known as UPI, in April 1963.)[31] Such a task is a formidable one for any student newspaper editor, especially at the beginning of the school year when recruiting has not yet filled out all the staff positions. Though the majority of the editors were appointed by the elected editor, the core of the reporting at *The Mississippian* was done by students in the journalism classes.[32] Until those students were far enough along in the program to produce stories, editors would have to cover the campus news themselves. That meant editor-in-chief Sidna Brower and managing editor Jan Humber would be doing the bulk of the news reporting. Other editors would handle sports and features.

As the school year began, the top story was the integration issue. It is unclear who wrote some of the stories because bylines were not always included. "Bylines were given when you really did original reporting," Humber explained, and not when it just involved rewriting news releases or other news stories.[33] Brower recalled that many of the stories about the coming integration in the first few issues were generated from regular meetings with administration officials. "I would have briefings with an administration official almost every day on what was happening, whether the governor was going to do something," she said. However, "the administration never told me what to write or what not to write."[34] She had reinforced that in an editorial a couple of weeks after the riot: "Again I must remind the people that I have not received any pressure or instructions from anyone as to what I should or should not write. I have recorded my own thoughts, mainly the theme that violent demonstrations do not aid the cause."[35] And then a week later, she reprinted an editorial from the *Crimson White* at the University of Alabama that discussed the editorial responsibility of the student newspaper, including the responsibility to be accurate and take a stand on important issues. Her editor's note once again touted the freedom of the press at the University of Mississippi: "Ole Miss is one of the few college newspapers that has no censorship. We hope to retain this freedom of the press with responsible editorials and objective news stories."[36]

Robertson echoed the same sentiment about his tenure in the editor's position: "I recall visiting roughly every two weeks with George Street [assistant director of development in September 1962][37] in the Lyceum. . . . I recall frequently he would tell me, always with a twinkle in his eye and a smile on his face, 'Now, Jimmy, we're not going to tell you what to print in the paper, but we think you should know what people are saying.' Then George would tell me what some fool alum had said, or the complaints of a legislator, whatever. I always had the sense that George was walking a tight rope (like so many were in those days) and he told me just enough so that he could report back, 'Yes, I talked to Robertson about that, and told him what you said.'"[38]

At least once in the fall of 1962 the administration asked the student editors to print specific stories. During the afternoon before the riot began, the administration met with student leaders, including Brower, to discuss "how we could keep the campus calm," Brower said. "And that is when the administration said they wanted to put out this special edition [of *The Missis-*

*sippian* on Monday morning], and I certainly thought that was a good idea."[39] Within a few hours, a riot that ended with two dead would change the focus of that special edition. If it had not, however, Brower was prepared to do as the administration requested and print just what they wanted. Even with the riot, the edition included the same letter from the chancellor that he had requested be printed.

Any professors serving in advisory capacities to the student editors also certainly would have some impact on the work the students do. Brower said the student newspaper did not have a designated adviser. The publisher, instructor Walter Hurt, dealt with publishing issues and did not offer any real editorial assistance.[40] Humber remembers him as a timid man, "scared of his own shadow. I think he was horrified of being adviser to the newspaper."[41] Brower also found Journalism Department Chair Samuel Talbert and journalism professor Dr. Jere Hoar to be willing listeners and advisers.[42] Humber, who had transferred as a junior from Stephens College in Missouri, found herself turning to her old newspaper adviser at Stephens College for help. "I talked to her all the time over the telephone," she said. Also, "Dr. Hoar was a very demanding professor, but he was someone I felt I could talk to. He was a source of moral support to me particularly."[43]

As in most university and college settings, professors in almost every area serve as mentors and unofficial advisers to students who may feel comfortable coming to them for advice of all kinds, not just academic. Brower found that kind of relationship with history professor James W. Silver and his wife, Margaret Thompson Silver, who worked in the Dean of Women's Office. Dr. Silver was a tenured faculty member who had been teaching on the Ole Miss campus since 1936. By 1962, when Meredith integrated the campus, Silver was known as a professor who spoke out against segregation. *The Mississippian* published one of his essays on states' rights the week after the riot with an editor's note that explained that the piece was an attempt to explain some of the issues at hand in an objective manner.[44]

In 1963, Silver "delivered a scathing attack on life in mid-twentieth century Mississippi"[45] in his resignation as the president of the Southern Historical Association. His expanded remarks became a book[46] and a journal article,[47] both published in 1964 and titled *Mississippi: The Closed Society*. They were harsh indictments of the state's inability to accept social change and to banish old traditions like segregation. Angry members of the White Citizens' Council demanded his termination from Ole Miss. Before anything could happen, though, he took a leave in 1965 to teach at Notre Dame and then later taught at the University of South Florida. Silver never returned to teach in Mississippi, and he died in Florida in 1988.[48]

But in 1962, Silver was trying to help at least two students navigate the treacherous waters of integration. Along with offering advice to Brower, Silver also acted as an unofficial adviser and friend to James Meredith.[49] He advised both students to avoid meeting. "He [Silver] did not want me to interview James Meredith," Brower said. "He did not want me to meet him because he felt that would just endanger my life and perhaps James Meredith's life. So I never met Meredith until like 40 years later."[50] A *Mississippian* story on the third day after the riot included Meredith's views on his treatment in the first days at Ole Miss, but Brower said the story was written from a press conference and did not come from an interview. The only interview with Meredith came near the end of the school year and was conducted by associate editor John Corlew.[51] Though the decision not to interview Meredith early in the year was part of Brower's effort to keep the campus as calm as possible—probably a wise decision on her part given the volatile nature of the situation—it was also the manifestation of the influence faculty can have over student editors and reporters.

Other factors certainly played a role in how the editors and reporters could write about the integration issues. Like all student journalists, the staff of *The Mississippian* faced constraints on their time available to do reporting work. They also had classes to attend, homework to complete, class assignments to fulfill, all requiring many hours. At times, school work had to take precedence over the student newspaper. Also, it would have been difficult at times to appropriately report all the facets of the situation simply because, before the riot, most of the action (such as meetings, governor's decisions, and court proceedings) did not occur on or near the campus. The court cases were being adjudicated in Jackson (more than 160 miles south) and New Orleans, Louisiana (more than 350 miles south). Without access to modern resources, such as the internet, fax machines, and cell phones (in fact, dial telephone service had only arrived in Oxford, Mississippi, the previous year),[52] students would have been hard pressed to have timely access, if any, to information necessary for complete stories. At the time, the newspaper did not subscribe to wire services such as Associated Press (AP) or UPI, thus further limiting their access to information. Still, with these limited resources, the newspaper staff attempted to report the key events happening at the capitol or in the courts as best they could.

Though, as Robertson pointed out, the newspaper was not expected to bow to pressure from alumni, complaints received directly or through campus officials could color how the student staff would approach a story. Neither Robertson nor Brower reported any threats from alumni, at least none that they considered serious, and neither tried to let such pressure affect their newspaper work. The reporting from the time does not reflect it either. Still, knowing that alumni or others are trying to exert pressure can influence how a staff would approach controversial stories.

*The Mississippian* editors did not shy away from the James Meredith story when they began to cover the issue, though apparently student reporters did not always understand the legal wrangling. For example, on January 25,

1962, the first time the newspaper wrote about the possibility of a black man entering Ole Miss, a large banner headline across the front page declared "MEREDITH GAINS SHORT CUT," with the kicker headline "Ruling 'favorable.'" That "short cut," however, was that a district judge had ruled previous testimony would be allowed in the current hearing, which might then only mean a shorter hearing on the matter and nothing approaching a "short cut" to admission. The students also were not able to follow the case as closely as the professional press. For instance, the ruling from that hearing announced on January 25, was not reported in *The Mississippian* until February 9, 1962, almost a week after it was made. Even then, it was only in passing because the case had been bumped to the United States Fifth Circuit Court of Appeals and a decision from the higher court was expected the next day, Saturday. The newspaper reported the Saturday decision (the judges refused to intervene to force Ole Miss to admit Meredith) in the next edition, Tuesday, February 13.

By then, though, *The Mississippian* was dealing with fallout from another story that also had appeared on the front page of the Friday, February 9 paper. That story had been a special report, minus any byline, that was a profile of James Meredith although no one interviewed him. Reporters had contacted officials at Jackson State College where Meredith was currently a student and also talked to people from his home in Attala County, located northeast of Jackson, in order to give students an idea of who this man was.[53] All those interviewed had spoken positively about Meredith. In rebuttal, anonymous individuals distributed a mimeographed paper titled *Rebel Underground* to the campus dorms on Monday morning. The two-page bulletin was critical of the campus newspaper's profile of Meredith, claiming that such reporting showed the newspaper supported integration when it should be supporting segregation. The unknown authors also personally criticized *The Mississippian* editor Jimmy Robertson, using the profile as an example of how Robertson had failed the student body that elected him to the position.[54] On the editorial page inside *The Mississippian,* on February 13, Robertson took the anonymous writers to task and challenged them to an open debate of any issue the newspaper had covered that year.[55] No debate ever took place, however, and apparently the identity of the authors of the *Underground,*[56] which published sporadically for the next year, was never known.[57] Typically, *The Mississippian* ignored most of the bulletin's criticisms in later issues.

Even with a smaller summer staff, *The Mississippian* continued to report the James Meredith case with a handful of stories. A skyline head above the flag on June 8, 1962, announced that Meredith had been arrested. The small deck head explained that he was accused of violating an oath, and the story reported that Meredith had listed Hinds County as his residence when he registered to vote in Jackson, where he lived and attended Jackson State

College, but he claimed Attala County as his home county in the federal law suit he filed to gain entrance to the University of Mississippi. The statement at the time of registering to vote would then be a lie, according to authorities, and he was arrested.[58] It was another of the delay actions that integration opponents used to try to keep Meredith out of Ole Miss.

Though *The Mississippian* only carried four more stories about integration throughout the summer of 1962, student editors did recognize that the issue brewing was an important one. Editors twice used skyline heads above the nameplate, making the non-bylined story the top story of the day. Finally, in the last integration story of the summer, students reported that a federal judge had told a district judge to order Ole Miss to admit Meredith. That story also included a few paragraphs about another black, a twenty-one-year old woman named Alfanette Marie B. Bracy, who had applied to attend Ole Miss.[59]

*The Mississippian* only had eight issues during the fall term before the deadly riot broke out, but the integration/segregation issue was mentioned in almost every one. The national and even international press started arriving on campus, and a press room was set up in the Lyceum administration building to accommodate them.[60] Brower thought most of the national print media did a good job in covering integration at Ole Miss and the ensuing riot, particularly the *Christian Science Monitor*. However, she had a poor opinion of the state press, particularly the *Jackson Daily News* and its columnist Jimmy Ward, who took Brower to task several times.[61] Brower's dislike was apparent early in the term. In the third edition of the new school year, *The Mississippian* ran a front-page editorial by Brower above the nameplate.[62] It was in response to a front-page editorial that had run the day before in the *Jackson Daily News* that had condemned the national press for slandering the people of Mississippi.[63] Brower blasted the *News* for using "screaming headlines and sensationalized stories" itself while at the same time castigating the national press for the way it covered the issue. "Perhaps the Jackson Daily News should reread their editorial and stories and 'practice what they preach,'" Brower wrote.[64]

The *News* did not let the attack go. Two days later, columnist Jimmy Ward invited *The Mississippian* editor to borrow information about a closed meeting between the governor and James Meredith that he said only the *News* had attended. He ended the entry with a snide, "You're welcome, Sidna."[65] Three days later, an unsigned editorial in *The Mississippian*, probably written by Brower, responded to Ward: "Although I don't care to start a verbal war with the editor of the Jackson Daily News, I would like to reply to his generous offer in Saturday's paper. I certainly appreciate his permission to reprint any or all of the inside information on the closed meeting between Governor Ross Barnett and government authorities and James Meredith last Thursday. However, the report was not so 'exclusive' that our reporter [Jan

Humber] could not obtain the information. We did not need to wait until Friday afternoon to learn of the proceedings [from the *Jackson Daily News*]; our front page for the Friday morning edition was complete and ready for the press by 10 p.m. Thursday." [66]

As the fall term began in 1962, Brower knew the integration issue was coming to a head. However, she did not make big plans to mobilize her small staff. After all, she did not suspect a deadly riot was coming. Instead, she decided to cover the story as it developed, sending whoever had time to do it. Each day she met with campus officials to learn updates. She sent Humber to cover stories, too. [67] An unsigned editorial in the fifth issue warned that the university would face closing if Governor Ross Barnett stuck to his promise to never integrate during his term. [68] Brower was particularly worried about that possibility or that the school's accreditation would be rescinded. "Frankly, as a senior—and I know other seniors—we were very concerned that we were about to graduate. Is this not going to count?" [69]

It finally became apparent that Meredith would be allowed to enter the college on Monday, October 1. The federal government had to get involved, however, to make it happen. Governor Ross Barnett was acting as registrar and had promised publicly to always keep up the fight against segregation, even threatening to shut down the education system in the state if necessary. However, privately, he made a quiet deal with President John F. Kennedy and Attorney General Robert F. Kennedy: the federal government would have to send troops to Ole Miss so Barnett could back down and save face with his supporters, claiming he was overwhelmed by the show of force. [70] The troops arrived on Sunday, September 30.

## REPORTING THE RIOT

Like most students, managing editor Jan Humber was not on campus that weekend. Many had gone to the football game in Jackson where the Ole Miss Rebels beat the University of Kentucky, 14–0. Humber, however, was at home in Clarksdale, about sixty miles west of Oxford. She received a call after church from Chancellor John D. Williams, asking her to return to campus as soon as possible and plan to put out a special Monday edition of *The Mississippian* that would include a statement he had prepared. His statement asked students to help keep the university operating by not participating in demonstrations and by reporting agitators to the authorities. [71] He told Humber that he had not been able to reach Brower, who had gone to Jackson to attend the football game, so he had called her instead.

Humber had planned to return to campus later that night with friends, but her father drove her to Oxford that afternoon and dropped her at the Tri-Delta (Delta Delta Delta) Sorority House where she lived. "As I walked out of the

Tri-Delta House to walk over to *The Mississippian* office to meet with Chancellor Williams, a truck drove by," Humber said. "There were men in the back of the truck who had on orange kind of flak jackets, and they had on white helmets. And, of course, I had no earthly idea of who they were or anything."

Her reporter training took over, and she followed the truck to the oldest building on campus, the Lyceum administration building, where the men got out and encircled the building. "I walked up to each one of them—I walked all the way around the Lyceum—and I asked every single one of them who they were and why they were there. No one would say anything to me at all. . . . I paid attention to what they had and noticed that they had tear gas projectiles and something that would fire tear gas, but no side arms whatsoever."[72] The leader of the group told her they were U.S. Marshals, but would answer no other questions. Later, pictures in other publications would show officers with pistols in holsters on their hips that Sunday,[73] but Humber maintained that there were none visible when the men first arrived. That became an issue when authorities tried to sort out who had been shooting that night. She also told that to the AP reporter when she was interviewed after the riot. Some newspapers and even the governor of the state claimed "the marshals came with guns, and they shot people, which was an absolute lie," she said.[74]

After speaking to the marshals, Humber left the area and went to *The Mississippian* offices to meet the chancellor, who obviously knew nothing about the marshals coming to campus until she told him. "As happened during this entire thing, the university and the chancellor and the university's leadership were the last to know anything. They were left out of the loop," Humber said. The chancellor left the letter he wanted printed and then gave Humber a ride back to the Lyceum. Except to eventually stow her camera in a nearby building, Humber did not leave the front of the Lyceum building until after the first round of tear gas was used. "So I saw everything that went on," she said.[75]

Her story that ran on page 1 of *The Mississippian* the next day reports the key things she saw that afternoon and early evening. She tried to keep it factual though the opening sentences were certainly her opinion: "Students started out yesterday by shouting slogans of their pride in Mississippi and ended up with nothing to be proud of. Last night the restraint and simple boisterousness that had marked most of the demonstrations in the Meredith situation degenerated into unrestrained hatred and violence." She went on to tell of watching as rioters attacked the car of a Movietone photographer and reporter, eventually tipping the car over and smashing the camera. Highway patrolmen rescued the two and took them to safety. She described the attacks on the marshals as the crowd threw lighted cigarettes and other burning objects (starting the canvas top of a military truck on fire) and eventually bricks taken from a construction site and Molotov cocktails. She told of angry adults flocking to campus, bypassing the entrances the officers closed, of rioters trying to commandeer a fire truck and a bulldozer, of injuries from both guns and tear gas being fired, of reporters being attacked and their cameras smashed. Her story also included that a French reporter had reportedly been shot and killed,[76] though she never saw the French reporter. The death toll in the end was two: the French journalist and a local repairman. Hundreds more were injured.

Humber did not report her own story in the paper, though. Like the students who had left town for the weekend, most of the professional reporters and photographers also were not on campus when the marshals arrived and surrounded the Lyceum. As one of the few reporters there at the beginning, Humber began taking pictures with a camera owned by the campus newspaper. She noted that the crowd's camera smashing probably started because of a rumor earlier in the year that the university was going to hire cameramen to film students participating in panty raids so the students could be caught and dismissed from school. At the time, she was not worrying about what the crowd was doing. "I climbed up on the hood of a car. I was looking through the view finder on my camera, and all of a sudden I heard this voice say, 'Jan, you idiot. Get down from there.'" The voice was Bill Street, a reporter for the Memphis *Commercial Appeal*, whom she had gotten to know through his coverage of the integration issue. It was then that she realized the car she was standing on was surrounded by an angry mob of men. Street told the group that Humber was with the student newspaper and helped her off the car. He warned her that the protesters were smashing cameras, so she put the camera under her jacket and took it to the nearby Old Y building (the second oldest building on campus and now the Croft Institute for International Studies building) for safe keeping.

Then she immediately returned to the front of the Lyceum administration building. "I was determined I was going to watch and see whatever else happened because I had already seen examples of so-called reporters who had reported things that had not actually happened," she said, pointing to a story in the professional press a few days before that told of students pulling down the United States flag and replacing it with the Confederate flag.[77] She was at the flag pole when this incident occurred. What really happened, she said, is that reporters and photographers were standing around the flag pole and one urged some students to pull down the U.S. flag and put up the Confederate flag. One male student grabbed the chain of the flag to do just that but stopped when Grey Jackson, student body vice president, intervened and cautioned the students not to play into the hands of the reporters and bring dishonor on the campus. "It appeared in print that Ole Miss students had pulled down the American flag in protest, which was a lie," Humber said. "I saw what happened. I was so disillusioned [by the false stories]. I was this idealistic journalism student, and all my heroes were journalists. I just thought most news people were for truth above all things. And then I saw so many things reported that didn't happen."[78]

Though Humber said the marshals did not fire guns, plenty of other people were carrying and firing them. Most of the people milling around were not students. She said most students had either attended the football game in Jackson the day before or had gone home, and most would not return until just before the midnight curfew. Who Humber saw "were some of the meanest looking people I've ever seen in my life, just streaming on campus. We found out later that there had been radio stations in Alabama that the day before had been urging people to come to campus and fight for the Southern way of life." At one point, she saw an individual with a rifle on top of a building near the Lyceum. She reported that fact to a highway patrolman: "He didn't even look up there. And he says, 'don't worry your pretty little head about that, little girl' and literally pats me on the top of my head! He walks away, again never even looks up, and he disappeared."[79]

National guardsmen were brought in as reinforcements. At least one of the trucks carrying the men was driven by a black soldier. People thought the man was Meredith in disguise and started throwing Molotov cocktails and other objects while the driver took cover in the Lyceum. At that point, about 8 p.m., the tear gas was fired, and Humber headed to *The Mississippian* office to start writing her story.

By that time, Brower was also at the office working on her editorial for the special edition. She had returned to the campus in the afternoon and had attended a meeting with campus officials and student leaders about what could be done to keep the campus calm, including a discussion about the special edition of the newspaper planned the next day. Then the riot started.

Brower had returned to work at *The Mississippian* office. "At one point there was a knock on the door, and I went up and there was a kid and I'm assuming his father," Brower said. "You could see the anger and the hatred in their faces. 'Where's that nigger? We're going to kill him' [they said]. At that point I figured I better lock all the doors, which I did."[80]

Brower said she allowed the professional journalists and photographers to use *The Mississippian* office equipment such as telephone, typewriters, and darkroom, so the office was abuzz with activity that night. "I was in the photo lab showing a guy our system," she recalled. "There was a knock at the door, and we were told that the French correspondent [Paul Guihard] had been shot, and the photographer said, 'Oh, my God. That's my man.' So he had to leave to go identify the body."[81]

Humber recalled that sometime during the evening the newspaper's business manager came running into the office, absolutely terrified, and told everyone to quickly leave the building if they valued their lives. He had been on Courthouse Square downtown when a bus from Alabama pulled over and the driver asked him for directions to campus. He told the editors that he had stood on the first step of the bus and looked inside. "It was filled with meanest looking men I have ever seen in my life. And every single one of them had a gun," Humber quoted him as saying. He then ran from Barton Hall, afraid that the coming mob would strike the newspaper offices first,[82] but the editors hunkered down to finish the next day's paper. No other incidents happened at the office that night.

With a chuckle, Humber remembered that the only time an administration official had ordered the newspaper staff to do something came that night and had nothing to do with content in the paper. Twice, Katharine Rea, dean of women, called the newspaper office and told Humber and Brower that they had to be back at their respective sorority houses before the curfew or they would face discipline from the campus judicial committee. The two complied, but Bill Street, the Memphis reporter who had pulled Humber off a car earlier in the evening, would not let Humber walk alone through an area of campus known as The Grove. Street, a combat veteran, gave Humber explicit orders to follow every command while he walked her to her sorority house. A UPI photographer escorted Brower.

As they hurried through the dark trees, people were streaming past them and onto campus, obviously bypassing the officers who had closed the roads onto campus. "We start hearing all these popping sounds," Humber said. "On one level I knew it was gunfire. On another level my mind didn't want me to admit there was gunfire." At one point, Street assured Humber that the sounds were cherry bombs, "but they were not cherry bombs; they were gunfire. Anyway, he was trying to keep us calm."[83]

Brower had not really been afraid while walking around the Lyceum at the beginning of the riot earlier in the evening, even when someone threw a Molotov cocktail. Only later did she consider that bullets had whizzed past her in the dark as she and Humber walked home. "At the time I didn't think about that bullet could have hit me."[84] One of the two killed that night, Ray Gunter, a twenty-three-year old repairman, was shot dead in The Grove. Neither woman knew if it had happened before or after they walked through on their way home.

## EDITORIALS: TAKING A STAND AGAINST VIOLENCE

The editorials brought Brower acclaim from around the country but also condemnation from the student senate. She noted in an editorial before the riot that "the Meredith case is the most serious event that the state has experienced since Mississippi's decision to secede from the Union" before the Civil War.[85] Yet, she still did not realize that she was participating in a historical event. "I just felt like I had a job to do and that was reporting what was happening and appealing to civility,"[86] she said.

A call for peace and civility was the focus of more than one editorial she wrote that semester, including the one that appeared the morning following the riot. The short, six-paragraph piece, titled "Violence will not help," urged anyone participating in the unrest "to return to your home. . . . No matter what your convictions, you should follow the advice of Governor Ross Barnett by not taking any action for violence." Seeking a peaceful campus was just one of her concerns, however. Rioting students could be jeopardizing their education, she pointed out. According to a note that immediately followed Brower's editorial on the page, "Any student caught participating in demonstrations or engaging in a riotous manner may be subject to expulsion, reminded Judicial Council Chairman Jack Lynch." And there was the image concern: "They [rioters] are bringing dishonor and shame to the University and to the State of Mississippi."[87]

Her editorial was picked up by various publications and won praise across the country. It was in sharp contrast to a few days earlier when she had commended students for their "mature behavior" and for exhibiting "intelligent logic and reasoning in most of their actions" as tension was building on campus. At that point before the riot, except for a few students who wanted to make trouble, "there were no demonstrations or loud outbursts of adverse opinions."[88] She feared that if students got out of hand, the governor would be forced to close down the university, which could jeopardize the educational plans of all the students.[89]

Even after the riot, Brower and her editors continued to plead with students to act peacefully. After denying charges that she had been brainwashed by the federal government, she wrote in an editorial, "it is sad, indeed, when supposedly educated people must be reminded that rioting and violence do not help any cause but bring humiliation to all concerned."[90] A week later the staff joined her in an editorial supporting the university officials and student body officers in condemning the violence and demonstrations. "The problem now at hand is one of academic nature—returning to the education of the student body as the ultimate goal of the University of Mississippi."[91]

By December, Brower had written thirteen editorials that she had signed with just her last name attached as a tag line at the end. Eight of these related to the behavior of students. She castigated students for poor behavior several times, and praised the faculty and alumni for doing more to help the university through the crisis. She touted a scholarship fund the newspaper was setting up to honor the dead French reporter. Near the end of October, she voiced her unflagging faith that the students had come to their senses. "The students, for the most part, have awaken and realized the damage that was done to the prestige of their University and do not wish for this to continue," she wrote.

Then, not for the last time, she responded to some of the criticism she was receiving in letters to the editor, particularly one that called her a traitor because of the editorial she wrote the night of the riot. "As I see and as I saw the situation, I am far from being a traitor to the South when I deplore the violent demonstrations that resulted in the death of two men and the injury of many others," she wrote. Then she stated the obvious: "Although many students do not approve of integration, the fact remains that the school has been desegregated with the entrance of James Meredith to Ole Miss. . . . more than likely Meredith is here to stay."

Finally, apparently responding to charges that she was acting at the behest of others, she declared, "I have not received any pressure or instructions from anyone as to what I should or should not write. I have recorded my own thoughts, mainly the theme that violent demonstrations do not aid the cause."[92] A week later, Brower again chastised protesters outside Meredith's dorm who continued to harass the marshals and soldiers who were stationed on campus to keep the peace, but she also chided the administration for not enforcing their "get tough" policy by letting these actions continue without consequences, noting that removing the few troublemakers would allow the campus to get on with more important matters.[93]

Brower did not write another editorial until just before Thanksgiving. "Just what rights do Ole Miss students have?" she asked as she began one of her longer pieces. Her editorial was also in part the only news report about an incident that had occurred the previous Thursday night. A group of students had eaten in the cafeteria with Meredith, and later two of them found their rooms ransacked and their clothing and other items destroyed. Again she chided the administration for not taking actions to stop the few troublemakers while an overwhelming number of students "are making an almost desperate attempt to study. But how can they study when they must live in fear of physical damage if they disagree to some extent with the rougher groups." Besides, she pointed out, "It seems that if Ole Miss is to remain a true university and keep its scholars, all students should have the right to associate with whom they please and be able to say what they please without the fear of being chastised."[94]

The editorial was the proverbial straw that broke the camel's back. That night, the Tuesday before Thanksgiving, the student senate considered a resolution to censure Brower.[95] Humber remembers that day as one of the worst in her life. Both she and Brower had been told to appear before the senate to answer questions about the newspaper and their coverage of the riot. Humber recalls being grilled by the senators. "To this day, if I get into a large gathering where people start to shout and become hostile, I will break out in a sweat," Humber said. "I will get very, very nervous. I still don't even like to talk about that night. I was screamed at. I was threatened. It was just an absolutely horrible experience." Finally, one of the senators, Gerald

Blessey, spoke up and called a halt to it. He then walked her back to her sorority house. "I just remember I was really almost in shock," Humber said. "I was terrified. It was absolutely horrible. To tell you the truth, I was more frightened that night than I was the night of the riot."[96] The senate took no action that night and the matter was referred to the Student Activities Committee for consideration.[97]

On the Monday after Thanksgiving, Brower attended the next meeting of the activities committee and once again found herself addressing criticisms of her work. Among the charges, the senators accused her of "committing a grave, reprehensible, almost inconceivable injustice to her fellow students," of failing to take a position on issues, of editorializing "contrary to belief," of "neglecting to stand up for the rights of the majority of the student body and with neglecting to fulfill her responsibility to the student body," and of printing only letters that were favorable to her position.[98] The senators were correct on one point: she had not taken a position for or against integration. "Even though I personally thought James Meredith had a right to be there, I did not see that saying that would help the situation," she said. "It would probably only make matters worse. Basically my editorials were appealing to law and order, saying 'don't riot boys.'"[99]

The complaint about the letters to the editor that the newspaper ran was certainly unfounded. Brower received more than a thousand letters from all over the country and only a few from Mississippi or campus. The overwhelming majority were supportive of her editorial position. Those that were unfavorable were almost always unsigned and often were obscene, so they could not be run because the newspaper had a policy against considering any letter that was too long, unsigned (though the name was withheld from many letters) or considered "immoral, indecent or libelous."[100] The committee demanded to see these letters and Brower agreed to bring them to a meeting on Thursday night. Complying with that request required an 80-mile trip to her home in Memphis, Tennessee. Because her desk at the newspaper office was in an open area and accessible by anyone who came into the office, Brower had started taking the letters to her room at the sorority house for safekeeping. When the stacks became overwhelming there, she took them home. She piled the letters into a large garbage can and brought them back to campus for the senate to peruse.[101]

The Thursday night meeting was too late for the Friday morning paper's deadline, so it was not reported until the next issue, Tuesday. The Student Activities Committee reframed the resolution and sent it on to the full Senate for review Tuesday night.[102] A report on that Tuesday meeting appeared in the Thursday morning paper. The lengthy meeting was even longer as the senators debated letting two TV cameramen in. Finally, they allowed everyone to attend. Senators voted 63–27 to reprimand rather than censure Brower, which many feared would be misconstrued as "censoring" the newspaper and

open the group up to criticism for doing so. The last sentence of the resolution was meant to allay that criticism: "This resolution is not to be construed
as being opposed to editorial freedom—this Senate upholds that privilege for
our campus newspaper—and recognizes the said editor's stand of deploring
violence as a right and just one." The resolution accused Brower of "failure
in time of grave crisis to represent and uphold the rights of her fellow students" by not protesting the use of tear gas, not countering the national press
that distorted what was happening on campus, and not taking a position on
integration. [103]

The real heart of the issue, Brower said, was that people were upset if the
newspaper presented both sides of an issue. "That I think is what caused the
censure," she said. "They didn't think I should be doing that. I should be
upholding Southern traditions, whatever they meant by that. I guess that I
should have supported segregation. Instead I was trying to get the students to
see what the outside world thought."

The idea that she should do something to straighten out the professional
media who got it wrong baffled her. "They were the ones causing the problem, not I," she explained. "I don't know how I could straighten them
out." [104] Almost three months later the student senate passed a bill that would
give them the power to impeach the student editor, though they never used it
with Brower. [105]

Following the reprimand, Brower only wrote a handful of editorials. One
in January appeared after Meredith announced he was leaving the university
because of the harassment. (He later changed his mind and graduated that
August.) She questioned Meredith's decision to get into the once all-white
school only to leave it a few months later. She ended with the question that
she had always hoped to answer if she had interviewed him: "What then was
James Meredith's purpose in entering Ole Miss?" [106] Fifty-five years later,
she still wonders.

## REPORTING INTEGRATION

Following the riot, *The Mississippian* coverage of Meredith, integration and
the hundreds of troops occupying the campus was minimal. Clearly the editors were taking a "less is better" approach: the less the newspaper focused
on it, the better the situation would become. The plan was evident in the first
issue after the riot. The whereabouts of Meredith—the subject of the riot in
the first place—was barely mentioned near the end of the main story. He had
been safely stashed in his dorm room with guards at the door throughout the
riot. [107] In fact, after the first couple of days, Meredith was seldom mentioned
in new stories during his entire time on campus though letters to the editor
discussed him. Tuesday's front page was entirely about the riot aftermath and

Meredith's first day on campus. It included a picture of him on his way to a history class. [108] A story accompanied the photo and detailed the names of the two dead, the continuing unrest, the current status of the campus, and the fact that most of those arrested were not Ole Miss students. It also included the report that Meredith attended his first history class the day after the riot even though most of the students who returned to campus stayed away, so many classes were canceled. [109] A second story described the troops searching any vehicle entering campus, which resulted in arrests and confiscation of weapons. [110]

The next day, a story quoting from a press conference Meredith held told his views on his treatment so far. [111] Mild disruptions went unreported in the paper. However, at the end of October, a large, one-hour demonstration outside Meredith's dorms made the paper. [112] The chancellor's response to the demonstration received top play two days later with a skyline head above the nameplate and a two-column story down the right side, warning students that swift, harsh action would be taken against anyone who participated in further violence. [113] The chancellor reiterated that warning in January after a student was suspended for protesting. [114]

A few stories addressed the concern that the accreditation of Ole Miss was in jeopardy because of what had been happening at the campus. A story after Thanksgiving announced that the accreditation had not been pulled but warned it was still possible. The full statement from the accrediting commission followed. [115] Two weeks later, the newspaper reported that the Association of American Law Schools was threatening the accreditation of the Ole Miss School of Law. [116]

After the riot on September 30, many people and organizations issued formal statements, such as a group of professors, the chancellor, the dean, student body officers, the academic council, and Mississippi congressmen. Rather than try to interpret the statements or create stories based on them, the editors chose to run most of the statements verbatim, allowing readers to figure out what it all meant. The practice was the result of the small staff the newspaper had putting out the paper every day. As the newspaper became more of a target, fewer students wanted to work on it. "We lost a lot of staff members. It was not necessarily a pleasant or safe thing to be on the newspaper staff. So we didn't have but a few staff members," Humber said. [117]

At least one story the students pursued never made the paper because it turned out to be nothing but a rumor. Humber said she received several telephone calls from students wanting to know why *The Mississippian* had suppressed a story about a coed being shot the night of the riot. The callers claimed the story had appeared in the student's hometown paper. Humber and fellow staffer Ed Williams started calling all the hospitals in the area and some farther away but could not find such a coed. Finally, Humber convinced someone in the registrar's office to give her the girl's home telephone number. When she called, the girl answered the phone and said she had been at home since before the riot and had decided not to return to campus. [118]

The newspaper seldom reported anything to do with troops on campus. Generally, anyone reading the paper without knowing the troops were there would think they had not stayed around campus after the September riot. In fact, the last troops left the campus the following June, [119] which was one of the few reports about them that ever appeared in the student newspaper.

Freedom of expression became an issue early in 1963. The controversy began when art professor Ray Kerciu had a showing of five of the works he had painted following the riot. The art pieces were inspired by the racial conflicts of the riots and included a Confederate flag. Complaints from the Mississippi Citizens Council and the United Daughters of the Confederacy forced campus officials to remove the oil paintings. Students protested the action, [120] including a law student who filed a lawsuit claiming the work was obscene and indecent as well as desecrating of the Confederate flag. [121] A number of letters followed, both for and against the artist's work. Brower tackled the issue in one of her longer editorials. She pointed out that the desecration claim was ambiguous and that Kerciu was only representing his own impressions. "If anyone violated the sanctity of the flag of the Confederacy, a nation which no longer exists except in the minds of men, the villain was the one who rioted on the night of September 30, 1962." She ended by questioning if the university planned to suppress all expressions that do not agree with certain groups. [122]

## REPERCUSSIONS

Though the letters of support poured into *The Mississippian* office from all over the country, not everyone on campus was thrilled with what the student newspaper was doing, and some made sure the staff knew about their displeasure. Humber and Brower never wrote about the repercussions they encountered, but they certainly remember them. The first came for Humber the night of the riot. When she finally arrived at her sorority house after putting the paper to bed, she found the other sorority sisters watching Governor Ross Barnett on television. "He was talking about what was happening on campus, talking about how horrible it was that these terrible marshals had opened fire on helpless coeds, and had come on with their guns, just a complete fabrication," she recalled. "I said, 'He's lying! That's not what happened. He's lying!'" A good friend, whose room was just across the hall from Humber's room, was appalled that she would call the governor a liar. Humber told her friend that the governor had been in Jackson the whole time and not on campus, so he did not know what was really happening. "She never spoke to me again," Humber said, noting that her friend and several other sorority sisters refused to ever sit at the same table for meals or have anything to do with her.[123]

Humber found herself in a similar situation during the Thanksgiving holidays. The false reports from the governor, other officials, and the media convinced her to stay on campus throughout the semester. "I did not leave the campus from the day of the riot until the Thanksgiving holidays because I was absolutely determined that I was going to stay there, and I was going to cover and to watch whatever happened. . . . I would bear witness to what actually happened because, as I said, I just saw so many things happening." She finally went home for the Thanksgiving break. Her father, who had tried after the riot to convince her to leave Ole Miss and finish school in Florida, talked to her again about leaving because the governor had made the conditions at the school seem so terrible. "I cannot believe that you would believe what this man said. I cannot believe you are standing up for a liar and a fool," Humber remembered telling her father. He raised his hand to slap her, then dropped it and walked out of the room. "I never again discussed with my father one thing that happened at Ole Miss."[124]

Brower also had problems at the Kappa Kappa Gamma sorority house where she lived. A couple of girls with rooms at the top of the stairs would spit on her when she was walking up to her room. "So I soon learned to just go up the back stairs," she said. At a sorority reunion a few years so, "one of the girls apologized to me and said if she had known then what she knows now, she would never have said the things about me that she did." Members of the Kappa Alpha sorority circulated a petition to impeach Brower as editor, and one night asked Brower's best friend, who was the Kappa Gamma president, to sign the petition and get others in the house to sign as well. No one at Kappa Gamma signed the petition.[125]

Both the women faced name calling and other reprisals when they were walking on campus. Humber said several members of the campus Senate would spit on the ground in front of her. One in particular went out of his way to do it. Anonymous, threatening phone calls in the middle of the night were also a problem.[126] One male student followed Brower around campus, yelling at her and making wild accusations about the NAACP paying her way at Ole Miss. Some of the harassment was from off campus, too. "One radio station down in Jackson was saying things like I was sleeping with James Meredith," Brower said. That made her father furious and he wanted to sue, but a lawyer talked him out of it.[127]

The Mississippi Citizens Council and other groups were not happy with the integration at Ole Miss. Brower saw that displeasure first hand. One day, in the middle of a history exam, she was called out by a man in uniform and escorted to the alumni house conference room where "a bunch of, to me, old white men" were sitting. She was led to believe they were members of the white supremacist Citizens' Council. They grilled her about what she had done, why she had written the editorials and other pieces, and she answered them honestly. Her history professor, who was not supportive of her work on the newspaper, refused to let her continue with the exam, and instead made her retake another exam on another day all by herself.[128]

Brower's parents were supportive of what she was doing, even though they worried about her and also felt some repercussions. The night of the riot, as they watched television news from their home in Memphis and learned about what was happening at Ole Miss, they saw a car on fire and feared it was their daughter's. The jammed phone lines made it impossible to connect with her until morning to make sure she was OK. They also got a number of nasty phone calls. Brower was concerned that what she was doing would adversely affect her father's dairy and food supply business, most of which was carried on in northern Mississippi. "He told me not to worry about it, write what I thought was right," she said. Years later, while cleaning out her parents' home, she found a bunch of letters from her father's customers, all agreeing with what his daughter was doing at Ole Miss but afraid to say so publicly because of the problems it would make for them. Generally, her parents did not tell her about any problems they faced though her father made sure to stop in to see her regularly on campus to make sure she was safe because he was more worried than he was letting on.[129]

Humber's parents were less supportive, however. After the riot, her father called her repeatedly, asking her to leave Ole Miss and transfer to the University of Florida where her uncle was the Dean of Men. But she would not leave. "My mother called me up during all of this and said, 'I'm very proud of you for staying there and for sticking by your guns.' She said, 'You do what you feel like you've got to do.'" She said she never knew if her father, who was a farmer, ever had problems because of what she did. After the Thanksgiving incident, "we never discussed it again."[130]

## DO STUDENT NEWSPAPERS DO A GOOD JOB?

One criticism often leveled against student newspapers is that they just do not do a very good job of covering the issues.[131] Even if such an assessment is true, students work hard to do the best job possible. Brower said she tried to make sure the issues were being explained in the stories and in her editorials.[132] Humber said the criticism is not valid for either of the two student newspapers she worked on, first at Stephens College and then at the University of Mississippi. "In both cases, the student writers and reporters really made it their business to be well informed, to know what was going on in the world around them, and then also to find out what was going on around campus." She acknowledged that it is often difficult for staffers to do the best job, especially when they are also trying to be good students. The students faced the challenge of not being taken seriously, which meant they were often not invited to official press conferences and briefings when their professional counterparts were. "I may not have done the very best job that anyone could do," Humber said, "but I did my darnedest to find out what was going on, and I did my darnedest to be there as an eye witness and honestly report what I saw."[133]

Brower won a number of honors for her work on the newspaper that year. The first came less than two weeks after the riot when the Scripps Howard newspaper chain awarded her an internship with any Scripps Howard newspaper in the country[134]; she eventually picked New York City.[135] In January, someone in New York nominated Brower for a Pulitzer Prize in editorial writing.[136] Brower said she was criticized unfairly for publicizing the nomination. In fact, it was other staff members who opened the mail and wrote the story. "I was shocked that I was even nominated," she said. "Actually, I kept praying that I wouldn't get it because I thought, here I am a college senior and if I get a Pulitzer Prize, where can I go from here?" She had to prepare a portfolio to submit to the judges, and in June 2011 she donated that portfolio, along with the hundreds of letters to the editor she had received in 1962, to the Ole Miss archives.[137] In February 1963 she won a distinguished service award in student journalism at the Fifth International Affairs Conference in New York City where she served on a panel about freedom and responsibility of the student press.[138] The newspaper also garnered praise that year, including being singled out in *The Publishers' Auxiliary* publication as "one of the most striking college dailies in the United States."[139]

## CONCLUSION

During a panel discussion to mark the 100th birthday of *The Mississippian*, former editors Sidna Brower Mitchell and James "Jimmy" Robertson both said they thought the *The Mississippian* was the freest newspaper in the state in the 1960s.[140] Though certainly not all the professional newspapers in the state supported upholding such Southern values as segregation, many did just that, probably because they believed that if they took any other stand, their readership would rebel and the newspaper would cease to exist. Because of the generally hands-off approach the administration at Ole Miss had with the student newspaper, *The Mississippian* editors thought they could push the boundaries that many of their professional Mississippi counterparts were reluctant to attempt. However, despite what readers might have been inferring from what appeared in the student newspaper, the editors never took a position on integration, even though they all had strong personal convictions about it. Their decision not to support nor oppose integration explicitly was seen by many as tacit approval. Certainly the student Senate thought as much when they reprimanded Brower. The senators held the belief that although Brower should be allowed to express her own opinions, she also had a duty as an elected representative of the student body to represent opinions of the general student body. That becomes a thorny issue, however. Truly representing student opinions on every small issue would require regular, comprehensive surveys, which would be impossible to manage, and surely there would never be total harmony on any one issue anyway. So perhaps representing student opinions then becomes a matter of representing any opinions of any students, and as one of the students, surely the editor's opinion was as valid as was her decisions on which letters-to-the-editor to run.

However, the student senate did not see it that way. There is no indication from the newspaper stories about the senate reaction to the letters after Brower brought more than a thousand letters she had received for them to peruse. Apparently they were not swayed by the overwhelming number that supported the newspaper's position and congratulated Brower. Nor did they seem to consider that few of the letters came from current students and again were mostly supportive. They went ahead with the reprimand. Forty years later, in 2002, the student senate lifted it. [141]

Though the editors thought they were free from being told what they could or could not write, they did face pressure in some ways. Administrators had an influence over what was written in the early issues of the paper during September 1962. Officials who met regularly with Brower could steer the discussion one way or another, providing information they thought students should know and holding back information they did not want the newspaper to pursue. Brower does not believe that was the case, but still, when judging the validity of a story, one must consider the sources as well as any agenda a source might have for presenting information in the way he or she does or for even omitting information.

The influence of one professor, Dr. James Silver, kept Brower from ever conducting an interview with James Meredith. She saw that as a wise move, one that would keep the campus calm in a time of crisis. Indeed, among her responsibilities as editor, Brower believed she had a duty to foster peace and civility on campus. She not only encouraged peace in her writing, she practiced it by making editorial decisions designed to promote civility. That included such moves as not voicing an opinion on integration, agreeing to publish the special edition that administrators had planned as a vehicle for calming the student body (but then later for reporting the riot) and then toning down the reporting afterward that might only cause more problems. At one point, Brower ran an editorial from another student newspaper that detailed the responsibilities of a campus newspaper, including the responsibility to take a stand on all issues important to the campus. Brower never did that and never regretted doing so. It was a decision that probably saved the campus from more violence and her from more reprisals than the ones she suffered.

Besides not interviewing Meredith and not reporting most of the harassment he suffered, the editors' low key approach included mostly ignoring the troops on campus and not questioning their continued presence. Surely, the mere presence of hundreds of uniformed men would have created or inspired many stories throughout the year, but only a few were ever written. Again, this decision not to actively pursue stories about Meredith, the marshals who guarded him at all times, and the troops stationed on campus was one that probably prevented further violence. Students regularly harassed the men in various ways, such as name calling, and if the newspaper had been reporting more about these things, such behavior would be encouraged not squelched. Still, it also meant student reporters were not digging more into the issues like the cost of keeping the troops on campus and not more fully reporting on the real impact integration had. It was a price the editors thought was worth paying to keep the peace.

Neither Brower nor Humber believe the repercussions they suffered affected their work or their decisions about the newspaper, but harassment they faced—from other students and even from the few people who wrote negative letters—had to increase the stress they felt. The student senate actions were particularly difficult for Humber, creating a situation for her that today would be labeled post-traumatic stress disorder. No other stories carried her byline throughout the year, though having a small staff required that she write a lot of stories. Interestingly, Brower, who had nightmares for years, wrote only a few editorials after the Senate decision. It may not have been a direct result of the reprimand as she became involved in other projects and spent a lot more time away from campus, but on the surface it appears there may be a connection. She was not the first editor reprimanded by the student Senate, either. During the previous school year, her predecessor, Jimmy Robertson, faced a similar situation because of his editorials, particularly those calling for an end to the "unwritten rule" that Mississippi all-white college teams could not play integrated teams and therefore could not participate in national championship games.

Outsiders looking in at *The Mississippian* can see a lot of flaws in the work of student editors and reporters, especially if one compares their work to professional journalists. It is, however, an unfair comparison, much like comparing apples and oranges; they may both be fruit, or newspapers in this case, but that is about all the similarity that exists. Like their professional counterparts, student journalists generally work hard to produce a quality newspaper with the best resources available. Still, they face issues that the professionals do not. For one, the time and space constraints were very different. Being newspaper staffers has never been a students' first job—they are students first and foremost, even though some might fudge on the class performance to do their newspaper work. Many student staffers were unpaid or received remuneration for their work. Brower recalled that she received about $100 a month as editor.

Access also became a key issue. Oxford, Mississippi, is a rather remote location when considering that much of the integration news was taking place in offices located in Jackson or courtrooms as far away as New Orleans, all far removed from the campus in a time when dial-up telephone service had just begun in Oxford. Also, until the following spring, *The Mississippian* did not have access to wire services, so they could not rely on that avenue for information. Even when events occurred on campus, the student press was often excluded or not informed about the meetings and press conferences. Thus, obtaining information about events first hand was not an easy matter for these students.

No matter the criticism that might be leveled at *The Mississippian* or the editors during 1962–1963, they certainly were practicing what Humber noted has become expected at Ole Miss: "*The Daily Mississippian* has a tradition of following their own drummer and trying as best they can to get the whole story and to get the truth. It has been an independent voice"[142] and remains one today.

* * *

Sidna Brower Mitchell went on to work in New York, London, and other areas after she graduated from Ole Miss. She and her late husband owned several weekly newspapers in New Jersey for twenty-five years. She retired as deputy director of New Jersey Council on Affordable Housing (COAH), a controversial state agency. Though she no longer owns any newspapers, she does continue to live in New Jersey and occasionally still writes cooking columns she started more than thirty-five years ago.

* * *

After graduation, Lillian Janette "Jan" Humber Robertson married James "Jimmy" Robertson, who attended law school at Harvard and eventually went on to become a Mississippi Supreme Court judge. They later divorced. She wrote for the *Delta Democrat Times* just before outspoken journalist Hodding Carter left there, did freelance work, and edited the Ole Miss Alumni Review as well as a magazine. She died November 16, 2014.

## NOTES

1. "What Press Censorship Looks Like," Foundation for Individual Rights in Education, accessed March 14, 2017 https://www.thefire.org/resources/student-press/.

2. Frank LoMonte, "Viewpoint: Student Newspapers Are Struggling with Their First Amendment Rights," *USA Today College*, February 1, 2017, accessed March 14, 2017 http://college.usatoday.com/2017/02/01/college-newspapers-free-speech/.

3. "The Legislation," *New Voices USA*, accessed March 14, 2017 http://newvoicesus.com/the-legislation/.

4. Wayne Overbeck and Genelle Belmas, "Freedom of the Student Press," *Major Principles of Media Law, Centgage Learning* (Boston, MA) 2013: 613.

5. Jan Humber, telephone interview by author, October 22, 2011.

6. "No Statement on Meredith," *The Mississippian* (Oxford, MS), September 18, 1962: 1.

7. Sidna Brower, telephone interview by author, September 15, 2011.

8. Examples include the following: Russell H. Barrett, *Integration at Ole Miss* (Chicago: Quadrangle Books, 1965); Frank Lambert, *The Battle of Ole Miss: Civil Rights v. States' Rights* (New York: Oxford University Press, 2010); Charles W. Eagles, *The Price of Defiance: James Meredith and the Integration of Ole Miss* (Chapel Hill: University of North Carolina Press, 2009); Henry T. Gallagher, *James Meredith and the Ole Miss Riot: A Soldier's Story* (Jackson, MS: University Press of Mississippi, 2012); Nadine Cohodas, *The Band Played Dixie: Race and the Liberal Conscience at Ole Miss* (New York: Free Press, 1997).

9. Walter Lord, *The Past That Would Not Die* (New York: Harper and Row, 1965), 251.

10. Humber, interview.

11. James W. Silver, "Mississippi: The Closed Society," *The Journal of Southern History* 30, no. 1 (February 1964): 7.

12. Ibid., 3–5.

13. Special to *The Mississippian*, "Meredith Gains Short Cut – Ruling 'Favorable,'" *The Mississippian* (Oxford, MS), January 25, 1962: 1.

14. Jacob Batte, "1911–2011: A History of *The Daily Mississippian,*" *The DM Online*, accessed June 15, 2011, http://www.thedmonline.com/article/1911–2011-history-daily-mississippian.

15. "Dates Changed," *The Mississippian* (Oxford, MS), October 17, 1961: 1.

16. Humber, interview.

17. Batte, "1911–2011."

18. David G. Sansing, *The University of Mississippi: A Sesquicentennial History* (Jackson, MS: University Press of Mississippi, 1999), 159.

19. Brower, interview.

20. Dr. Jere Hoar, telephone interview by author, November 8, 2011.

21. Humber, interview.

22. Batte, "1911–2011."

23. Brower, interview.

24. Humber, interview.

25. "Campus Paper Lauded: Only College Daily," *The Mississippian* (Oxford, MS), June 7, 1963: 7.

26. James Lawton, "Jimmy" Robertson, email to author, September 15, 2011.

27. James Lawton "Jimmy" Robertson, "Mississippian at 100 – 1950s and '60s" panel discussion, accessed September 15, 2011, http://blip.tv/mcast/mississippian-at-100-panel-1950s-and-60s-5357428.

28. Brower, interview.

29. "Campus Paper Lauded."

30. Ibid.

31. "Paper begins UPI service," *The Mississippian* (Oxford, MS), April 9, 1963: 3.

32. Brower, interview; Robertson, email.

33. Humber, interview.

34. Brower, interview.

35. Sidna Brower, "Editor Comments," *The Mississippian* (Oxford, MS), October 23, 1962: 2.

36. "Editorial responsibility," *The Mississippian* (Oxford, MS), October 30, 1962: 4.

37. Barrett, *Integration at Ole Miss*, 156.

38. Robertson, email.

39. Brower, interview.

40. Ibid.

41. Humber, interview.

42. Brower, interview.

43. Humber, interview.

44. "Silver Writes on States' Rights: Faculty Opinion," *The Mississippian* (Oxford, MS), October 9, 1962: 2.

45. "Mississippi: The Closed Society," *Time* magazine, November 15, 1963, accessed September 26, 2011, http://www.time.com/time/magazine/ article/0,9171,873156,00.html.

46. James W. Silver, *Mississippi: The Closed Society* (New York: Harcourt, Brace & World, 1963).

47. Silver, "Mississippi: The Closed Society."

48. "James W. Silver, 81, a Professor Who Fought for Racial Equality" obituary, *The New York Times*, July 26, 1988, accessed September 26, 2011, http://www.nytimes.com/1988/07/26/obituaries/james-w-silver-81-a-professor-who-fought-for-racial-equality.html?src=pm.

49. See Barrett, *Integration*; "UM tribute set for Professor James W. Silver," *Zing*, accessed September 26, 2011, http://zing.olemiss.edu/um-tribute-set-for-professor-james-w-silver-2/; Brower, interview.

50. Brower, interview.

51. "Meredith Speaks Out: U.M. Negro Gives Views," *The Mississippian* (Oxford, MS), May 10, 1963: 3.

52. "Oxford Prepares for Dials as Telephone Company Expands," *The Mississippian* (Oxford, MS), January 12, 1961: 1.

53. "Meredith the Man," *The Mississippian* (Oxford, MS), February 9, 1962: 1.

54. "Rebel Underground Attacks Newspaper," *The Mississippian* (Oxford, MS), February 13, 1962: 1.

55. "Rebel Underground?" *The Mississippian* (Oxford, MS), February 13, 1962: 2.

56. The University of Mississippi Library, Integration of the University of Mississippi digital collection, includes several issues of the *Rebel Underground*. The description: "The Rebel Underground stressed segregation and states' rights. The anonymously, irregularly published paper typically attacked James Meredith, Russell Barrett, James Silver, the federal government, Civil Rights groups, Communication and *The Daily Mississippian.*" Accessed September 29, 2011, http://clio.lib.olemiss.edu/cdm/search/collection/integration.

57. Brower, interview.

58. "Meredith Jailed in Jackson: Accused of Oath Violation," *The Mississippian* (Oxford, MS), June 8, 1962: 1.

59. "Path Cleared for Mandate: Federal Court Tells District to Clear the Way for Negro," *The Mississippian* (Oxford, MS), July 18 1962: 1.

60. Sidna Brower, "Editorial Questioned," *The Mississippian* (Oxford, MS), September 20, 1962: 1.

61. Brower, interview.

62. Ibid.

63. "Let the Adjectives Flow," *Jackson* (MS) *Daily News*, September 19, 1962: 1.

64. Brower, "Editorial Questioned."

65. Jimmy Ward, "Covering the Crossroads with Jimmy Ward," *Jackson* (MS) *Daily News,* September 22, 1962: 1.

66. "Editor's Comment," *The Mississippian* (Oxford, MS), September 25, 1962: 4.

67. Brower, interview.

68. "Editor's Comment," September 25, 1962.

69. Brower, interview.

70. See Barrett, *Integration*, 125; Walter Lord, *The Past That Would Not Die* (New York: Harper & Row, 1965), 167.

71. "Chancellor Issues Plea," *The Mississippian* (Oxford, MS), October 1, 1962: 1.

72. Humber, interview.

73. "Marshals Wore Revolvers," *The Clarion-Ledger* (Jackson, MS), October 3, 1962: 1.

74. Humber, interview.

75. Ibid.

76. Jan Humber, "Death, Injuries from Campus Rioting," *The Mississippian* (Oxford, MS), October 1, 1962: 1.

77. The story was repeated in Lord, *The Past That Would Not Die,* 153.

78. Humber, interview.

79. Ibid.

80. Brower, interview.

81. Ibid.

82. Humber, interview.

83. Ibid.

84. Bower, interview.

85. Brower, "Editor's Comments," September 25, 1962.

86. Brower, interview.

87. Sidna Brower, "Violence Will Not Help," *The Mississippian* (Oxford, MS), October 1, 1962: 2.

88. Sidna Brower, "To Ole Miss Students," *The Mississippian* (Oxford, MS), September 21, 1962: 1.

89. Brower, "Editor's Comments," September 25, 1962.

90. Sidna Brower, "Editor's Comment," *The Mississippian* (Oxford, MS), October 10, 1962: 2.

91. "Mississippian Staff Supports Statements," *The Mississippian* (Oxford, MS), October 16, 1962: 4.

92. Brower, "Editor Comments," *The Mississippian* (Oxford, MS), October 23, 1962: 2.

93. Sidna Brower, "UM 'Get Tough Policy' Appears Lost in Crowd," *The Mississippian* (Oxford, MS) October 31, 1962: 2.

94. Sidna Brower, "Editor's Comments – on Students' Right," *The Mississippian* (Oxford, MS), November 20, 1962: 2.

95. John Corlew, "Senate Discusses Editor: Postpone Action," *The Mississippian* (Oxford, MS), November 27, 1962: 1.

96. Humber, interview.

97. Corlew, "Senate Discusses Editor."

98. John Corlew, "Senate Committee Discusses Editor," *The Mississippian* (Oxford, MS), November 28, 1962: 1.

99. Brower, interview.

100. Corlew, "Senate Committee Discusses Editor."

101. Brower, interview.

102. John Corlew, "Decision on Editor to Come Tonight," *The Mississippian* (Oxford, MS), December 4, 1962: 1.

103. "Text of Resolution," *The Mississippian* (Oxford, MS), December 6, 1962: 1.

104. Brower, interview.

105. John Corlew, "Senate Votes 33–19 on Impeachment Bill," *The Mississippian* (Oxford, MS), February 28, 1963: 1.

106. Sidna Brower, "Editor's Comments," *The Mississippian* (Oxford, MS), January 8, 1963: 4.

107. Humber, "Death, Injuries," 4.

108. "First Day in Class," *The Mississippian* (Oxford, MS), October 2, 1962: 1.

109. Sidna Brower, "Troops Surround Ole Miss," *The Mississippian* (Oxford, MS), October 2, 1962: 1.

110. "Troops Conduct Auto Searches, Make Arrests," *The Mississippian* (Oxford, MS), October 2, 1962: 1.

111. "Meredith Gives Views on Treatment So Far," *The Mississippian* (Oxford, MS), October 3, 1962: 1.

112. Ed Williams, "Mob Demonstrates at Meredith's Dorm," *The Mississippian* (Oxford, MS), October 31, 1962: 1.

113. "Chancellor Speaks Firmly: Men Hear Talk Promising Action," *The Mississippian* (Oxford, MS), November 2, 1962: 1.

114. "Chancellor Requests Ending to Agitation," *The Mississippian* (Oxford, MS), January 16, 1963: 1.

115. "Commission Gives UM Extraordinary Status," *The Mississippian* (Oxford, MS), November 29, 1962: 1.

116. "Group Question Law School Standing: Hearing During Holidays," *The Mississippian* (Oxford, MS), December 18, 1962: 1.

117. Jan Humber, interview by author, November 11, 2011.

118. Humber, interview, October 22, 2011.

119. "300 Troops Removed from UM Campus," *The Mississippian* (Oxford, MS), June 12, 1963: 3.

120. "Pickets Protest Art Ban: Removal of Paintings Stirs Student Protest," *The Mississippian* (Oxford, MS), April 9, 1963: 1.

121. "Blackwell Files Against Kerciu for Paintings," *The Mississippian* (Oxford, MS), April 9, 1963: 2.

122. Sidna Brower, "Editor's Comments," *The Mississippian* (Oxford, MS), April 9, 1963: 4.

123. Humber, interview, October 22, 2011.

124. Ibid.

125. Brower, interview.

126. Humber, interview, October 22, 2011.

127. Brower, interview.

128. Ibid.

129. Ibid.

130. Humber, interview, October 22, 2011.

131. Clifford Wilcox, "Antiwar Dissent in the College Press: The Universities of Illinois and Michigan" in *Sights on the Sixties,* Barbara L. Tischler, ed. (New Brunswick, NJ: Rutgers University Press, 1992).

132. Brower, interview.

133. Humber, interview, October 22, 2011.

134. "Sidna Brower Earns Award for Journalism," *The Mississippian* (Oxford, MS), October 10, 1962: 1.

135. Brower, interview.

136. "Brower Nominated for Pulitzer Prize," *The Mississippian* (Oxford, MS), January 11, 1963: 1.

137. Brower, interview.

138. "Editor Receives Award: Student Conference," *The Mississippian* (Oxford, MS), February 28, 1963: 1.

139. "Campus Paper Lauded: Only College Daily," *The Mississippian* (Oxford, MS), June 7, 1963: 7.

140. Sidna Brower Mitchell and James "Jimmy" Robertson, "Mississippian at 100 – 1950s and '60s" panel discussion, June 18, 2011, accessed October 22, 2011, http://blip.tv/mcast /mississippian-at-100-panel-1950s-and-60s-5357428.

141. "Integration-Era Editor of Student Newspaper Donates Letters, Other Memorabilia to UM," *Zing,* accessed November 14, 2011, http://zing.olemiss.edu/integration-era-editor-of -student-newspaper-donates-letters-other-memorabilia-to-um/.

142. Humber, interview, October 22, 2011.

*Chapter Three*

# The Campus Conscience

J. N. Heiskell, owner and editor of the *Arkansas Gazette*, saw his newspaper win two Pulitzer's in one year for the same event: covering desegregation in Little Rock, Arkansas, in 1957. Despite his own personal belief in segregation, he also believed the newspaper must be the conscience of the community, and as such the newspaper must sometimes take stands that are right but not necessarily popular with readers.[1] Tammy Dunn, editor/general manager/ publisher of the *Montgomery Herald* in Troy, North Carolina, had similar feelings about doing the right thing when she and an assistant editor wrote a mission statement for the newspaper in the late 1990s, which states that the newspaper should be "The conscience of the community, a recorder of its history, a voice for all citizens and an advocate for good."[2]

Being the conscience of the community and doing the right thing are not always easy. And certainly that's what the staff of *The Daily Californian* found out in 1964–65 when protest came to its campus.

## COVERING THE FREE SPEECH MOVEMENT
## AT UC BERKELEY—1964

Student reporter Peter Benjaminson was in *The Daily Californian* office in Moses Hall (Old Eshleman), talking to night editor Jim Branson on October 1, 1964, when he learned about the protest in Sproul Plaza nearby. "We were going like 'what the hell? They're actually going to do it,'" Benjaminson recalled. After three weeks of fairly mild demonstrations against the administration's more strict guidelines for political activism on campus, University of California-Berkeley students had taken the most serious action so far. They had surrounded a police car brought onto the plaza to transport former student Jack Weinberg to jail for violating the activism rules. For the next

55

thirty hours, the car—with Weinberg inside—did not move. The Free Speech Movement had begun.

Benjaminson immediately went to work. He and other reporters at *The Daily Californian* student newspaper remained at the forefront of reporting on the various protests and responses for most of the school year, writing about the Free Speech Movement throughout the fall and later what was dubbed the Filthy Speech Movement in the spring term.

Through it all the student reporters and editors worked diligently to be factual and accurate, and as objective as possible. That is what fall editor Susan Johnson believed was the highest standard of good journalism, an ideal she tried to instill in her staff.[3] At the end of the semester, she identified the newspaper's role throughout the Free Speech Movement in the final editorial that she wrote as editor. She said that although she had not realized it at first, she now knew that the newspaper had been the conscience of the university—pointing out the good as well as the bad on all sides of the issues as it diligently worked to write objective news stories about the movement. Her final piece criticized both administrators and protesters for failing to communicate without strings attached, but heaped most of the blame on the students behind the Free Speech Movement because they made the administration a "faceless mechanistic bureaucracy." It was more typical of editorials throughout the semester that had often seemed skewed toward the administration even if they did not offer outright support. Johnson's final words were those of a loyal student who urged others "to keep the University in the best shape possible for student, administration and faculty alike. . . . Each of us has an investment in this University. The investment extends far beyond the four years we spend here and far beyond the corner of Bancroft Way and Telegraph Avenue."[4]

Johnson's desire to present all sides of an issue—to be the conscience of the campus—was apparent on the editorial page as well but actually resulted in more ambivalent and indecisive editorial positions. Examination of all the editorials shows the hesitancy the editors had most of the time in taking a strong stand to support the free speech issue or to get solidly behind the administration. However, they regularly called for both administration and protesters to communicate better. The three top editors who approved the editorial each day often did so without consensus. Editor Johnson and managing editor Justin Roberts usually went for the conservative position, with Roberts as the more conservative of the two, whereas assistant editor Jim Willwerth was more liberal and often disagreed with the other two. The majority overruled him.

Then a few weeks before Christmas, the paper finally took a strong stand and asked the Board of Regents not to approve unrestricted speech. Johnson and Roberts wrote the editorial piece and, in an unusual move, signed their names at the bottom. Willwerth would not go along. When a group of disgruntled staffers who sympathized with the movement approached him, Willwerth asked Johnson for permission to write a dissenting opinion that was published the next day. It is perhaps through this publishing of many viewpoints that the newspaper was able to truly become the conscience of the student community.

This chapter considers how *The Daily Californian* provided that conscience to the Berkeley campus, particularly through the daily editorials, during the Free Speech Movement of the 1964–1965 school year. This chapter also considers the news coverage of the events and tells the story of *The Daily Californian* during that time through the memories of six editors and reporters: Justin Roberts, fall managing editor and spring editor; Jim Willwerth, fall assistant editor; Peggy Krause, fall city editor and spring managing editor; Jim Branson, fall night editor/reporter and spring city editor; Peter Benjaminson, fall reporter and spring assistant city editor; John Oppedahl, spring reporter. Susan Johnson, who was editor during the fall when the movement was at its height, died in 2006 before this book was begun. Her husband, Cebe Wallace, was her boyfriend at the time she was editor and shared his remembrances of her experiences as editor.

## UNIVERSITY OF CALIFORNIA, BERKELEY

The Berkeley campus of the University of California is the flagship of the state's multiversity system. Its history begins in 1869 when the university first opened its doors in Oakland with forty students. In 1873, the university moved to Berkeley, located north of Oakland and across the bay from San Francisco. By fall 1964, the Berkeley campus enrolled more than 25,000 students. The university became a statewide system when the University of California–Los Angeles (UCLA) began in 1914. Today, the University of California has ten campuses[5] serving about 220,000 students.[6] A president, who answers to the twenty-six-member Board of Regents, sits at the head of the University of California while chancellors run individual campuses.[7] The chancellor position was created in 1952, and professor Clark Kerr, who would serve as UC president during the Free Speech Movement, was named the first chancellor at Berkeley.[8]

The Free Speech Movement in 1964 was not the first student movement the university had encountered in the twentieth century nor was it the first time the university had regulated activism. In the 1930s, a movement influenced by communism had begun. UC President Robert Gordon Sproul, who had been selected to pull the university system out of near bankruptcy during the Great Depression and who ran the university for twenty-eight years, chose to squash that activism by banning political activity from campus. Student activists handled the banning by simply moving off campus a short distance. At that time, Sather Gate with its adjoining footbridge over Straw-berry Creek was the south entrance to campus. Moving their tables outside the gate along Telegraph Avenue between Sather Gate and Bancroft Way seemed to cause little problem for the activists; they could still reach most students who passed through the area on the way to and from school every day. Even President Sproul's ban on using campus buildings for candidates' speeches did not pose much of a problem as a YMCA-owned hall nearby was readily available. Bookstores along Telegraph provided interested students with all kinds of political material, even Communist Party literature.

Then the campus began to change. Eventually, the Berkeley campus pushed its boundaries south, buying up the land along Telegraph between Sather Gate and Bancroft Way. The administration building, named Sproul Hall, was built in that area on the east side of Telegraph in 1941, and a student union was added on the other side in 1961. The road between the two buildings was closed off and became Sproul Plaza. Now Sather Gate was well inside the campus, but even that was not much of a problem because activism had died down.

Kerr, who took over the presidency of the campus in 1958, was known as a more liberal leader but still opted to enforce the old rules regarding political bans. The rules regulating political speech became known as the Kerr Direc-tives.[9] By 1964, activists had again set up outside the campus entrance, this time where Telegraph now dead-ended into Bancroft at the south entrance to campus.

The campus climate was also beginning to change in the early 1960s with the issue of power at the crux. While administrators worked to maintain the control they had tightly wielded over the university, the students were push-ing against the envelope. For decades, the concept of *in loco parentis* (literal-ly, in place of the parent) had been rigidly enforced with curfews for stu-dents, punishment by the university for civil offenses, and careful supervi-sion of extracurricular activities. "In consequence much student political activity was reminiscent of outlaw cells meeting in secret under a repressive regime,"[10] one author wrote of the time.

In 1960, one of the most notable power struggles involved *The Daily Californian* student newspaper. Of course, that was nothing new for the student newspaper that for many years had battled the Executive Committee of the Associated Students of the University of California (the student government body) over the right to print what it wanted. The ASUC wanted more control. After all, a portion of student fees that the ASUC collected was designated as a subscription fee for the student newspaper, which was then made available for free to students. The students on the newspaper staff maintained they had a duty to keep the student body informed no matter what the administration or ASUC wanted, and the ASUC believed that not be-smirching the reputation of the university should be of primary importance.

As far back as 1947, the ASUC Executive Committee had tried to control the newspaper through the creation of an advisory board that it wanted to manage the editorial and news policies of the *Daily Cal.* The newspaper fought the action at that time and won, though the issue reared its head again in 1950 when the ASUC tried once more to create an advisory board and install an adviser at the newspaper.[11]

Still battling for control in the summer of 1960, the ASUC Executive Committee, with *Daily Cal* editor Dan Silver agreeing, made changes in the newspaper's bylaws, which set up a consultative board while the Executive Committee retained the right to reject any editors selected by the Senior Editorial Board. That fall, though, the newspaper continued writing strong editorials that slammed compulsory military training for male students, the Kerr Directives, and the House Un-American Activities Committee that had been investigating Communism since the committee's creation in 1938.

Then, the day before the fall ASUC elections, the newspaper endorsed a candidate from the radical student group SLATE for the representative-at-large position in the ASUC, an unheard-of action that required at least seven of the ten-member editorial board to agree on the endorsement; the vote had been unanimous. A week later, the ASUC called a meeting to suspend both the bylaws of the newspaper and the Senior Editorial Board, claiming that the bylaws did not stop irresponsible behavior on the newspaper even though the students had carefully followed the bylaws in endorsing the candidate. The Judicial Committee halted the meeting because all the editors had not been given appropriate notice to attend. Two days later, the Executive Committee convened again to take up the matter of the newspaper. This time, fifty-six of the fifty-eight editorial staff members resigned, including the entire Senior Editorial Board.[12] The striking staffers started their own publication, *Independent Californian,* but without a sales staff and no financial backing from ASUC, it folded after a month. Less qualified students kept *The Daily Californian* afloat.[13]

By the time school started in the fall of 1964, a lot of recent changes had occurred among the Berkeley student body that led to feelings of alienation for many students. With enrollment up by about 7,000 students in a four-year span, the university was overcrowded. Salaries had slipped to the point that about one-fourth of the faculty had left. Temporary employees were filling in, and graduate teaching assistants shouldered even more of the teaching burden. Grad students made up more than one-third of the student body, and the needs of the undergraduates were neglected. The multiversity system encouraged students to begin their college education at smaller community colleges, but many still started at the universities. At Berkeley, freshmen attended large classes with several hundred other students. The number of students participating in fraternities and sororities declined by almost half of what it had been six years earlier. Instead, many students chose living ar-

rangements that supported more individuality not community. All these factors combined to further alienate students. [14]

The Civil Rights Movement had also captured the attention of student
activists at Berkeley in the early 1960s. The city itself was struggling with
racial issues involving school segregation and discrimination over jobs and
housing. Even though one-fifth of the city population was black, few blacks
were seen shopping downtown or on the Berkeley campus. The white majority in the community was fairly open about its anti-black feelings. In 1963,
Berkeley voters stopped an open-housing ordinance that would have protected black renters. In 1964, the city's school board was almost recalled
over desegregation. In response to the racial concerns in the city, the students
created the Berkeley chapter of the Congress of Racial Equality (CORE), and
the group regularly picketed various establishments in the Bay area that it
decided did not hire enough blacks, including targeting the *Oakland Tribune*
and car dealerships in San Francisco. [15]

## THE FREE SPEECH MOVEMENT

At least two events occurred during the summer of 1964 that served as
catalysts for more vigorous protesting at Berkeley and eventually the creation
of the Free Speech Movement. First, a group of Berkeley students spent the
summer in Mississippi as part of the Mississippi Summer Project—often
called Freedom Summer. Mario Savio, who became the main voice of the
FSM, was among that Berkeley group who traveled to the Magnolia State.
He worked registering voters in Holmes County and then teaching at a Freedom School in McComb. He related one experience in Mississippi where he
and a friend were beaten before they were able to fend off their white attack-
ers. Experiences like these changed them. When the Berkeley students returned to campus, they were different. They were not afraid of continuing the
fight for social justice on another front. [16]

The second event during that summer was the National Republican Convention in San Francisco where Barry Goldwater became the party's presidential nominee. Jim Branson, night editor at *The Daily Californian* that fall,
recalled that William Knowland, publisher of the *Oakland Tribune* and a
former California senator, brought his Republican friends who were in town
for the convention to see the "crown jewel of the East Bay," the Berkeley
campus of the University of California system. "There, to his horror, were all
these scruffy kids collecting money for the Civil Rights Movement," Branson said of the tables that were lined up along the entrance to the campus at
Bancroft and Telegraph. "There was some outrage among the Republican
hierarchy over this, and they put some pressure on the UC Berkeley administration. When the kids came back to school in the fall of '64, there was a new

rule that no fundraising would be allowed on campus for political movements."[17] Three months later, Knowland denied that he had ever personally exerted pressure on the administration to make any changes.[18] Also, the tables from which students distributed political materials were banished from along the campus entrance on land the university claimed it owned. The administration tightened rules about campaigning and recruiting members for groups interested in off-campus issues and continued a ban on those same groups meeting on campus. Mostly, however, the rules were vague and inconsistent and were inconsistently enforced.[19]

The administration's plan to enforce the activist regulations hit the front page of the student newspaper from the beginning of the semester. In its third issue of the semester on Thursday, September 17,[20] *The Daily Californian* announced that on the following Monday the administration would be enforcing the Regents' political policy that included removing the tables set up at the Bancroft/Telegraph entrance to campus and ending the soliciting that went along with them. The announcement angered the student political group SLATE. It was already itching for a fight. In its new *Supplement to the General Catalog* (one of the earliest attempts at evaluating classes and professors on a college campus), SLATE had called for students to rebel during the semester: "SPLIT THIS CAMPUS WIDE OPEN!"[21]

On Friday, the newspaper reported that the free speech issue could come to a head on Monday when administrators promised to start enforcing the rules; sixteen groups expected to ignore the campus rules anyway and set up tables in the banned area.[22] On Monday, the administration said it would return the area to the students but with conditions such as material handed out there could be informational only without advocating a position, but absolutely no fundraising. Student activists from at least twenty groups rejected any conditions on their activism.[23] That same refusal permeated through every protest, picket, and sit-in that the students sponsored. They demanded complete freedom of expression.

Pickets and discussions continued for several days. The ASUC got involved, asking students to support a petition to end the rules. They also proposed buying the Bancroft-Telegraph area from the university so students could use it freely. A debate on the free speech issue was scheduled and canceled. Students conducted an all-night vigil on the steps of Sproul Hall (the administration building). At a press conference, university President Kerr condemned the protests. Chancellor Edward Strong eased restriction on distributing political material (it could now advocate "yes" or "no" votes), but he still banned soliciting.

On September 30, the newspaper reported that the administration had had enough; a showdown was coming.[24] It started at 3 p.m. that day. After eight students had been called into the dean's office for defying the rules, almost 700 students crowded onto the second floor of Sproul Hall and refused to leave when the building closed. They finally left about 3 a.m. the next morning, but they were not done protesting. Tables returned to the banned area by noon. That is when Jack Weinberg, a non-student manning one of the tables, was arrested. A thirty-hour sit-in around the police car followed, with thousands of students participating, many coming and going throughout the day and night.

When the sit-in around the police car began, reporter Peter Benjaminson immediately went into reporter mode. "I went down to find out what was going on and in fact climbed up on top of the police car," he said. A photo taken at the event shows him sitting on the car, scribbling in a notebook as he talked to one of the protesters. He had already written several stories detailing the students' complaints about the new rules and had interviewed several of the key protest promoters; many like Art Goldberg and Mario Savio would become the driving force behind the FSM. "Art Goldberg was my main contact, and I was often quoting him in the paper," Benjaminson said. "When I went down there [to the police car], I saw him. There were hundreds of students sitting around the car, preventing it from moving. Goldberg or someone on his staff wanted me to come up there and sit on the hood. I somehow made my way through the sit-down strikers, which was difficult because they were all crammed together. I had to step over and between them without falling on them, which was somewhat difficult."[25]

Benjaminson was one of several student reporters who provided information for the stories in the student newspaper the next morning. The main story that appeared on page 1 was a compilation of all the reporters' efforts. "I was appointed the rewrite guy," night editor Jim Branson recalled. "We had like 10 reporters on it. They were rushing into me and giving me different bits of information. I was sitting there . . . typing furiously. We typed our stories on half sheets not a full sheet of paper, on these old stand-up Royal typewriters, one paragraph on a half sheet. I was juggling these half sheets around [to organize the story]. We were fighting like hell to get this out, and finally rushed down to the printer at, I don't know, two in the morning to get this story out. The story that appears about that sit-in the next day has no byline on it, but I wrote it."[26]

The sit-in finally ended when university officials struck a deal with the leaders of the protest. The pact called for the creation of a committee made up of administrators, faculty, and students (including protest leaders) to make recommendations for managing political activism on campus. In return, students agreed to stop all protests against the regulations. The administration promised to not pursue charges against Weinberg and to let a Student Conduct Committee of the Faculty Academic Senate deal with students already found in violation of the regulations. A short-lived peace returned to campus. It was not long before the FSM was complaining about the way members were selected for the Committee on Campus Political Activity (the administration chose the student members), how the suspension of the eight students was being handled (six were reinstated whereas Savio and Goldberg were treated differently because they were deemed instigators of the sit-in), and how the administration was controlling negotiations.

Finally, on December 1, the FSM issued an ultimatum, joined by the Graduate Coordinating Council, who planned a teaching-assistant strike: drop charges from the sit-in around the police car, make rules that allow only the courts to regulate political speech, and stop disciplining students for political activity. The next day, when the administration had not acted on the demands, students once again crowded into Sproul Hall and refused to leave. Outside the building, about 635 uniformed police prepared to force the students to leave. Beginning about 4 a.m. the next day—on the governor's order—the officers spent twelve hours clearing the building, dragging out students who refused to walk. About 800 were arrested, and their trials dragged on through the next semester.

On January 3, 1965, acting Chancellor Martin Meyerson announced that students would be allowed to use Sproul Hall steps for rallies and to set up tables for any purpose, including soliciting funds and support. The FSM had won and the next day sponsored its first legal rally on the steps of Sproul Hall.

Then in March, according to *The Daily Californian*, a man who was not a student, was arrested at the Bancroft-Telegraph entrance to campus because he "held a small sign upon which was painted a four-letter word for sexual intercourse. Beneath the blue four-letter word, the word 'verb' was written in parentheses."[27] Similar signs appeared, and speeches filled with that F-word and other curse words rang out over Sproul Plaza. Thus began the Filthy Speech Movement, which lingered through the rest of the semester. The controversial, crude *Spider* magazine that students produced and tried to sell on campus also helped keep the topic of regulating expression in the news that semester.

## THE DAILY CALIFORNIAN

Throughout the controversy, *The Daily Californian* staffers covered as many aspects of the protests, negotiations, and meetings as time and space allowed. It was the same job the newspaper staff had been trying to do since 1871 when the paper, then the *University Echo,* first began as a stock-controlled company owned by campus fraternities. In 1874 it merged with a campus literary magazine and became the *Berkeleyan.* By 1897 it went daily, and the name changed to *The Daily Californian.* ASUC bought the stock in 1910.[28] It became independent in 1971, published by the Independent Berkeley Students Publishing Company, Inc., and operated solely on funds from advertising.[29] However, like professional newspapers, *The Daily Californian* suffered heavy losses of revenue in the late 2000s. As of April, 2012, the newspaper was attempting to get students to return to subsidizing the paper by approving a $2 fee to keep the 141-year-old newspaper afloat.[30]

As is the case for most student newspapers, *The Daily Californian* has always required a great commitment from already busy students who want to work on the staff. It was no different in 1964. Most serious reporters and editors saw their grades suffer. "There was a lot of work involved," said John Oppedahl, who joined the staff in spring semester 1965 and covered much of what became known as the Filthy Speech Movement. "I didn't go to class that much, and I suffered the consequences. . . . The commitment for spending time at the paper was overwhelming. You didn't have much time to socialize. I was never home. You studied, you went to class, you worked at the *Daily Cal.* And if there was some time where you could get a hamburger, great. I bet I worked harder there than almost any other time in my professional life, and I was a reporter and editor for 36 years."[31]

Justin Roberts, who was managing editor in the fall of 1964 and editor the following semester, also remembers the long hours. "As it turned out, *The Daily Californian* became my second life," he said. "I was literally spending 12 hours a day, every day that we published, working on the *Daily Cal,* essentially full time. And my grades, unfortunately, showed it." A C-average student when he graduated, Roberts credits a good word from university President Clark Kerr for him even being accepted to law school.[32] Peggy Krause, who was the city editor in the fall of 2004, recalled the demands of the newspaper: "One night I was there so late that I went in the women's restroom on a leather couch and slept there all night."[33]

Working at the newspaper was hectic, Oppedahl recalled. "Sure we covered the pom-pom contest, and we covered the theft from the campus vending machines, but we were also writing these really important, thought-provoking stories involving the biggest political figures in the state and sometimes in the country because everyone wanted to weigh-in on what was going on at Berkeley. It was a supercharged atmosphere. It was heady stuff, and it was great fun."[34]

*The Daily Californian* published Monday through Friday whenever school was in session. Writers were unpaid. Only editors received a small stipend for their work. Students interested in working for the newspaper did not automatically get to do so; they had to try out first, even Jim Willwerth who had already been a student newspaper editor during his time at College of Marin and had worked summers for professional newspapers. "It was not as simple as coming over and saying 'I want to be part of this,'" he said of his experience in trying out for the staff. "I was surprised at how professional they were. They didn't take just anybody. The standards of reporting were very, very high. You were expected to write well, and you were expected to report honestly. None of the news pages were going to have stories in them that appeared to be public relations efforts of any kind. You were expected to do your job just the same way a professional newsman would do his or hers."[35]

Students found *The Daily Californian* was an excellent place to learn to become that professional journalist. "It was the greatest training you could have," said Jim Branson, who went on to spend about thirty years as the managing editor for an Oakland television station. "Here we were kids, and we were covering real news. [The editors] taught us principles of journalism that I carried with me all my life. They were the best. We really got terrific training. It served me well the rest of my life."[36]

Jim Willwerth, who was honored in 2004 as Alumnus of the Year for his career of thirty-three years at *Time* magazine, also praised his time at *The Daily Californian*: "Certainly my education as a journalist began at the *Daily Cal*. . . . You might have been young and foolish and full of silliness at one time or another, but you either had to be a journalist or you couldn't stay. *The Daily Californian* said this is how journalism works, and this is what you have to do. I was always grateful for that."[37]

Oppedahl, who was the publisher of the *San Francisco Chronicle* when he retired, recalled that the student newspaper was a good training ground for him: "I probably learned more as a reporter that spring than I learned in my career later. You went out of your way to be even more scrupulous about being fair and quoting everybody and trying to be as balanced and thoughtful as possible. As an educational experience, I think all of us who were involved learned more about basic reporting, how to be fair and how to be thorough. . . . You learned a lot right away."[38]

Peter Benjaminson also began his journalism career at *The Daily Californian*. He later worked as a reporter, an educator, and a spokesman for various groups as well as writing several books.[39]

Students who worked on the newspaper did not have to be journalism majors or plan to become professional journalists. Managing editor Justin Roberts, who went on to become a lawyer, started reading the newspaper as a freshman and decided he wanted to become involved. He never took a single journalism class. City editor Peggy Krause took a few journalism classes to learn the style of writing but majored in education and taught school after graduation. Editor Susan Johnson was a sociology major.

Students with aspirations to be an editor first had to prove themselves as reporters one semester and then as one of five night editors the next semester. As one of the night editors during the fall of 1964, Jim Branson was also a reporter who usually covered student government meetings. In his night editor duties, he was responsible for getting stories edited and headlines written for the next morning's paper. Just like in a vintage movie, Branson would sit in the center or slot of a horseshoe-shaped table that sat in a bay window, doling out stories to the cub reporters who sat around the rim of the table, editing and writing headlines.

He then took the edited paper copies of each story down the hill from campus to Johnny Trench's letter-press print shop where it would be printed some time after midnight. The night editor stayed at the shop to supervise the building of the pages and approve the final designs. The copy was set by grizzled, old Linotype operators who deftly operated large keyboards of ninety characters (upper and lowercase letters had separate keys) that were arranged in order of how frequently they are used rather than like a traditional typewriter or computer keyboard. Following the design outline or dummy prepared by the managing editor, the print shop workers built the pages using the pieces of lead type composed by the linotype machines, hammering the type into frames.[40] "If the story was too short," Benjaminson said of his time as night editor, "they'd yell at the night editor to 'gimme another graph.' So you'd add something. If it was too long, they'd throw the extra lead at you, and you'd try to dodge it. They didn't really hit anybody—it was a joke. But there was actual flying lead down there."[41]

Typically, the students had to have the copy down to the press for typesetting in the early evening, usually no later than about 7 p.m., so the presses could begin running by midnight. The old rotary press took six to seven hours to print 27,000 copies of the eight- to 16-page newspaper for distribution on campus early the next morning. The night of the sit-in around the police car, deadlines went out the window. Reporters and editors were trying frantically to get as much in the paper as possible. Branson said he remembered being at the print shop well after midnight with the latest stories. That delayed everything down the line, including the printing. It was late morning the next day before students could read *The Daily Californian* on campus.[42]

After a stint as a night editor, a student could apply to work in other editor positions. The full staff box during fall semester 1964 listed six editors covering news: Susan Johnson, editor; Justin Roberts, managing editor; Jim Willwerth, assistant editor (editorial); Peggy Krause, city editor; Stanley Schmidt, news editor; and Nancy Tolbert, assistant city editor. Separate staffs handled sports on the editorial side and advertising on the business side of the newspaper. After serving in a mid-level news editor position for a semester, a student could ask to be considered for one of the top three editorial positions: editor, managing editor and city editor. Several students spent a semester as assistant editor, then became the city editor, managing editor, and finally the editor. The top positions each semester were nominated by the outgoing Senior Editorial Board and approved by the Publication Board that included members from administration, faculty, and student editors. In 1964, the Senior Editorial Board consisted of the editor, managing editor, city editor, assistant editor, news editor, sports editor, and two assistant city editors.[43] The editor was the face of the newspaper and wrote some of the editorials but had little to do with day-to-day management of reporters and story flow. The managing editor—with the help of the city editor, news editor, and assistant city editor—planned the news copy and made sure stories were assigned and written. The assistant editor was responsible for the editorial page and wrote most of the editorials under the direction of the editor.

## THE EDITORIAL PAGE

Editorials, as well as the other items that traditionally appear on editorial and op-ed pages, play the vital roles of providing information, analysis, and forums for public discussion. These help readers to make decisions about issues and then take appropriate action.[44] Though editorials certainly are not expected to provide the objectivity required in news stories, they can provide meaning "by keeping in view the central values of our age despite the tides of passion and propaganda that swirl about and obscure them."[45] The editorial and the editorial or opinion page of any newspaper should be the community's conscience as well as a sounding board.[46] They give meaning to what is happening in the world, fight for the rights and needs of citizens, dispel myths, and provide a daily forum for discussion.[47] Indeed, editorials should help people make sense of the world and at times point out issues and concerns that its readership may have failed to understand or take into account, a kind of inner voice as Johnson said *The Daily Californian* had been as it served as the campus conscience.

The job of writing the first draft of most of the editorials during the Free Speech Movement fell to Jim Willwerth, who was the assistant editor. He, Johnson, and Roberts would discuss what the editorial position would be, and Willwerth would usually write it though they seldom agreed on the focus. "We divided along ideological lines," Willwerth said. Roberts was an ardent, conservative Republican whereas Johnson was more moderate and middle-of-the-road but less sure of herself and usually accepted the more conservative, pro-administration position favored by Roberts. Willwerth was undecided about the speech issue in the beginning, but as the protests continued he took a stand. "I thought the students were right, so I became the liberal who supported the students who were rebelling," he said. That led to many intense discussions and even arguments in the newsroom, especially if Willwerth found out the other two had changed his original editorial, often to be more supportive of the administration.[48]

Finally, for only the second time during the fall semester, a signed editorial appeared on December 9. Johnson and Roberts put their names to the position they took, a position Willwerth could not endorse. The editorial filled two columns on the editorial page. The piece described the Free Speech

Movement as "pre-occupied with the means of civil disobedience and disre-spect for authority," calling the protests a "ludicrous spectacle." The FSM's demand for open discussion is not the way to becoming a greater university, they argued, and some regulation of speech is imperative for the campus. They urged the Board of Regents, who was considering how to deal with political activism at the university, to not throw the campus wide-open to political expression.[49] Though the editorials throughout the semester had criticized both sides for various actions, it was the first time the editors had taken such a direct stand on the issue of free speech. It was difficult for Johnson to do, too. Her husband, Cebe Wallace, who was Johnson's boy-friend during this semester, said his late wife had developed a strong journa-listic sense that she had to remain impartial, a standard she learned from her father and an uncle who were both journalists. So expressing opinions did not come easily to her. "She thought her job was to be a presenter of facts, an honest broker of events, and not an advocate," he said. "Everyone wanted her to take a position. It was hard to be what she thought a good journalist should be."[50]

Several staff members, who had been unhappy with the regular pro-ad-ministration editorial position, finally approached Willwerth, concerned that the views of so many of the staff were not being represented in the editorials just like the one Johnson and Roberts published. So Willwerth did something that was not common at the newspaper at the time; he penned a dissenting position, which Johnson allowed to run on the editorial page the next day. In it, Willwerth endorsed a faculty proposal sent to the Regents. That proposal favored no restrictions on free speech issues on campus. Willwerth was adamant that the campus should enjoy "full campus freedom of ideas" with-out regulation, while at the same time not condoning illegal activities of protesters. Thirteen other editors and reporters joined Willwerth in signing the piece.[51] Afterward, Willwerth said, he received a note from President Clark Kerr. "It was a note of congratulations that I had framed the issues well and exercised my first amendment right," he said.[52]

More than half of the daily editorials in the *Daily Cal* dealt with some aspect of what would become the Free Speech Movement. Early in the se-mester, it appeared the newspaper might be more supportive of the students, particularly after an editorial that appeared the first week of the semester that was critical of the Board of Regents. During the previous semester, the Regents had turned down a request to allow the students to start an FM radio station. Now the editorial bristled when it recounted how one Regent had suggested that the board did not need another student voice like the student newspaper that they could not control. The editorial went on to urge students to support the ASUC president's quest to continue seeking approval for the radio station.[53]

In the beginning of the semester, it was evident the editors did not have a well-defined position on the free speech issue. They would present both sides of whatever had happened, sometimes presenting the administration in a negative light, but then they would fill the final sentences with ambivalence or criticism about what they had just praised. The day the administration said it would begin to enforce the regulations on political activism that would only allow informational not persuasive leaflets, the editorial ended with two questions: Is there really a difference between *information* and *persuasion* in politics? And just how does the administration plan to enforce the rules?[54] The next day, the editorial started out strongly against the Regents. It said the Regents had misinterpreted the state Constitution when they applied the requirement for political independence at the university to political speech. The Constitution had only meant to keep politics out of the appointment of administrators, it maintained. "Campus administrators are making a mistake" in enforcing the activism rules on students. Students picketing and conducting vigils were within their rights to do so, it added. Then, in a kind of about-face, the editorial ended with a warning that pressure tactics to get the administration to capitulate were not the answer.[55]

Almost three weeks later, and after the sit-in around the police car, another editorial considered the state Constitution again, this time showing that the Regents and administration were acting within the power granted to them by the Constitution to manage the university, but noted that it was not yet clear that the right decisions had been made in managing the free speech issue.[56] Near the end of the semester, Johnson joined with editors of *The California Aggie* at UC-Davis and *Daily Bruin at UCLA* in a joint editorial that blamed the FSM for problems and then ended with an admonition to President Kerr to step up to the plate and really try to understand students.[57]

As the semester went on, the editorials became more critical of the movement though not necessarily more supportive of the administration. They often condemned one side while not supporting the other. The day after the first sit-in inside Sproul Hall that lasted until about 3 a.m., the editorial was light-hearted and short, noting that it was too early to judge the situation. "We admire the intrepidity and old fashioned persistence of the mixed political groups, despite a certain amount of rashness creeping into their methods. The time is not ripe for an observer's assessment of the controversy, since its face and facets change daily. Earlier this week, we thought it had ended." The editorial concluded with the hope that students got at least a little sleep before facing the realities of schoolwork.[58]

A day later, with student protesters surrounding the police car, the newspaper ran no editorial. In its usual place on the editorial page was a statement from ASUC President Charles R. Powell calling for the demonstrations to cease. He said the rules the students were protesting were mandated by the state Constitution and not the administration, and further demonstrating would only jeopardize the Open Forum Policy that allowed for speakers of all persuasions to present on campus (with some restrictions).[59] Allowing the ASUC statement to replace the editorial was a kind of tacit approval of the statement.

The next editorial—"We Plead for Peace"—was a lengthy piece that filled two columns when it appeared on Monday after a pact between the FSM leaders and the administration had halted the sit-in around the police car. The editorial tried to balance the blame for what had happened: "No one was completely right, none were completely wrong." As the editorials usually did, it summarized much of what had happened—in this case it was the mistakes made by each side in the fracas. Still there was more praise for the administration as it several times pointed to President Clark Kerr as the one who acted with courage. It ended with an echo of the ASUC statement: stop demonstrating or lose freedoms already enjoyed.[60]

At times it was difficult to determine which position the newspaper supported. It often appeared to side with either side at various moments, sometimes playing devil's advocate. When the ASUC talked about buying the Bancroft-Telegraph area at the entrance of campus to create a free-speech zone, the newspaper opposed it. After all, the editorial pointed out, the ASUC is ultimately responsible to the administration and Regents, who could still exert some control. Even deeding the property to the city of Berkeley would not solve the problems because then the city would be controlling the actions on the property, and the city had not been eager to support the student protests so far. "The plan, we hope, will be short lived."[61]

The next day, the newspaper came close to endorsing the Free Speech Movement when it criticized a city councilman for saying free speech that threatens the country should be controlled. Such a position "is contrary to every principle of democracy," it pointed out.[62] But the following day, it was back on the administration's side. FSM leaders were claiming the administration had acted in bad faith when it entered into an agreement with protesters the week before in order to end the sit-in around the police car. "We do not believe that the administration has shown 'bad faith,'" concluded the editorial that filled two columns after reiterating the points of the agreement and the process of the negotiations before offering some suggestions for handling the situation.[63]

Then, a week later, the editorial verged on supporting the protesters again even though it insisted the editors were not trying to condemn any one side. Still, "if the students had not protested loudly, visibly and illegally, this campus would not have questioned the ban" on student activism. Now, "we must not relax. We must bend every effort to earn the right of a real open forum now denied this University but granted to other state schools of higher education."[64]

The next editorial about the free speech issue was one of criticism and resignation. First, it blasted the chancellor's latest statements on maintaining the current rules as being "ill-timed and ill-thought prejudgments," then ended with a what-is-the-use shrug because "the chancellor has already made a decision."[65] Then a secondary editorial that same day took sides with a student group, Particle Berkeley, which was threatened with losing campus status if members did not stop participating in the FSM and stick to its goal of furthering scientific research. "Certainly even the organizations whose purposes are not strictly political should be allowed to participate in the entire spectrum of campus affairs," the editorial maintained.[66] With decisions looming about how the administration would handle discipline for students cited in the early protests, two editorials in a row reminded students that protesting before the decisions were made was really just finding the administration guilty without a fair trial, something the students were demanding for themselves.[67]

Though the newspaper's allegiance seemed to sway between both sides of the free speech issue, it certainly did have one position that never changed: Everyone needs to work for a solution that would come with improved communication,[68] cooperation and especially the involvement of the Academic Senate (faculty) and ASUC Senate (students).[69] At times, the editorials pointed out that the current protesting was unnecessary, such as the vigil students planned to coincide with a meeting of the Regents, a move the editors said was "as useful at this stage of the game as holding a wake for a man gone for years."[70] One editorial pointed out that students had staged a rally demanding change for something the chancellor had already changed.[71]

Many times it seemed the editorial was more against a proposal or action than for the opposing side. They did it by pointing out problems with whatever plan was being considered and encouraging more discussion before making decisions. That was the tenor of the editorial on the same day the newspapers ran full statements from the FSM supporters, President Kerr, and a faculty group that made recommendations for regulating activism. The editorial pointed out that those recommendations included requirements that would be stifling to speech just because groups could not easily comply with them.[72] Editorials criticized the Regents for the way they were handling things,[73] the legislature for considering getting involved,[74] the students for forcing the governor to step in to end the Sproul Hall sit-in,[75] the FSM for being too reliant on Mario Savio for leadership.[76] Another editorial praised the Academic Senate for considering both students and administration in liberal proposals it made to the Regents, and then concluded by warning that a completely open campus was not the answer.[77] One editorial recognized that the 800 students facing court action for the Sproul Hall sit-in would likely feel the impact of their civil disobedience for some time, and encouraged the administration to extend some mercy or have 800 martyrs on campus, which would only prolong the conflict. [78]

The editorials also echoed the feelings of many students, whether or not they were protesting. One pointed out that the Berkeley students were not being treated the same as students at other state colleges on the speech issue, a condition that made students feel even more alienated. [79] Editors added their approval to a long piece from nine political science professors that replaced the editorial in early December. The professors said it was time to return to class and serious academic studies. They also commended the majority of the student body who did not participate in the protests. [80] As the campus prepared for Christmas break, another editorial told of the challenge students would have in explaining to their family and friends at home what had happened that semester. [81]

The editorial pages also featured columns and Letters to the Ice Box (letters to the editor). The daily columnists wrote about many topics, including the free speech issue. Eric Levine, the most prolific on the topic, wrote ten columns about free speech during the fall semester. (Willwerth, who edited all the material for the page does not remember Levine. *Daily Cal* alumni records show Levine is now deceased.) Levine usually didn't offer much background about the issues—he assumed students knew what was going on. Instead he plowed headlong into his opinion and pointed fingers, usually at the administration. In his first free-speech column, he made connections between the students picketing the hiring practices at the *Oakland Tribune* and the administration suddenly deciding that the area outside the main gate of campus was not the city's property to control but the university's. Without naming *Tribune* publisher Knowland, Levine claimed complaints from the newspaper prompted administrators to ban political activity in the area because picketers were recruiting others to help their cause. [82] A few days after the sit-in around the police car, Levine reiterated some of the history of free speech on campus from the 1930s to the present, and then applauded the FSM for becoming "a legitimate political force." [83] He generally sided with the FSM, found the administration's various rulings confusing, and criticized the faculty for not fighting for more control. After the 800 arrests in the Sproul Hall sit-in, Levine accused the administration of going to war against the students. [84]

Dozens of letters addressed the free speech issue as well, both for and against what was happening. Willwerth said letters usually had to be cut to fit the space, but now does not remember much controversy with them. No letter writers waged wars with each other or generated any controversy on their own. Willwerth said he has few recollections about the letters as being passionate or defining in any way. He said he printed most of what was submitted though "I would look for letters that actually were thoughtful if I could find them." [85]

In the spring semester, the editorial policies made a marked change. Roberts, who had taken over the helm as the editor of the student newspaper, decided from the start that whoever wrote the editorial would add his or her name at the end as a tagline. "This created something different," he recalled. "Generally, the person who was the editor at the *Daily Cal* was never really known. But with my name on the editorial, I instantly became known as the editor of the *Daily Cal.*"[86] He wrote most of the editorials that semester.

His pieces often voiced stronger positions than the newspaper had seen the previous semester. During the first month of the term he wrote mostly about other issues. Then in March, just after the first obscenity arrest, he christened the Filthy Speech Movement in the final sentence of his editorial.[87] He penned fourteen editorials that dealt with what was essentially the aftermath of the fall's Free Speech Movement. Personally, Roberts said, he supported the issue of free speech but abhorred the group's tactics, "the way the FSM confronted the university, to call for strikes, to call for boycotts, to call for sit-ins. All of this created a hell of a lot of bad publicity for the University of California. . . . What we went through for many months, topped off by the Filthy Speech Movement, why we were the laughing stock of the nation." The administration wasn't guiltless either. "It's sad that the university took a position that essentially dared the students to have sit-ins and strikes and boycotts and so forth."[88] In print, Roberts supported the Meyer report to the Regents on political activism,[89] but criticized a second report to the Regents because it favored the FSM.[90] He supported *in loco parentis*[91] and thumbed his nose at the possibility of a renewed surge by FSM leader Mario Savio.[92]

Another editorial policy Roberts changed was to allow the publication of more dissenting opinions. During the fall semester, he had been concerned when the newspaper had endorsed Lyndon B. Johnson for U.S. president, something no one could remember ever happening before. He disagreed with the endorsement and argued with editors Susan Johnson and Jim Willwerth to write a dissenting position. In it, he supported the Republican candidate, Barry Goldwater. "I'm telling you, the shit hit the fan," he said. "He [Goldwater] was not regarded well in the liberal community. I was like a traitor." Roberts did not view himself as a strong political person: "I wasn't even eligible to vote at that time." So when he had the power to make changes in how the student newspaper ran, he did. Student reporters and editors would no longer have to fight to air a dissenting opinion. Several times during the semester, other editors joined in group editorials that Roberts did not support, and he was OK with that. It kept the staff happy and still allowed him to get his thoughts out there as well.[93]

## NEWS COVERAGE

Student reporters wrote about the Free Speech Movement almost every day. In fact, all but two issues of the fall semester featured stories related to free speech. By the end of the term in January, though, the FSM was running out of steam. Still, only a handful of editions during spring semester did not report something related to the free speech issue, especially after it morphed into the Filthy Speech Movement in March. Its life did not last as long nor engage students as vigorously as the Free Speech Movement of the previous semester. Still, along with stories about a controversial magazine that students tried to sell on campus, the Filthy Speech Movement kept the topic of regulating expression as the dominate theme in the student newspaper for the remainder of the school year.

When the movement began, none realized the true importance of the movement. "We just covered it," Roberts said, noting that as the fall semester began, it seemed as if the administration was making a lot out of nothing. The tables at the entrance to the campus, along with the soliciting, were more of a nuisance than a serious problem. As managing editor, he had a lot of work to do in organizing the coverage of the various events and had little time to actually watch what happened. But when about 800 students jammed into Sproul Hall in early December, he decided to cover some of it himself. "I got myself inside to see what was going on," he said. "I can't remember how I talked my way in, but I did. I saw them all sprawled out on the second floor and in the stairwell also. And I was there when they started to haul them out and put them aboard buses to take them off to Santa Rita Jail."[94]

Curiosity drew Jim Willwerth to the sit-in around the car, where he spent time observing and soaking up the atmosphere whenever he had time. "I was very drawn to it, even though I would not have joined it," he explained. "Reporters don't join; they just report." He decided to write a column describing the experience around the car. "It was just color and a lot of feeling in it, what people were talking about. Some coed handed me an apple in a kind of sharing thing, stuff like that. Meanwhile, Mario Savio was up on top of the car. He was a very, very impressive orator. And Jack Weinberg, of course, was inside the car, pissing in a coke bottle. So I had a lot of great color there."[95]

Peter Benjaminson wrote many of the FSM stories throughout the fall semester. He wrote about the first protests before the sit-in around the car, but "I didn't even see it as the beginning of anything, just a giant incident." Only in hindsight did he realize the events were an important part of history. He attended many of the FSM meetings, whether he was covering them for the newspaper or not. "I went to some just out of interest and told the people I wasn't there for the *Daily Cal*. I just wanted to see what was happening," he said. The meetings often lasted many hours as the students discussed the fine points of the agreements that were at times many pages long. All students were allowed to speak, which lengthened the meetings. "It was a political thing in the sense that the movement wanted to give everyone the chance to express themselves so they wouldn't feel left out," Benjaminson explained. The FSM leaders wanted to "get the real low-down on the public opinion—that is the public opinion of their followers, to see what they wanted." The student newspaper did not cover every meeting either, but the FSM never complained about the amount of coverage that fall. After all, they were front page news every day.[96]

One moment after the sit-in around the car stands out in Benjaminson's mind: "I was walking through the center of campus, which you could hardly avoid doing most days, and [FSM leader] Art Goldberg saw me from maybe 200 yards away and started running toward me. It was like one of those scenes in a slow motion movie. He wasn't running in slow motion, of course, but I remember it in slow motion. He was running toward me and he was saying 'the committee has rejected the settlement.' It was the precursor to the Sproul Hall sit-in [where 800 were arrested]. I don't remember his exact words but he was implying heavily that this would get much worse. That's why I remember it in retrospect as being a great thing. So I took notes of what he said and went over to the *Daily Cal* office and wrote a story about it. By that time, I realized we were in a historical setting that people would look back on. I saw him [Goldberg] as the prophet of the future, which he was. By that time, I believed the threats."[97]

Accessing information was one of the biggest challenges for the newspaper, according to John Oppedahl, who joined the staff in the spring semester. "We were not professionals, so we sometimes had difficulty finding out what was going on with the Regents," who ultimately would be deciding how the activism rules would change. He remembers frustrating discussions late at night as the editors tried to find out what the FSM leaders were doing because they did not always allow reporters to attend their meetings.[98]

Oppedahl was one of the main reporters writing about the Filthy Speech Movement when it sprung up on the coattails of the Free Speech Movement. The lead on one of his stories about that part of the movement remains one of his favorites to this day: "____, ____, ____, ____, and ____" were entered into evidence yesterday in the trial of nine persons arrested last month on campus for obscenity.[99] "We never printed the word," he explained, noting that typically newspapers from the '40s into the '90s reflected the parameters of mainstream society, the limits of polite society. Avoiding public profanity was the norm for that time and the newspaper followed suit. "It wasn't that we were afraid of anybody. We could have printed the word, and we would have been criticized. But we weren't afraid of retribution. Our stance was that it was in poor taste to use words like the ones they were using on campus in our newspaper. . . . We talked about it. Our view was, 'No, we don't do that stuff. We're not putting naked girls in the paper. We're not putting crude language in the paper. We're not putting Nazi symbols in the paper.'" As a professional editor and publisher, he banned profanity from every newspaper where he worked. "'We have a higher standard here,' I would say. 'That standard is that we don't use profanity.'"[100]

Students worked hard to maintain objectivity in the news stories they wrote. Jim Willwerth found out early on that just accurately reporting an event could be perceived as not being neutral, depending on how one side's position might appear. One of his first assignments at the newspaper was to report on a civil rights demonstration by CORE at a local grocery store. As he started the assignment, he expected to talk to both sides of the issue and find that the CORE people were heroic in their protest for equality. Instead, he found demonstrators who were not just marching with signs or chanting or singing songs. "They were going into the store and vandalizing the store, throwing whole shelves of things on the floor, stuff like that, which struck me as not being in the tradition of Martin Luther King Jr.," he said. They also threatened to destroy the store. Then he talked to the grocery store management, who said they had not expected to be treated this way but had hoped to enter into civil negotiations with the protesters. Afterward, Willwerth wrote the story exactly as he had seen and heard the demonstration. CORE was angry. "All I had done was go there and see what was happening and then report it. Of course, when I reported it, [CORE] didn't look very good." CORE members claimed the student newspaper really had two editorial pages—one on the front page and the traditional one inside.[101]

Despite similar challenges throughout the Free Speech Movement, the newspaper continued to work for objectivity in its reporting of the issues. "You went out of your way to be even more scrupulous about being fair and quoting everybody and trying to be as balanced and thoughtful as possible," John Oppedahl said, noting that these basic principles should always continue in journalism. "I really do believe there is something you can aspire to called objectivity and balance. I know there are a lot of people who would disagree with that, but I think they're wrong. You don't get it all the time, but you do aspire to it. You try to get as close to being as objective as you can. I still think that is a goal and model for what a reporter does."[102]

Generally, FSM supporters seldom complained about the coverage. However, Justin Roberts recalled one incident during the spring semester when FSM leader Mario Savio stormed into the newspaper office to complain about an editorial Roberts had written that criticized the FSM. Roberts said he did not think the piece had been groundbreaking in any way, but it still struck a chord with the FSM leadership. Savio told him that he had no right to publish such a position and started arguing with Roberts about the piece. "The idea of Mario Savio, the leader of the Free Speech Movement, coming into my office, complaining about an editorial, slamming the newspaper down on my desk and telling me I have no right as an editor to write that—I thought it was just incredible," Roberts recalled. "It always got me as being indeed ironic." Some twenty years later, Roberts had the opportunity to visit with Savio and reminded him of the encounter at the *Daily Cal*. "He put his hands on his face and he said, 'I said that?' And I said, 'you sure did. I have never forgotten it.' And he said, 'Oh, my god, that's not something I should have said.'"[103]

## GETTING ALONG

Unlike many other student newspapers, *The Daily Californian* had few challenges at that time with the administration trying to control what it printed. Some of the staff remembers the administration as sometimes being difficult to work with, particularly Richard Hafner, who was the public affairs director at the university. "Dick Hafner had a contentious relationship with us, even though he was a member of the Publication Board," recalled Jim Branson. "He was constantly on us to try to bend the coverage in his direction, which is what spokesmen do."[104] Peter Benjaminson remembers Hafner as not being offensive but friendly in his approach with the newspaper. Hafner always tried to make sure that he had made the administration's position clear though he never tried to force the newspaper to write anything.[105] Justin Roberts also said working with Hafner, a former *Daily Cal* editor himself, was not contentious. Indeed, he was one of the people Roberts would talk to about troubles or concerns at the paper.[106]

John Oppedahl found the administration to be helpful even though Hafner would let the staff know if he thought any position was unfair or erroneous. However, Oppedahl learned early on that he needed to find someone to trust, someone who would tell the truth about what was really going on. That was Ray Colvig, another public relations representative at the university. Colvig provided background information to help really understand the issues. "Once in a while he would close the door, and he would say something like 'we didn't have this conversation, and here's what the administration is trying to do.' This was way off the record. You talk about Deep Throat. Well, this was Deep, Deep Throat. He would tell me what the administration was really trying to do, compared to their public statements. I would go back to the office, and I would never quote him. But I would be better able to frame my story in a more sensible way." Oppedahl was not alone in his frustrations over understanding what was really going on with the administration. "Even professional newspapers couldn't figure it out," he said. Colvig helped him understand that perhaps the Regents were exerting pressure or that the Regents were split on a decision.

Few major conflicts occurred among the *Daily Cal* staff members. Benjaminson remembers that some staffers got along and others did not, as in any workplace. "I was fairly prickly myself," he said. "Certainly [night editor] Branson and I had arguments about whether a story I had written should be used," he said. One incident in particular, regarding a series of stories Benjaminson wrote about foreign student political rights on campus, stands out. "We got into a big row, desk pounding and shouting," Benjaminson said. "We were friends later that day, and I still call him occasionally."[107] Branson no longer remembers the argument.

Peggy Krause remembers a staff that all worked together and taught each other. "I didn't go on in journalism," she said, "and I had not had any journalism before [working on *The Daily Californian*] so they taught me what I needed."[108]

Jim Branson remembers less agreement than the others do. "There was a lot of conflict on the paper about how to cover and how to comment on the protests that were going on," he said. "We [newspaper staff members] wanted to be more supportive of the movement than the paper was as a whole. The administration was trying to stifle free speech, and it was pretty clear who was right and who was wrong."[109]

Jim Willwerth remembers some intrigue at the newspapers with plots to get more power over how things were done, to get better assignments and to get more space in the newspaper. "It really produced an atmosphere that was just full of all the great stuff that goes on whenever the social fabric is being torn—just all that good stuff starts happening when someone raises the temperature or makes the pot boil over."[110]

## CONCLUSION

As one would expect, the Free Speech Movement was the main topic of discussion around the campus and in the student newspaper during the 1964–1965 school year. The reporters and editors extensively covered the movement but do not believe their work fueled it in any way. They just covered as much of what happened as they could and as many sides of the issue as they could. Occasionally, they also reported on how the movement had spread to other college campuses, but the bulk of the news coverage was about what was happening at Berkeley: the interminable FSM meetings and actions, the court trials and official campus proceedings that protesters faced, the Regents' and administration's responses.

A true campus conscience would have been found on the editorial page, and sometimes it was indeed there. Often an editorial that praised one side might also criticize that same group for something or urge it to consider other points as well. A piece that castigated one group may also criticize the opposing group. Almost always the editorial writer did an excellent job of summarizing the various issues, even though most of the space might be that summarization with just a few sentences of real opinion. Still, very few editorials took hard, fast positions, which made the opinions seem more ambivalent and less decisive than a strong conscience would have provided. Yet, when it came to finally taking a clear stand, the opinion supported some regulation of speech on campus, a position a number of the staff did not support. In many ways, the editorials show the struggles the three top editors had in agreeing on point of view the newspaper would put forth as the staff's opinion. According to most of the reporters and editors interviewed, most of the staff did not support the editorial positions of the newspaper that fall. However, they only wrote dissenting opinions a few times throughout the entire year.

The Free Speech Movement only seemed to encompass spoken speech, even though the written word was also imperiled when the sale of the crude *Spider* magazine was banned from campus. Still, student newspaper editors and reporters never feared that the sanctions might extend to them as well. The Free Speech Movement was not "exactly about speech," Jim Willwerth said. "It was about the right to be political, which of course at the bottom is free speech, the right to be political in a public arena, and the right to be controversial. In other words, the First Amendment contains the right to be controversial. And those students [at Berkeley] were not being allowed to be controversial."[111]

For many students involved in the turmoil, the movement was the highlight of their college careers. "I basically remember it as a good time to be a journalist," recalled Peter Benjaminson. It was anything but that for editor Susan Johnson. Her husband Cebe Wallace recalled many teary phone calls and letters she wrote him while he was stationed away from the area during his Air Force service, telling him about pressure from the governor and student groups who all telephoned her at home. Being torn like that was difficult. "For many people, it was the high point of their lives," Wallace said of the FSM. "For her, it was anything but the glory days. It was terrible." She was reluctant to relive those days when various people writing articles or books about the FSM contacted her throughout the following decades, he said, and she seldom participated in interviews.[112]

Still it was a history-making time, John Oppedahl said. "What was exhilarating about it was that most of the stories that I covered were big stories, and they were also handled by the professional press, so our competition wasn't just the campus radio station. We were competing for reportage with all of the pros. That was pretty heady stuff. It was great fun as a young journalist to be tossed into this sort of maelstrom."

\*          \*          \*

Susan Johnson Wallace graduated in sociology, worked in various jobs before becoming a full-time mother who later in life worked as an ESL teacher. She died November 20, 2006.

Justin Roberts went on to law school at Hastings College of the Law in San Francisco and for more than forty years practiced law in California, specializing in medical malpractice.

James Willwerth graduated from Berkeley with a bachelor degree in Journalistic Studies (a combined journalism and political science degree) and then spent a year in a journalism master's program so he could be the Berkeley campus stringer for *Time* magazine. Five years later he finished his master's thesis on war correspondents in Vietnam. His stringer position turned into a full-time job with *Time* that lasted thirty-three years, working in such places around the globe as Asia, Central America, Los Angeles, New York, and San Francisco. He has published five nonfiction books.

Peter Benjaminson graduated in political science at Berkeley and the School of Journalism at Columbia University. His varied professional career included stints at several newspapers (*Detroit Free Press, Atlanta Journal Constitution,* and *Chief Leader*). He did a fellowship at Princeton, wrote several books (including the how-to book *Investigative Reporting* that he co-authored with Dave Anderson), acted as a spokesman/public information officer in New York City, taught journalism classes, and was a claims examiner and investigator for the New York State Department of Labor. He continues to write books in retirement.

James Branson graduated from Berkeley but returned to work as a copy editor and managing editor of *The Daily Californian* for several years before becoming managing editor of KTVU Channel 2 News in Oakland for thirty years. He is now retired.

John Oppedahl earned a bachelor's degree in political science from Berkeley and a master's in journalism from Columbia University. He was a reporter and/or editor at the *San Francisco Examiner, The Detroit Free Press, Dallas Times Herald, Los Angeles Herald Examiner,* and *The Arizona Republic.* He was the publisher at *The Arizona Republic* and *San Francisco Chronicle* before he retired in 2003.

Peggy Krause McCormick taught social studies and ESL after she finished college.

Benjaminson and Oppedahl both ended up at Columbia University as graduate students when the 1968 student protesters there occupied various campus buildings. The two were walking across campus one day and saw the tear gas canisters flying around, Oppedahl recalled. "We just walked over to the journalism school and looked around and we thought, 'yeah, it's a pretty good demonstration but not quite up to the level of Berkeley.'"[113]

## NOTES

1. Donna Lampkin Stephens, "The Conscience of the *Arkansas Gazette*: J. N. Heiskell Faces the Storm of Little Rock," *Journalism History* 38 (Spring 2012): 35.

2. Tammy Dunn, telephone interview by author, May 18, 2017.

3. Cebe Wallace, widower of Susan Johnson Wallace, telephone interview by author, May 21, 2012.

4. Susan Johnson, "The Last Stand," *The Daily Californian* (Berkeley, CA), January 8, 1965, 14.

5. "History of UC Berkeley," University of California, Berkele, accessed May 7, 2012, http://berkeley.edu/about/hist/foundations.shtml.

6. "It Starts Here: UC at the Frontier," University of California, accessed May 8, 2012, http://www.universityofcalifornia.edu/aboutuc/.

7. Division of Business Operations, University of California, accessed May 8, 2012, http://www.ucop.edu/busops/.

8. W. J. Rorabaugh, *Berkeley at War: The 1960s* (New York: Oxford University Press, 1989), 11.

9. Ibid., 11–15.

10. David Lance Goines, *The Free Speech Movement: Coming of Age in the 1960s* (Berkeley, CA: Ten Speed Press, 1993), 63.

11. Karen Spencer, "*Daily Cal*–Part 1, 1947–1960," in Michael Rossman and Lynne Hollander, *Administrative Pressures and Student Political Activity at the University of California: A Preliminary Report* (University of California, 1964), accessed May 7, 2012, http://www.cdlib.org.

12. Larry Marks, "*Daily Cal* – Part II: The Strike of 1960," in Michael Rossman and Lynne Hollander, *Administrative Pressures and Student Political Activity at the University of California: A Preliminary Report* (University of California, 1964), accessed May 7, 2012, http://www.cdlib.org.

13. Goines, *The Free Speech Movement,* 276–277.

14. Rorabaugh, *Berkeley at War,* 12–18.

15. Ibid., 18–19.

16. Goines, *The Free Speech Movement,* 97–98.

17. James Branson, telephone interview by author, April 4, 2012.

18. Ben Nyburg, "Knowland Interview: 'Never Talked to Kerr," *The Daily Californian* (Berkeley, CA), December 4, 1964, 5.

19. "The Grievances of the Students," in Michael Rossman and Lynne Hollander, *Administrative Pressures and Student Political Activity at the University of California: A Preliminary Report* (University of California, 1964), accessed May 7, 2012, http://www.cdlib.org.

20. Pete Benjaminson, "Politics Banned at Bancroft Entry," *The Daily Californian* (Berkeley, CA), September 17, 1964, 1, 3.

21. Jim Branson, "SLATE Supplement Appears, Letter Asks for Rebellion," *The Daily Californian* (Berkeley, CA), September 16, 1964, 1.

22. Pete Benjaminson, "Political Groups May Defy Dean," *The Daily Californian* (Berkeley, CA), September 18, 1964, 1.

23. Pete Benjaminson, "Bancroft Groups Refuse Conditions," *The Daily Californian* (Berkeley, CA), September 22, 1964, 1.

24. "University, Political Groups Look to Possible Showdown," *The Daily Californian* (Berkeley, CA), September 30, 1974, 1.

25. Peter Benjaminson, telephone interview by author, April 3, 2012.

26. James Branson, telephone interview by author, April 4, 2012.

27. Andy McGall, "Obscene Sign Causes Arrest; Protest Rally Called For," *The Daily Californian* (Berkeley, CA), March 4, 1965, 1.

28. "Many Changes in Daily Cal Over the Years," *The Daily Californian* (Berkeley, CA), October 1, 1964, 6.

29. *The Daily Californian* History, accessed May 15, 2012, http://www.dailycal.org/about/.

30. Tomer Ovadia, "The High Cost of Independence," *The Daily Californian* (Berkeley, CA), April 11, 2012, accessed May 15, 2012, http://www.dailycal.org/2012/04/11/the-high-cost-of
-independence/.

31. John F. Oppedahl, telephone interview by author, May 9, 2012.

32. Justin Roberts, telephone interview by author, April 6, 2012.

33. Peggy Krause McCormick, telephone interview by author, April 5, 2012.

34. Oppedahl interview.

35. James Willwerth, telephone interview by author, April 3, 2012.

36. Branson interview.

37. Willwerth interview.

38. Oppedahl interview.

39. Benjaminson interview.

40. Branson interview.

41. Benjaminson interview.

42. Branson interview.

43. "Senior Editorial Board Controls Daily Production," *The Daily Californian* (Berkeley, CA), October 1, 1964, 6.

44. Ernest C. Hynds, "Editors at Most U.S. Dailies See Vital Roles for Editorial Page," *Journalism Quarterly* 71, no. 3 (Autumn 1994): 573–582.

45. John Hulteng, *The Opinion Function: Editorial and Interpretive Writing for the News Media* (New York: Harper & Row, 1973), 10.

46. Steven M. Hallock, *Editorial and Opinion: The Dwindling Marketplace of Ideas in Today's News* (Westport, CT: Praeger, 2007), 9.

47. Gayle A. Waldrop, *Editor and Editorial Writer* (Dubuque, IA: Wm. C. Brown Company, 1967), 4–5.

48. Willwerth interview.

49. Susan Johnson and Justin A. Roberts, "An Appeal to the Regents," *The Daily Californian* (Berkeley, CA), December 9, 1964, 8.

50. Wallace interview.

51. Jim Willwerth, et al., "Dissenting Opinion: Faculty Proposal Endorsed," *The Daily Californian* (Berkeley, CA), December 10, 1964, 6.

52. Willwerth interview.

53. "What Kind of Fools Are We?" *The Daily Californian* (Berkeley, CA), September 18, 1964, 12.

54. "The Finish Line," *The Daily Californian* (Berkeley, CA), September 21, 1964, 12.

55. "The Long, Long Line," *The Daily Californian* (Berkeley, CA), September 22, 1964, 8.

56. "The Legal Basis," *The Daily Californian* (Berkeley, CA), October 12, 1964, 8.

57. "We Need a Leader," *The Daily Californian* (Berkeley, CA), December 4, 1964, 12.

58. "The 'Sleep-In,'" *The Daily Californian* (Berkeley, CA), October 1, 1964, 10.

59. "ASUC Statement," *The Daily Californian* (Berkeley, CA), October 2, 1964, 12.

60. "We Plead for Peace," *The Daily Californian* (Berkeley, CA), October 5, 1964, 8.

61. "The Act of Deeding," *The Daily Californian* (Berkeley, CA), October 7, 1964, 8.

62. "On Free Speech," *The Daily Californian* (Berkeley, CA), October 8, 1964, 8.

63. "Bad Faith," *The Daily Californian* (Berkeley, CA), October 9, 1964, 12.

64. "Peace, We Hope . .," *The Daily Californian* (Berkeley, CA), October 16, 1964, 12.

65. "Strong Statements," *The Daily Californian* (Berkeley, CA), October 21, 1964, 8.

66. "Particle Off-Campus," *The Daily Californian* (Berkeley, CA), October 21, 1964, 8.

67. "Decision Before the Trial," *The Daily Californian* (Berkeley, CA), December 2, 1964, 8; "During the Course of Action," *The Daily Californian* (Berkeley, CA), December 3, 1964, 6.

68. "Promising Start," *The Daily Californian* (Berkeley, CA), November 6, 1964, 12.

69. "Back at the Start," *The Daily Californian* (Berkeley, CA), November 11, 1964, 8.

70. "The Regents Know," *The Daily Californian* (Berkeley, CA), November 18, 1964, 8.

71. "Cal's Strange Creatures," *The Daily Californian* (Berkeley, CA), September 30, 1964, 8.

72. "A Matter of Record," *The Daily Californian* (Berkeley, CA), November 14, 1964, 12.

73. See "Too Complicated," *The Daily Californian* (Berkeley, CA), November 23, 1964, 6; "On Shaking Ground," *The Daily Californian* (Berkeley, CA), December 10, 1964, 6; "Tomorrow's Decision," *The Daily Californian* (Berkeley, CA), December 17, 1964, 12.

74. "New McCarthy Era," *The Daily Californian* (Berkeley, CA), January 6, 1965, 8.

75. "We Need a Leader," *The Daily Californian* (Berkeley, CA), December 4, 1964, 12.

76. "Feathered Super-Men," *The Daily Californian* (Berkeley, CA), November 24, 1964, 12.

77. "A Reasonable Solution," *The Daily Californian* (Berkeley, CA), December 8, 1964, 6.

78. "The Quality of Mercy," *The Daily Californian* (Berkeley, CA), January 7, 1965, 8.

79. "Where Do We Belong?" *The Daily Californian* (Berkeley, CA), November 19, 1964, 8.

80. "Return to Class," *The Daily Californian* (Berkeley, CA), December 7, 1964, 12.

81. To Grandmother's House," *The Daily Californian* (Berkeley, CA), December 14, 1964, 6.

82. Eric Levine, "Free Speech Now!" *The Daily Californian* (Berkeley, CA), October 1, 1964, 10.

83. Eric Levine, "Free Speech's Odd History," *The Daily Californian* (Berkeley, CA), October 6, 1964, 6.

84. Eric Levine, "War with the Students," *The Daily Californian* (Berkeley, CA), December 2, 1964, 8.

85. Willwerth interview.

86. Roberts interview.

87. Justin Roberts, "For the Courts Only," *The Daily Californian* (Berkeley, CA), March 5, 1965, 12.

88. Roberts interview.

89. Justin Roberts, "A Welcome Philosophy," *The Daily Californian* (Berkeley, CA), May 6, 1965, 8.

90. Justin Roberts, "A $75,000 Bluebook," *The Daily Californian* (Berkeley, CA), May 13, 1965, 8.

91. Justin Roberts, ". . . in loco parentis," *The Daily Californian* (Berkeley, CA), April 20, 1965, 8.

92. Justin Roberts, "Whose Honeymoon is Over?" *The Daily Californian* (Berkeley, CA), April 23, 1965, 12.

93. Roberts interview.

94. Roberts interview.

95. Willwerth interview.

96. Benjaminson interview.

97. Ibid.

98. Oppedahl interview.

99. John F. Oppedahl, "'Word' Presented at Obscenity Trial," *The Daily Californian* (Berkeley, CA), April 21, 1965, 1.

100. Ibid.

101. Willwerth interview.

102. Oppedahl interview.

103. Roberts interview.

104. Branson interview.

105. Benjaminson interview.

106. Roberts interview.

107. Benjaminson interview.

108. Krause interview.

109. Branson interview.

110. Willwerth interview.

111. Ibid.

112. Wallace interview.

113. Oppedahl interview.

*Chapter Four*

# Two Faces of Journalism

When protesters at Howard University planned a takeover of the administration building in March 1968, student newspaper editor-in-chief Adrienne
Manns was one of the key organizers. She considered herself a crusading
journalist. "That's what I wanted to be and kind of patterned myself that way,
making sure the facts were correct but always looking for a way to improve
the world through journalism," she recalled. "That was my ideal." During the
five-day sit-in, she only left the protest to negotiate with administrators.
Other editors handled the duties of publishing the weekly *Hilltop* student
newspaper. [1]

When protesters at Columbia University took over several campus
buildings, including the administration building, about a month later, protest
organizers asked student newspaper editor-in-chief Robert Friedman to participate. "There was a moment for me, the very first day of the building
occupation, where I was asked to join the coordinating committee and I
declined," Friedman said. "I said I couldn't do that and be the editor of the
newspaper. We all in our own ways kept our distance, or found some way of
separating ourselves from the actual protests even though we were essentially
in support of them. We saw ourselves as journalists and that was our mission.
The most important thing was to be in a position where we could write our
stories and get the [*Columbia Daily Spectator*] newspaper out." [2]

The two young editors, both working to define themselves as journalists
at the same time and in very similar experiences, grappled with the same
question that journalists have been facing for decades: "Should I be an advocate or an objective observer?" Each made a different choice. Yet their college newspaper experience ultimately guided their career path just as it has
for so many journalists. Manns, frustrated by an inability to make significant

change in the world after graduation, reluctantly left journalism. Friedman made his career in journalism.

For many who are planning careers as professional journalists, student newspapers at colleges are their training grounds and as such are the places they learn about what it means to be a journalist, what role journalists play in society and what impact the objectivity/advocacy question will play in their careers. The student press allows young people the opportunity to practice writing and reporting skills while at the same time molding their ethical viewpoints and their ideals about journalism. Even though students will likely model their work on that of the professional press, the student newspaper is the place many of them will begin to make self-defining decisions, just as Manns and Friedman did, about the kind of journalism they would practice when they graduated. The college newspaper experience, then, is an important time in the development of future journalists. This chapter considers not only how these two editors and other student reporters and editors at *The Hilltop* and *Columbia Daily Spectator* did the job of reporting events but also studies their journalistic goals and beliefs about objectivity and advocacy in journalism. Eight former reporters and editors participated in interviews to tell the story of what happened: three from Howard and five from Columbia. Though some at both schools had short journalism careers after college, only two of those interviewed—one from each school—continue in those fields today. Four of the eight now have careers in law (three attorneys and one judge). One editor went into higher education, and another is a private equity investor and theatrical producer. Additional staffers from both schools could not be located or did not reply to requests for interviews.

Considering the development of advocacy/objectivity ideals within the context of the 1968 student protests also addresses two important areas in journalism history: the understudied student press during the turbulent protest years of the 1960s and the personal development of journalistic ideals.

## ADVOCACY VS. OBJECTIVITY: HOWARD AND COLUMBIA—1968

Objectivity in journalism is "the apparent value-free impartial reporting of observable or verifiable factual data from a detached, impersonal point of view." Some of the elements of objectivity in news reporting actually go back to the first newspapers when the colonial printers promised to report in a factual, truthful, and impartial manner. It was a lofty goal but one few could realistically meet simply because the individuals funding the newspapers controlled the point of view. Colonial printers may have considered themselves to be impartial, but it became almost impossible to attain as the American Revolution loomed.[3]

Impartiality and objectivity are not the same even though *impartial* is part of the definition for the word *objective*. An objective news story is impartial, but a piece of writing that is impartial may not be detached and impersonal or even factual.[4]

Researchers have found no clear point when objectivity entered into the world of journalism though one of the earliest press criticism books in 1859 castigated newspapers of the time for failing to be factual and impartial, both elements of the definition for objectivity, hinting that newspapers should therefore be objective.[5] Most of mainstream journalism had adopted the standard of objectivity in reporting by the mid-1900s. It was the core of the Code of Ethics for the Society of Professional Journalists that was first adopted in 1973.[6] Certainly by 1968, society had an expectation of the practice of objectivity in the professional press. Indeed, objectivity was seen as a key value of the responsible press.[7]

Advocacy journalism has perhaps deeper roots that stretch to the earliest days of newspapers when it was common for the writing to reflect the opinions and bias of whoever paid for the printing. Through the more than three centuries that newspapers have been published, advocacy journalism has been part of the mix in various ways. At times it has enjoyed a resurgence, even to a certain extent in more mainstream newspapers. The popular idea of civic journalism in the 1980s or investigative journalism into government wrongdoing like the Watergate scandal of the 1970s are such examples. Today, advocacy journalism has morphed into something more along the lines of the muckrakers of a century ago when journalists exposed various abuses in big business and corruption in government. Advocate publications are often left leaning and not apologetic about what they do, like *Mother Jones*, which is happy to be called left, liberal, and progressive as its reporters "cheerfully investigate any people or entities of any political persuasion, right, left, or center, if their behavior warrants it."[8]

Both forms of journalism have been able to find a place in society and have drawn students to their ranks throughout the decades. It is not surprising, then, that student journalists in 1968 found themselves considering these same issues.

## THE YEAR OF PROTEST AND VIOLENCE

The entire year of 1968 was a turbulent one in the United States, marked by protest, death, and violence both on and off college campuses. Most of the protests centered on civil rights/African-American concerns or the unpopular Vietnam War. On February 8, three black college students were killed when police officers fired into a crowd of South Carolina State College students who were protesting a segregated bowling alley near the campus of the historically black college in Orangeburg. More than two dozen others were injured by the bullets, many in the back as they tried to flee. Afterward, Howard University student Tony Gittens went to Orangeburg to see the situation first hand. He wrote about it for *The Hilltop*, which also included a picture Gittens took of a demonstration that followed the shootings. One demonstrator in the photo held a hand-lettered sign that read, "Bullets make excellent substitutes for tear gas and water hoses."[9] Large civil rights protests were launched around the country in response to the deaths, notably at the University of Wisconsin at Madison and the University of North Carolina at Chapel Hill.

Almost two months later, April 4, civil rights leader Martin Luther King Jr. was assassinated in Memphis, Tennessee, touching off demonstrations of all kinds throughout the country. In the aftermath of King's death, Black Panthers and Oakland police squared off in a shootout that left several dead or injured. Meanwhile, a double explosion in Richmond, Indiana, killed 41 and injured 150. Two months after that, presidential candidate Robert F. Kennedy was assassinated. In late August, the Democratic National Convention in Chicago was rocked by massive anti-war protests where hundreds of people, including bystanders, were beaten by thousands of police and National Guardsmen. Organizers of the protests, known as the Chicago 8, faced federal charges of rioting and conspiracy to riot.

In the midst of all this protesting, Howard and Columbia universities saw students take commonplace demonstrating to a new level: occupy campus buildings for several days and close down the school. Howard University in Washington, D.C., was the first to do so for five days in March, demanding a change to a more Afro-centric curriculum. New York's Columbia University followed a month later, pressing for an end to university involvement in an organization that conducted research to benefit the Vietnam War as well as an end to the construction of a new gymnasium that raised racial issues. Occupations and strikes at many universities occurred in the following months of 1968 and into the next year. Among these were students at San Francisco State College, who in November began what has become the longest strike in college history, and Harvard University and Boston University, where students occupied buildings in April 1969.

Although the protests at Howard and Columbia had dissimilar specific issues at the heart, both shared more than many might realize. Both were elite schools: Howard was known as the Black Harvard; Columbia was an Ivy League school. The 1968 sit-ins were not a spontaneous event at either school; issues that had stewed for a year or more had begun to boil and finally spilled out, taking the form of a takeover of the administration building at Howard and five buildings at Columbia. Race and war played a role in both protests, though certainly not in the same way. Protesters at both schools also found the administrations to be out of touch with students' changing needs and desires. When the takeovers occurred, neither administration was willing to budge much or work seriously for a compromise. Both university presidents stayed away from the university during the protests and kept themselves away from the student press. Before the Columbia sit-in, demonstrators from the New York-based university met with Howard protest leaders to learn how they had done it in Washington, D.C. [10]

Howard University was the first campus to have students occupy a building that spring, but Columbia University often becomes the *face* of the takeover student protests of 1968. A book devoted to discussing all the events around the world of just that one year gives Howard University's protest two sentences, and oversimplifies the underlying issue as "a lack of black history courses." [11] (The deaths at South Carolina State College do not even rate a mention in the book.) In contrast, the discussion about the demonstrations at Columbia University included details such as the development of the Students for a Democratic Society (SDS) organization that spearheaded the protest. It featured seventeen pages devoted to explaining the issues and the events that occurred. [12] Enterprising newspaper students from both universities went on to publish books about the events on their campuses that spring. Tom Myles, a photographer and writer for *The Hilltop* student newspaper at Howard University, published a 133-page book in 1969 that he subtitled a "photographic and narrative account." [13] Eight staffers from *Spectator* banded together to create a group called Members of the Board Associates. They worked through the summer in order to get their 307-page book to publishers that fall. [14]

## THE HOWARD UNIVERSITY PROTEST

Howard University is named for founder and Civil War Hero General Oliver O. Howard. The U.S. Congress chartered the university in 1867 as an institution for the education of African-American students and since 1879 has provided at least some of the funding. In 2016, the federal appropriation was 28 percent of the school's $783 million budget, with 10,002 students attending in fall 2015. [15] Among its thirteen schools and colleges today are a medical school, law school, and dental school. [16] In 1960, James M. Nabrit Jr., a renowned civil rights and constitutional lawyer in Washington, D.C., and dean of the Howard University School of Law, became the second black president of the university. He left in 1969. His tenure included the 1968 takeover of the administration building and the events that led up to it. [17]

Though it may seem easy to summarize the main issue behind the 1968 protest as a demand for black history classes as one author did, [18] it was anything but that simple. Rumblings "that the university [must] become more relevant to the needs of black people" had been fomenting for a few years before the five-day takeover in 1968. Black students had become increasingly aware of the role education was playing in the "continuation of the so-called 'niggerization' of black people," a process that involved "depreciating self-worth and encouraging black people to look outside of themselves for solutions to their problems" while putting them through a four-year "white-wash" at Howard that prepared them "to disappear into the white main-stream."[19] It was also becoming clear that proportionately more black sol-diers were dying in the Southeast Asia war, and this added more fuel to the fire.[20]

Author Tom Myles pointed to protests in spring 1965 as perhaps the beginning of the unrest that became the takeover in 1968. That spring is when Students for Academic Freedom (SAF) conducted rallies to protest the firing of professors they liked. The protests were unsuccessful, but it encour-aged students to think about banding together to address concerns. Other events compounded the students' desires to work for change. A due-process issue involving student discipline in 1966 was the impetus behind the found-ing of the Student Rights Organization, which was concerned that the univer-sity "was promoting and supporting a social and psychological frame of reference known for de-energizing and vitiating potential leaders of the black community." Members of SRO were also becoming more dissatisfied with some long-standing campus practices, such as compulsory Reserve Officer Training Corps (ROTC) for all males and a required freshman introductory course that equated a cultured education with, among other things, European and classical music while ignoring African-American music and culture. Some of the newspaper staffers were also members of SRO. "Needless to say, the newspaper was very important in creating a new positive framework for black students."[21]

Myles's *Centennial Plus 1* details the events that led up to the 1968 protest. The frequency of the demonstrations increased in the semesters prior to the takeover because of various administrative policies and actions, but the administration made few changes to address student concerns, opting instead to wait out the complaining students, who would graduate and take the issues with them. Then the Black Power Committee (BPC) arrived "and from that time on, the campus was literally 'on fire.'"[22] The BPC was born a year before the takeover, the day after an incident on March 21, 1967, when students rushed onto the stage as a Project Awareness lecture was beginning and disrupted the proceedings. The lecturer was the director of the Selective Service, General Lewis B. Hershey, who was to address students about the Vietnam War. The BPC's philosophy was basically that the administration would not make any changes unless forced to by a crisis situation. In their opening press conference the day following the Hershey incident, BPC members promised "to revolutionize black universities and to defeat the colonialist administrators who ruled on behalf of the white power structure, and to create universities to serve black people." Several students were ordered to appear for disciplinary hearings after the incident, but the hearings were postponed several times, including once when students stormed the hearing room. Shortly after that, President Nabrit announced a policy that the administration would be controlling and regulating all demonstrations and student-sponsored press conferences in the future. During this turmoil, the BPC sponsored at least two speeches by men refusing to go to Vietnam, including Heavyweight Champion Muhammad Ali. They also targeted ROTC, the top grievance for freshman males who were required to participate. Several started wearing Afro hairstyles and refused to cut it to meet ROTC standards. (ROTC participation became voluntary on February 1, 1968.)

Student demonstrations became stronger in February 1968, according to Myles's book. "We're going to get things straight in '68" was the mantra when angry members of the UJAMAA student group took action. UJAMAA, a Swahili word meaning togetherness, had been founded the previous fall when several campus groups joined forces, with Anthony Gittens as the director. About 500 students had gathered in mid-February to express support for the students killed and injured in Orangeburg, South Carolina. Then Gittens and Howard University Student Association President Ewart Brown announced demands they had for the administration that included resignations of the president, vice president, and liberal arts dean as well as changes toward a more Afro-centric curriculum. Following the speeches, students removed the U.S. flag flying nearby and took it and the list of demands to President Nabrit's office. They asked for an answer to their demands by February 29. Later, protesters removed a portion of a controversial fence near the women's dorms, along with the U.S. flag that flew there, and delivered them to Dean Frank Snowden Jr. When no response from Nabrit came, students disrupted the 101st Charter Day forum on Friday, March 1, 1968. Just as Nabrit was conferring honorary degrees, students mounted the stage and tried to take over the microphone. The sound system was immediately turned off and the meeting concluded, though protesters continued to shout to the audience. The administration sent letters to students believed to have participated in the Charter Day protest, ordering them to appear for disciplinary hearings. The action spurred students to rally and then stage the five-day sit-in at the administration building, March 19–23.

The takeover shut down the university. Students at the sit-in basically had four demands: drop charges against students named for disrupting Charter Day, reopen the university before students leave the administration building, restructure curriculum with more commitment to Afro-American thought, and give student leaders more freedom to handle their own business. They also asked for administration resignations.

The Board of Trustees and administrators did not capitulate completely on any of the demands. They did agree to work harder to become more relevant to students, but fell short of promising a major shift in the curriculum. They also would allow more student control over student affairs (they let *The Hilltop* be independent, for instance), would set up an ad hoc tribunal to deal with the Charter Day demonstrators, but would only resume classes when the building was cleared. If the building was not damaged, no charges would be leveled at the occupiers. As to the call for administration resignations, they reminded students that they are not in charge of deciding who runs the university.

Just after midnight on Saturday, March 23, the students accepted the administration's offers and ended the takeover.[23] Though the Vietnam War was not listed as part of the students' grievances, it was part of the backdrop of issues that angered students and part of the discussion throughout campus.[24]

The newspaper clearly supported the protesters from the beginning. Reporters positively covered speeches and meetings that called for promoting black pride,[25] finding black identity,[26] and even "a mild revolution."[27] A front-page editorial on March 8 explained that "it is the responsibility of *The Hilltop* to present issues and suggest solutions." A long list of suggestions followed: provide a more Afro-centric curriculum in many areas of the university, begin classes in jazz and other modern music, make all Afro-American newspapers available on campus, establish an Afro-American Research Institute, create a work-study program that put students out in the community, reorganize academic affairs on campus to give professors control, reinstate professors fired for political activism, free student government and the student newspaper from administration control, abolish curfews for women, ensure fair disciplinary hearings for students. Lastly, "all administrators who wish to retain the present non-democratic, non-black interest policy of the university should resign."[28]

Adrienne Manns was intimately involved with both the Charter Day demonstration and the subsequent administration building takeover. "Tony Gittens and I were the first ones to get up on the stage and interrupt the [Charter Day] proceedings," she recalled. "Tony got up and then I got up with him. I was really afraid because the security people were there with guns. But Tony was pretty fearless, so I got up when he did. . . . That's the first time I had participated in any demonstration." Along with the others, she received a letter ordering her to appear before the judiciary committee, the act that prompted students to plan the takeover of the administration building.[29]

## WRITING FOR THE *HILLTOP*

Manns was also the editor-in-chief of *The Hilltop*, the student newspaper with a history that stretches to 1924 when it first began publishing. In 2017 it had a circulation of 7,000 and published Monday and Tuesday.[30] In 1968, *The Hilltop* was a weekly newspaper that hit newsstands on Fridays. Manns recalled that students had to have stories and photos ready on Wednesday with proofreading on Thursday night. Students did the layout and helped with the paste-up work involved in preparing the pages for the offset press.[31] Pearl Stewart, a freshman reporter in spring 1968, was not involved in the production of the paper until her later college years, but she recalled weekly trips to the production shop in Maryland and staying up half the night "putting the paper to bed."[32] Both women worked at the student newspaper the entire time they were in college, beginning as reporters before they worked their way up to editor positions. Manns served as an editor beginning in her sophomore year and was the editor-in-chief in 1968. She recalled that the top editor received tuition as compensation, which was $550 a semester at the time. The managing editor received $250 a semester and other editors $200–250 for a year.[33]

Manns almost did not become the editor-in-chief for her senior year. The top editor position was determined by a publication board of administrators, students, and student government representatives. The board was unhappy about Manns's satirical column "Coon's Corner" that regularly criticized the administration, so they rejected her application for the job and proposed hiring a student with no newspaper experience. *The Hilltop* staff then rallied behind Manns. By her senior year, Manns already had some professional experience that included working as a stringer for the *Washington Post* and doing general assignment reporting at the *Daily News* in Washington during the summer of 1967. The staff went to the publication board, which eventually relented and hired Manns. She then chose the other editors who served with her. She managed a mostly volunteer staff with an $11,000 yearly budget from student fees, but that did not cover all the cost of publishing the newspaper. A business manager generated advertising to supplement the budget.[34]

Manns counts herself as a student of the muckrakers and the pioneer journalists. As a youth, she became a great fan of the *Chicago Defender* when she visited family in Chicago. The *Defender* was a daily newspaper at the time aimed at African-Americans. She also admired the work of writer Langston Hughes, who had been a reporter there in the 1920s. "Our family tradition, though I don't know if it was true or not, was that my great-grandfather had been a member of the staff of the *Defender*. I read it avidly and just thought that kind of newspaper had a crusading spirit. A crusading journalist—that's what I wanted to be," she said. Howard University's *Hill-*

*top* newspaper seemed a good place to start. "The newspaper was kind of a hot bed of radical thinking among students. When I came to Howard, there were members of the staff who were against the draft; they were against mandatory ROTC. Some of them were SNCC members [pronounced *snik*, the Student Nonviolent Coordinating Committee was a prominent civil rights organization at the time] or at least they were sympathizers. So when I walked into the office to work, I walked into a center of controversy. They were already activist journalists." The transition from observer to participant probably occurred for Manns during the summer of 1966 when she went to Harvard and heard civil rights activist and SNCC leader Stokely Carmichael speak about black power. Then working with voter registration "politicized me," she said.[35]

She aspired to become a professional journalist who could change the world and tried to do just that for a few years after she graduated from Howard. "But I left [journalism] because it seemed hopeless. I was so disillusioned and frustrated. . . . I was looking for a way to make a difference," she said. She was one of only two black journalists at the *Washington Post* at the time, sitting across from Carl Bernstein who would later become famous for breaking the Watergate scandal. She left *The Post* to work at the *Washington Afro American* where she was the acting city editor when she was just twenty-three years old. Manns decided she could not be a crusading journalist there, so she returned to *The Post* but found herself stuck working for the style section. Then she tried graduate school, returned to *The Post* again, and finally left Washington, D.C., in 1976. During another graduate school stint, this time at Hopkins, where she got deeper into African studies, she had the chance to teach temporarily at the University of Maryland and fell in love with teaching college students. She has spent most of her career in higher education. "I gave up journalism. That was emotionally one of the hardest things I've ever done," she said. "At heart I am probably always going to be a writer."[36]

But in 1968, Manns the editor was also one of the takeover organizers. She stepped back from the day-to-day operation of the student newspaper, letting other editors produce the newspaper for a few weeks and not interfering with what the reporters wrote. "I was able to detach myself pretty much from my two roles," she said. "I was able to compartmentalize to the point that I was able to say accurately what happened or didn't happen." Besides, she had surrounded herself with a hard-working staff that got along well, so it was not difficult to turn it over to them. "We were pretty much on the same page. The only difficulties we had were basically meeting deadlines. I was a little bit of a task master. I pushed people hard about making deadlines. But for content of the paper, we were mostly in agreement. . . . We spent a lot of time talking about issues, how much emphasis we would put on what. The only time I got upset was with Oswald [Ratteray, managing editor] because he used an expletive in a headline, a curse word, you know, the F word." The incident occurred at another time when Manns had been away from campus and had put Ratteray in charge. His "Fuck War" headline had gotten Manns called into the dean's office. "I had to stand by him, for loyalty sake," she explained. "I couldn't tell that he slipped this in on me, but he did." Privately, though, the staff had several conversations about the action and it never happened again.[37]

Manns's role during the takeover was less visible than the other organizers, and she preferred it that way. She led the negotiating team and issued statements to the press but never spoke at the rallies. With the deaths in South Carolina still fresh, she constantly feared for her safety: "Maybe it was my idealism at the time that this had to be something worth dying for because I knew students had been killed at Orangeburg; we were focused on what happened in Orangeburg. So we had to make a decision. We wanted to do everything to prevent violence—confrontation with law enforcement—but we knew it could happen." She said she had come to understand the gravity of protests while covering the now-famous October 1967 march at the Pentagon for *The Hilltop*. She saw the thousands of anti-war protesters confront 2,500 armed troops guarding the Pentagon. Though no protesters were shot, many were arrested. The experience was a reality check and helped her make a choice. "It was a decision I made to die if I had to," she said. "I don't know what I would have done if it actually happened, but I decided if it came to that, I guess that's what we would have to do. I feared for other people who may not have understood that could happen."[38]

In the end, when the protest leadership team decided the takeover was done so students should leave the building, Manns was disappointed. "I wanted to come out, but I wanted to have a boycott of classes until we got our demands met. But they overruled me." Exhausted and emotionally drained, Manns agreed to stand by the other leaders—Tony Gittens and student body President Ewart Brown—as they declared victory. "I remember that most vividly. I learned from that, that you have to back down sometimes. You can't always speak your truth. They weren't speaking my truth; they were speaking their truth. But I had to back off because it would have been very bad to lose our unity at the end. So, for the sake of the unity of the group, I didn't say anything."

Still, she learned an important life lesson about making real changes in the world: "It takes a long time. Tony said that. He said, 'you can't expect us to do in a week or a month or even four years what we are trying to accomplish.' He was right." Afterward, she had stress nightmares and felt frustrated that the takeover had failed. Her grades also suffered.[39]

*The Hilltop* covered the Charter Day event and the takeover protest. Two of its reporters were at the Charter Day event; Clyde W. Waite wrote a story for the student newspaper and Pearl Stewart's piece appeared in the freshman newsletter, *The Dialogue*. Stewart remembers seeing the students get up on the stage to interrupt the proceeding, and then the microphone was turned off. "As I recall, I was trying to take notes and I couldn't hear. I went up and approached the stage with my notebook," she said. "My involvement was to be there as a reporter." However, she ended up being on the list of students who allegedly caused the disturbance. "My parents contacted me and told me that they had received this letter from the university saying I was one of the people who had disrupted the normal processes of the university and that I would be dealt with accordingly," she said, noting that she also received a copy of the letter at her campus address. She was never disciplined. [40]

Waite recalls trying to be impartial as he covered the Charter Day event: "I remember the forlorn look of James Nabrit, the president, who was so besieged by the students, and I remember feeling a bit of sympathy but also disdain for him. As a reporter you try to see both sides of things. I know that Nabrit was under pressure from the establishment. The funding for the university in large part came from the federal government, and he had to placate the funding sources while at the same time try to be responsive to the students." [41]

Waite's story appeared on page 2 of the paper a week after the event. Written in chronological order, much like the minutes of a meeting, the story did not get to the student protest until the second column of the article, which filled most of three of the five columns on the tabloid-sized page. Several stories in the newspaper followed this same style rather than emulating professional news writing that would likely have used inverted pyramid style reporting with the most important elements of the story leading out the piece. Editors, often too busy getting the paper out to do much work on articles, apparently did not rewrite the piece either, opting to let it run as written. Both the writing style and editing may be a reflection of not having a journalism program at the school. Stewart said students could minor in journalism by taking a few classes, but no journalism major existed at the time. [42] There was little training for reporters. "It was pretty much on-the-job training," Waite explained. [43]

Waite tried to maintain an open mind about the protests throughout that year and never participated in any demonstration or rally. His view of what was happening was perhaps not the typical student view because he was not the typical student. He had not planned to attend college when he traveled from his small hometown of McKeesport in western Pennsylvania to Washington, D.C., after high school graduation. Then, while apartment hunting a few weeks later, he saw what he thought was an apartment building full of girls and went inside to apply for an apartment, thinking this would be a fun place to live. Instead it turned out to be a women's dorm at Howard University. The experience got him thinking about attending college. It took him two years to earn the money he needed to get started, so he was older and more mature than the typical freshman. Throughout his time at Howard, he also maintained a part-time job at the Library of Congress, which provided him with a different view than those students who mostly spent their time on campus. "I could see the more establishment view of achieving things through compromise, through participation," he said. "I just had a difficult time understanding the attitude of tearing up the social structure to rebuild something to replace it." He had joined the newspaper staff because fellow debater Adrienne Manns and others worked there. He was a reporter but never an editor.

By spring 1968, he was preparing to graduate, yet Waite was not unaffected by the social turmoil of the time. "There was a dynamic tension that was going on, not only throughout the country, from a social status standpoint, from a racial standpoint," he said. "It seemed that everything was in flux at the time. I was terribly conflicted. You could probably see some of that in my reporting, which was factual, what took place in the conflict between the administration and the students. . . . I know that there was the conflict between the practicality of achieving results and the destructive behavior that I saw that was hard for me to reconcile."[44]

Waite asked to write the main story about the takeover after it began. "I had a great interest in it," he explained, "and I was not inclined to be a demonstrator myself, but I was interested in the issues that both sides had raised. I don't believe I got assigned to do that. It was something that I felt the need to do." He went in and out of the building many times during the protest. "There was this anticipation that there was going to be tear gas; there were going to be people dragged out and arrested and all the rest of that," he said, though that never happened because eventually students left on their own.[45] Once again in chronological order, his story on March 22 explained how the protest developed, quoted some of the speakers at the rally that preceded the takeover, and finally described some of the scene inside the occupied building.[46] "These stories that we were writing, they were all first person [accounts]," Waite said. "They were all what we saw, what we were doing."[47]

Stewart, on the other hand, was among the takeover demonstrators and spent a few nights sleeping on the floor inside the administration building. "People slept. People talked. There was a lot going on. It was kind of like camp," she said. "I remember feeling very passionate about the issues concerning black studies. The mantra was 'Howard should be a black university,' which sounds ridiculous now because it was majority black [at the time], but the curriculum did not reflect that. The issues were very real and very important." She also felt it was important to report on the event. Being a participant journalist was not an issue at Howard where the newspaper staff had no code of ethics that reporters were expected to abide by. It was not unusual for the time, she said, noting that student newspapers throughout the country in general supported the student protesters on their campuses. "You wouldn't find many [student newspapers] that would editorialize against the protests," she said. She was elected as vice president of the sophomore class for the next year, continued to work for the student newspaper, and continued to cover campus issues. [48]

Stewart also had a close connection to the demand for a Black Studies Program. As a sociology major, she sat through some of the social science classes that she said were Euro-centric, which many students saw as a big problem, "even for students who had no interest in majoring in Black Studies but who didn't see any relevance to their lives or the lives of black people throughout the country," she said. "I remember walking out of a sociology class where the professor was having a discussion that involved [white movie stars] Elizabeth Taylor and Richard Burton and their lifestyle, and I just thought, 'this is so absurd.' I remember walking out of the class and getting out of that major." She later was one of the first students to graduate in Afro-American studies when it was finally added to the Howard curriculum. [49]

Stewart's report on the takeover in the March 22 paper was a front-page sidebar to Waite's main story and was filled with quotes from other protest participants. [50] These were the only two stories about the takeover on the front page of the issue, which was the only paper published during the event. Editors devoted about half the front page to the demonstration, including a photo. A campaign speech by presidential hopeful Eugene McCarthy and a preview of the coming visit of civil rights leader Martin Luther King Jr. filled the rest of the page. Inside, one page was devoted to the takeover event, including the jump from Waite's front page story, along with one other story on a third page, and pictures of students manning the campus telephone switch board and studying in an administration building conference room.

The rest of the eight-page, tab-size paper contained normal college newspaper fodder: announcements of coming events, sports, and opinion pieces. The usual columns and commentary filled the op-ed page but did not address the takeover. Instead, a long open-forum piece commemorated the 1960 Sharpeville massacre in South Africa where police killed sixty-nine people when they fired into a crowd of black demonstrators. Two regularly student-written columns addressed other racial issues. One of the letters to the editor offered support from students at George Washington and American universities.

The editorial, titled "The Motley Crowd," said the demonstration was the result of "101 years of stifling plantation rule" that students had finally decided to throw off. The Motley Crowd referred to the students who received letters for disrupting the Charter Day program. (The editorial indicated thirty-seven students received letters. However, Waite's story reported it was thirty-nine students, and Myles's book said it was thirty-eight.) The editorial points out that student government leaders were not among those cited on Charter Day, noting the move was the administration's failed attempt to "divide and rule." Instead, student leaders joined in the takeover protest. The piece concluded by urging UJAMAA members and other students to stick together because "you have nothing to lose but your chains."[51]

The March 22 issue was typical of *The Hilltop* reporting throughout the year. Most of the news pieces read like modern blog entries filled with opinions and observations about life, politics, and any other topic on the writer's mind. "It was a student newspaper, and it was perceived by the staff as an advocacy publication as far as student rights and student protests were concerned," Stewart explained. "There was an effort to cover the facts. If we ever got a response, say from the administration, it was in the story."[52] Waite said he could see the competing interests the newspaper faced. Newspapers, even those published by college students, "are supposed to operate as a news gathering operation, to report the things that are going on, to inform the student body," Waite said, "but the newspaper was looked to as an organ of the movement. There was a lot of pressure to involve the newspaper as an advocate of a position as opposed to one that just reported."[53]

The protest ended Saturday, March 23, between issues of *The Hilltop*. The next paper, March 29, had more coverage of the five-day event, including a full-page chronological account of the last two days of the takeover,[54] and another shorter piece that included more quotes from sit-in participants.[55] However, it was another college's protest that garnered the top spot on page 1. Written by Waite, it told of ninety Howard students traveling to Bowie State College, twenty miles northeast in Maryland, to help students there who were conducting a boycott of classes in an attempt to force administrators there to deal with their demands for improving the quality of everything from the condition of the dorms to the food and the registrar's office.[56] Another story that was almost as large dominated the bottom of the front page. Though not designated as an analysis, it did just that by examining the development of protests at Howard that finally culminated with the takeover.[57]

A strongly worded March 29 editorial chastised the administration for doing nothing, not just during the takeover but for some time leading up to the demonstration.[58] Though Manns does not remember if she wrote the editorial, she said it reads like something she would have written at the time. Specific word choice in the piece is an interesting example of what she said was an "attitudinal terminology" at the time.[59] When referring to the students or African-Americans in general, the author uses the word "black," but administrators or people who did not support the students' cause are called "Negroes" or "coloreds." The opening sentence shows the difference: "Black students at Howard, like black people in urban areas, are becoming the subject of intensive studies by irresponsible Negro tokens. . . ." Further down in the editorial appears references to "those Negro[es] who operate Howard," "colored nationalists," and "defending Dean Snowden as a colored hero," all showing the students' disdain.[60] "That was our thing. I take responsibility for that," Manns said, though she points to human rights activist Malcolm X as probably the person who started the practice of using the terminology this way. "We were saying the old guard, that they wanted to be known as Negroes, and they wanted to be known as coloreds, . . . that they were for promoting the status quo and getting along and fitting in." Referring to African-Americans as "black" was a sign of militancy, of a willingness to embrace racial identity, of a desire for change. It was meant to send a message to the administration and the administration knew it, she said.[61]

*The Hilltop* appeared to have no more problems than other student newspapers when it came to getting along with the administration. Campus officials were upset with some of the things the students published and did not say much about others. Sometimes, though, "it was pretty rough," Manns recalled. Her satirical pieces got her in the most hot water with the campus officials. Once she had accused Howard's president of tap dancing for Congress, equating the need to procure federal funding to a black person dancing and entertaining to get favor. The staff had even superimposed President Nabrit's head on the body of a ballerina. The president was angry, and the dean called, demanding an apology for the obscene portrayal. Manns replied that the piece was satire, and since the ballerina was clothed, it was not obscene. She did not apologize.[62]

One incident in particular stands out for Manns because of the heat she took for it. In a March 1, 1968, editorial, the newspaper chastised Howard law professor Patricia Harris, the administration, and the Board of Trustees for not speaking out publicly about the Orangeburg shootings. Harris, who served as the first black ambassador from the United States from 1965 to 1967, had the opportunity to speak out, the editorial maintained, because she served on the Human Relations Commission at the United Nations and, just four days after the shootings, conducted a press conference where she could have addressed it but did not.[63] Harris made an angry call to Manns about the "scurrilous attack" because she was not presently a member of such a commission (the correct name was Human Rights Commission, Harris said), and she had not conducted a press conference. The newspaper reported Harris's response in a correction story the next week, also on the editorial page. The newspaper apologized for the errors but tempered it with a call for action: "We apologize for the misstatements, but in doing so we do look forward to her speaking out as a fellow Afro-American."[64]

## THE COLUMBIA PROTESTS

When Columbia protest organizers decided they were going to take over buildings in New York City, they contacted some of the Howard students for advice on how to do it. Manns remembers meeting with some Columbia students to explain how they had managed the takeover at Howard. She was proud of the civility students maintained at Howard because, despite the crush of students piled into the administration building, students kept the building clean and did not vandalize the premises.[65] Students at Columbia were accused of just the opposite when police ended the eight-day occupation, though many students and faculty claimed the damage was caused by the police and not the students.[66]

Like Howard University, the Columbia protest did not just happen one day. It was the culmination of several issues, some that stretched back several years, in an environment that was ripe for something big to happen. The story is documented in the book *Up Against the Ivy Wall: A History of the Columbia Crisis,* which is the source for most of the information used here about the protest. It was written by members of the *Spectator* staff. Just as students had been expressing for several years at colleges and universities across the country, many of the Columbia student body felt the administration was not responding to their desires for change and a place at the decision-making table about issues that affected their academic lives. They also raised concerns about the university's continuing expansion that throughout the decade was taking big bites out of neighboring Harlem and evicting blacks and Puerto Ricans who made up 85 percent of the area.

While unrest over the unpopular Vietnam War was only part of the backdrop of the Howard protest, it was one of the key issues at Columbia. A little more than a year before the building takeovers, the *Spectator* student newspaper confirmed that the university was affiliated with the Institute for Defense Analyses, a research group started in 1956 to evaluate weapons and conduct other research for the Department of Defense. In 1967, Columbia's president, Grayson Kirk, and a Columbia trustee were on the IDA board.[67] Students saw the office on campus as Columbia's complicity in the Vietnam War that so many hated. Later that year, on October 23, 1967, SDS delivered a letter to Kirk demanding that Columbia sever all ties with any defense-related research. Eventually, the university did just that although Kirk continued as an individual on the IDA board. On February 23, 1968, SDS also stopped campus recruiting by Dow Chemical, one of the chief producers of the flamethrower fuel napalm and the defoliant Agent Orange, both used in the Vietnam War. On March 27, 1968, members of SDS protested inside Low Memorial Library, which served as the administration building at the time. The demonstration was two-fold: protest involvement in IDA and flout the new campus rule that forbade protests inside campus buildings. Six protesters, who became known at the IDA 6, were later ordered to appear before the dean but wanted an open hearing; the dean refused and placed them on probation.

The construction of a new gymnasium sparked the second key issue in 1968. The university was finally starting construction on the building that had been planned since 1960 when the city leased part of Morningside Park to the university. The plan called for the Black Harlem community to have access to the facilities as well. To do that, the community's entrance was designed to be on the lower level on the back side of the building—basically a back door. Community members, who felt they had not been part of the planning process, found the door solution to be a symbolic return to the days of blacks being required to enter through the back of a building. The community would also be able to use only about 12 percent of the building, another sore point for critics. The day after construction began in February 1968, twenty people staged a sit-in with twelve arrested. The next week, 150 protested and twelve were arrested.

The two issues came together on Tuesday, April 23. SDS protesters, upset about how the IDA 6 were treated, staged a rally at the gym construction site, joined by black students. SDS leaders were expected to attend a discussion with university officials in the McMillan Theater following the rally. Police converged on the construction site, and the crowds moved back to regroup at the sundial, located in the center of College Walk on the campus. Rather than meet with the administration in the theater, protesters then decided to take over the Columbia College administration located in Hamilton Hall until six demands were met: drop action against the IDA 6, with general amnesty for protesters; drop the ban on protests inside buildings; stop construction on the gym until appropriate community involvement could be accomplished; provide open hearings and due process for future student discipline issues; get out of the IDA; drop charges from previous protests at the gym site. When Columbia College Dean Henry Coleman came into the building to talk to the protesters, the students decided to hold him hostage until their demands were met though they allowed him to leave the next day.

The takeover spread to other buildings in the following days, and the university shut down. In the early morning hours the next day, black students in Hamilton Hall, members of the group Student Afro-American Society, asked all the white students to leave. Although the black students were also opposed to the gym, they had a different agenda that also included a demand for more Black Studies classes. The white protesters, directed by SDS leaders, marched to Low Library and broke a window in a door in order to enter. They commandeered President Kirk's office and rifled through his drawers and cabinets. Architecture students took over Avery Hall to protest the architecture program. Graduate students took over Fayerweather Hall. Other students took over Mathematics Hall. The students barricaded the various entrances to keep police or others from entering. To gather supplies, students entered and left the buildings through the windows.

The administration made feeble attempts to diffuse the situation by offering disciplinary warnings instead of probation. They did not want to give in on any of the demands. A faculty group's proposal, called "the bitter pill," would not give either side everything it wanted but called for working toward change. The administration finally called in the police. They came during the early morning hours of Tuesday, April 30. Officers, both in and out of uniform, cleared the buildings and arrested 695 people. Then they swept through the campus, beating anyone they met—including innocent bystanders—to force them off the grounds. Students followed up the takeovers with a class strike that about 6,000 students respected. Professors planned alternative ways to end the semester, and students were allowed to take passing grades rather than a letter grade. A second round of protests occurred May 17–18. This time students protested in the neighborhood at a building that the university had purchased and then had evicted tenants in preparation for expansion. Students also took over Hamilton Hall again, continuing the protest of the IDA 6 discipline.[68]

## COLUMBIA DAILY SPECTATOR

The student newspaper began as *The Columbia Spectator* in 1877. It published twice a month until fall 1896 when it went weekly for three years, then biweekly from February 1899 to June 1902. Daily publication during the regular school year began October 6, 1902, with summer publication beginning in 1916. In 1880, it was published in a small two-column format. Subscriptions cost $2 for a year of eighteen issues. It bears little resemblance—in looks or content—to its successor, the *Columbia Daily Spectator.*

Independent since 1962, the newspaper was completely run by students in 1968 with no faculty or administration oversight. Advertising paid for publication, and no one was paid for their work. The editors, chosen by the outgoing managing board of editors, typically served for one year, beginning in March of what was usually their junior year.[69] As protesting started to heat up at Columbia in spring 1968, a new set of editors was moving into leadership roles. At the annual Blue Pencil Dinner in mid-March, ten men were named to run the newspaper, including Robert Friedman as editor-in-chief with Michael Rothfeld as managing editor and Oren Root Jr. in the newly created executive editor position with the responsibility to coordinate editorial and business policy as well as plan and write editorials.[70] That same night, more than forty staffers were promoted to various news boards, including reporters Michael Stern and Robert Stulberg, who had both been covering the different protests occurring on campus.[71]

All of these five men had been with the *Spectator* staff since the beginning of their college careers at Columbia. As freshmen, though in different years, Friedman and Stern had shown up at the newspaper office, got an assignment, and kept coming back, which was the typical way people got started at the newspaper. Stern's first assignment was a review, but he soon was writing about community affairs, including the controversy about Columbia's expansion into Morningside Heights.[72] Rothfeld started because someone at the dorm where he lived suggested checking it out.[73] Stulberg followed in the footsteps of the first female *Spectator* editor, Eleanor Prescott, whom he had known when both of them were growing up in Detroit. "She really didn't try to sell me on the *Spectator*," Stulberg recalled about telling Prescott he was considering debate instead. "She looked kind of disbelieving that it would even be a choice in my mind." And, of course, *Spectator* won out.[74] Root remembers clearly his first byline as a freshman with a story he had written about a student athlete who had been reclassified as 1A for the draft, making him eligible to go to Vietnam despite his student status. His editor completely rewrote the entire piece with hardly any of Root's original wording, but Root still got the byline. As an editor, Root tried to truly just edit and leave the rewriting to the reporters.[75]

The *Columbia Daily Spectator* published each weekday, including Saturday and Sunday during the takeovers. Though it was scheduled to be available each morning at 8 a.m., it sometimes hit stands in the afternoon. "We used to joke that we were New York's second largest afternoon newspaper even though we were supposed to come out in the morning," said Stulberg, who was one of the lead reporters that spring.[76] Typically, the students published 10,000–15,000 copies of the tabloid-sized paper, usually eight pages, Monday through Friday. It was distributed free around campus.

Producing the paper required a mixture of production techniques common at the time. Using what was known as *cold type* or offset printing, students set copy with a Friden typesetting system that turned out long strips of copy that had to be cut and then affixed to the layout sheets with wax, which allowed for repositioning of the blocks of copy. Headlines were created on a linotype machine—*hot type*—run by a professional operator the newspaper hired. After assembling all the page elements—known as paste up—the students would grab a taxi and take the completed pages and artwork to the press in Brooklyn. The goal was to finish by 2 a.m. and then visit the West End Bar for a drink before it closed at 4 a.m. However, it stopped serving food at 3 a.m.[77] "The question was," Root recalled, "would we get the paper to bed in time to get to the West End to get my favorite sliced egg sandwich on rye with mayo and lettuce?"[78]

Putting out the newspaper required a lot of commitment. Work began early afternoon each day, including Sunday, with Saturday off. Most of the editors and reporters tried to squeeze classes into the morning hours and then spend the rest of the day at the *Spectator*. Many of the staff, all volunteers, spent 75–80 hours each week there. "I ended up majoring in *Spectator* rather than academic subjects," said Rothfeld, who was the managing editor when the takeovers began. "I went to classes, and I did OK on my grades and stuff, but I really loved *Spectator*."[79] It was the one-week break at midterm and two weeks before finals when the newspaper did not print that saved Friedman's grades. "That's when I did all my school work," he said.[80] Stulberg immersed himself in newspaper work so much that by the end of his first semester he was ill.[81]

Throughout the protests, the staffers worked to maintain objectivity and professionalism in their writing. "Most of the reporters and editors were sympathetic to the strike, but I would say none of them were actually participants," Friedman said, noting that he and most of the staff saw their role as journalists as "simply to tell the story as truthfully and tellingly as possible. And make sure we got the paper out every night. I think we kept a very high standard of journalism in reporting what was going on and we got a lot of praise for it from our colleagues in the professional press."[82]

Objectivity can be an elusive concept to try to embrace, but it was something the staff always strove to achieve. "We definitely tried to write coherent stories," Root said. "We had standards we tried to live up to in terms of the appearance of the paper and the way we wrote headlines. I look back on it, and I'm proud of what we did, even through the prism of forty-four intervening years."[83]

Stulberg recognized that complete objectivity was really not achievable: "We talked often about the canard that journalists are somehow bound to report objectively as if to say there was an objective truth from which the true reporter would emerge in the newspaper, when in fact every reporter at every newspaper had certain subjective views of what was going on and brought ideas about that to the table as they approached any event. So we talked about the importance of accuracy, the importance of care, the importance of fairness—giving multiple sides of the controversy [an] opportunity to express a view."[84]

The editors and reporters also thought they should not become participants in the protests because it would jeopardize the credibility and status of the newspaper. "The newspaper was highly regarded as a source for campus information by faculty, students and administrators," Friedman said, and the staff wanted to keep it that way.[85]

The *Spectator* staff worked hard to be professional. "[The editors] had very high expectations of distinguishing what we knew and what we didn't know and how we knew and how we determined that we knew it and how we would demonstrate it to others," Rothfeld said. After a story was researched, reported and written, the reporters had to defend it to the editors. It was a

rigorous process. "It was run like a professional, metropolitan daily newspaper, and everybody took it very, very seriously," he said.[86]

The staff also tried to emulate *The New York Times*. "The *Times* is what
we aspired to," Root said. "There were quite a few *Spectator* alums who
went to the *Times*, and in a grandiose way that's what we tried to measure
ourselves to."[87] Rothfeld remembers copying the *Times* style of making
headlines complete sentences and ranking stories by placement on the page
just as the *Times* did.[88] "All of our standards had been formed by the *Times*,"
Stern said. "We tried to be fair and balanced in reporting unless it was a news
analysis, which was a classic *Times* distinction of the '60s."[89]

However, none of the editors or reporters was impressed with *The New
York Times'* coverage of the protests and especially a front-page opinion
piece that castigated the student protesters. "When we saw the *Times* write
what we thought was a beyond-the-pale opinion piece on the front page, we
were pretty scandalized," Root said.[90] Stern recalls the *Times* reporting the
news stories about Columbia like a typical police story. "They really missed
the story," he said. "The issue was about the role of the university in society
and its relationship to the war, and that was what the student movement was
about in the '60s. . . . The [entire] student movement was covered as a police
story. That's what we resented, really."[91] The *Times* was not alone in covering it this way. "There was a strong tendency in the mainstream press to
focus on this as some sort of youthful acting-out," Stulberg said, noting that
it was rare for any professional media to "even mention the underlying issues, which had moved people to support the protests, including most especially the war in Vietnam and the racial issues raised by the construction of
the gym in the adjoining park. . . . We took the politics and social impacts of
the events quite seriously rather than view this as just some sort of exuberant
boxing match between contending sides. I think that was a fairly sophisticat-
ed view, given that we were student journalists."[92]

When the takeovers, strike, and subsequent protests occurred, the *Spectator* editors began an ongoing conversation about how to cover what was
happening, making sure they really tried to express the underlying issues and
explain them to readers. "It was not a complicated story to cover," Friedman
said, especially with everything happening right on campus. "What was complicated was figuring out what we wanted to write and getting it all done on
schedule. In the first three days I didn't sleep but a couple of hours. The
protests were going on twenty-four hours a day. We would double back to
the office about six o'clock in the evening and try to make sense of what had
happened that day and try to write our stories and get them edited over the
next eight hours."[93]

Reporters did not find the requirements for covering the protest to be any
different than their other assignments. "The goals during the crisis were the
same goals the newspaper always had, which were to research and report

with care and accuracy," Stulberg said. "In a sense, an additional imperative during the protest was to try as best we could to report on and illuminate the underlying grievances to the protests, the underlying political social issues." So the reporters spent time explaining the issues in many of the news stories. "The act of reporting them itself had an advocacy quality about it because we were saying to the reader it's important that you know about these; it's important that you think about them; it's important that you have the information you need to evaluate them."[94]

The first night of the takeovers, several staffers were up all night, covering the story or trying to get the paper out. Rothfeld had been at McMillan Theater, waiting to cover the SDS meeting with the administrators. When the SDS leaders did not show up, he went outside, just in time to see the protesters entering Hamilton hall.[95] *Spectator* reporter Mark Jaffe had gotten inside Hamilton Hall with the protesters but had to leave early the next morning when the white students were asked to take their protest elsewhere. Stulberg was on the plaza as the white students streamed out of the building. "I can just picture right now, the groups kind of contesting about what should be done next," he said. He interviewed protesters as they headed for Low Memorial Library and the president's office.[96]

Root and Rothfeld were working in the *Spectator* composing room on the fourth floor of Ferris Booth Hall when they saw the white students leaving Hamilton and heading toward Low. Both grabbed notebooks and went to report on what was happening. Root watched as students broke a window in the door to get into Low Library and went into the president's office. "I was there and witnessed the beginning of that substantial expansion of the building occupation," he said.[97]

Rothfeld met Provost David Truman at Low Library. Truman, half dressed, had rushed to the campus when he heard of the occupations. He asked Rothfeld to talk to the student protest leaders, who were now sitting in the president's office, and try to get them to leave. Rothfeld told Truman that he was there as a journalist and did not think it was appropriate, but Truman finally persuaded him to do it. Rothfeld spoke to SDS leader Mark Rudd, who only responded with a lewd remark. Rothfeld then returned to the entrance and urged Truman not to call in the police at this point because he thought it would only escalate the situation. In hindsight, removing the students from the building immediately would have been the wisest move, Rothfeld said. Instead, when the police did come to campus, the situation had been allowed to fester for days, and the police were ready to take out their anger on "these rich white kids" who were disrupting the university.[98]

Rothfeld also was appalled at what was going on at Hamilton and Low. "To me, philosophically, the taking over of buildings, the shutting down of classrooms, the disruption of the education process, those were things that I abhorred," he said. He opposed the Vietnam War but not for the same rea-

sons SDS members did. His view of a university's role included expression
without violence. "A university should be the one place in society where all
points of view can be presented and discussed and analyzed. And people
should be allowed to make up their own minds about developing their own
views." He was not happy when the newspaper editorial stance was in support of the protesters and portrayed the administration as "basically a bunch
of hoods" when he knew from his reporting time covering the administration
that it was not true. While he was opposed to any building occupations, he
sympathized with the black students, who, he believed, had "tangible issues"
with the "blatant racism" in the gym construction and thus had a positive
goal. The other protesters, however, were making "a negative, amorphous
attack on society." The black students had been willing to negotiate with the
administration but the other protesters had not. "They [white students] not
only disrupted an open-university process, but also employed the tactics of
totalitarian governments," Rothfeld said.[99] He also saw a slant creeping into
the news stories that also supported the protesters.[100]

## THE EDITORIAL POSITION

Rothfeld continued to attend the daily editorial meetings where the seven
student editors would hash out what the stance would be in the next day's
editorial, but he was not always happy about the position they adopted. Only
a majority of editors need to support an editorial for it to run. The editors had
a policy that if any editor did not support an editorial and felt strongly about
it, a dissenting tag line could be added to the piece, listing the editor who
disagreed. On the seventh day of the takeover, Monday, April 29, the dissent
line read, "Michael Rothfeld took no part in the determination of this editorial."[101] The next day, Tuesday, for only the second time during the protest, the
editorial page had space for a staff box; Rothfeld's name was missing.

Rothfeld said he had resigned Friday. It was a tough decision. "I had
worked hard for two and a half years to get onto the editorial board and to be
the managing editor," he said. "I had two philosophical differences with my
colleagues on the editorial board, whom I respected as people and liked as we
had all worked together for almost three years. First, I could not agree with
their active advancement of the white students' views and actions as well as
the polemical language of the editorials. Second, I could not agree with the
political spin that had entered *Spectator's* news reporting. The prospects of
endless 'dissent' lines under editorials and the futility of trying to change the
reporting slant made me decide to resign and do other things with my time."

After Rothfeld's resignation, two of the editors asked him to reconsider,
but Rothfeld held fast. One day he met SDS leader Mark Rudd on campus,
and Rudd said, "'Well, Rothfeld, I hear you got fired because of me.' This

was typical of the self-importance on the part of the SDS leaders. 'No, Mark, I didn't lose my job; I quit because I disagree with what you guys are doing,'" Rothfeld said.[102]

Rothfeld was not the only one who took issues with various editorial points. Sports editor Andrew Crane had dissented from a front-page editorial the day before, Sunday, which called for the administration to grant amnesty or close the university and noted the use of force to end the occupation that was entering its sixth day was "abhorrent and suicidal."[103] The business manager, advertising manager and comptroller did not sit on the editorial board and had no input on editorial policy, but they apparently wanted that made clear on May 2 when a tag line below the staff box and above the editorial noted their non-involvement.[104] The dissents were indicative of the varying opinions among the editors. "It was very contentious during that period," Friedman said. "There were a lot of dissents in those editorials, but we managed through the process and reached consensus."[105]

From the beginning of the takeovers, the "consensus" in the daily editorials, even if it was not strong, was generally critical of the establishment—first the administration and eventually the police. Even before the takeovers, the newspaper had a cool relationship with the administration. "They looked at us with wariness. We often published things that they did not like," Friedman said. "I should say, to their credit, they never made an effort to interfere with what we did or censor what we wrote or shut us down or anything like that. They might have wished they could have, but they didn't."[106]

The morning after students first occupied Hamilton Hall, the *Spectator* editorial blamed the administration for causing the unrest because of its refusal to give students a say in their education and then recommended that the faculty act to take control, especially of disciplinary action for students. It also supported severing ties with IDA, getting rid of the indoor protest ban, halting work on the gym, and withdrawing trespass charges against those who demonstrated at the gym. The protesters did not get away unscathed, either. It condemned some of the acts of the demonstrators, especially those holding Dean Coleman hostage, those resorting to violence at the gym site, and those allowing non-students to play a leading role in the Hamilton Hall takeover.[107]

The next day, the editorial attacked the administration again, this time for waiting until afternoon before talking to students about the dean's safety, for calling in police to wander around campus but do nothing, for locking campus buildings to ward off some possible community assault that never came. It also chastised the faculty for missing its opportunities to help, which essentially was an abdication of its role at the university. The only alternative to ending the protest, the editorial maintained, was to halt the gym construction and negotiate with the black students in Hamilton Hall.[108]

When a faculty ad hoc committee finally acted, the editorial praised them first for stepping up,[109] for being the only ones who appeared to be able to do anything to solve the crisis,[110] and then for crafting proposals for settlement that the editorial board encouraged all faculty and protesters to support as well.[111]

As the takeover entered its seventh day, Monday, April 29, the editors had plenty of criticism for all sides of the controversy: The Board of Trustees were out of touch; the administration was at the end of its rope with an exhausted faculty that was about to drop the tether; the protesters were losing sight of why they were demonstrating, seeking immediate action instead of real long-term change. Once again it laid out terms everyone should accept, some that were new this time: faculty must get behind the suggestions from the ad hoc committee and quit their jobs if the administration would not budge; the gym construction must stop; the IDA affiliation must end; and all protesters should receive the same punishment. (The tag line read: "Michael Rothfeld took no part in the determination of the editorial.")[112]

After police swept through the campus in the wee hours of Tuesday, April 30, arresting and beating students, the editorial that day was a two-column blank space with a wide black border and only the staff box, now minus Rothfeld's name. "I think probably the best editorial I wrote was the non-editorial," Friedman said, "because that [marked] the moment in the history of Columbia that they would call the police and arrest 700 people."[113]

The next day, Wednesday, May 1, the editorial called for resignations of President Kirk and Vice President David B. Truman for worrying about their authority more than what was best for the university, trustee Chairman William Petersen for paralyzing negotiations with protesters, and graduate faculty Dean George Fraenkel for undercutting the faculty. It called for a reorganization of the university, including the transfer of power from the trustees to the faculty, and it urged a strike until changes occurred.[114] The editorial on Thursday, May 2, addressed having police on campus, pointing to police presence as only fueling more student resentment and possible violence. Until the administration removed the police, it said, the campus could not begin to rebuild.[115]

When the student strike began the next week, the *Spectator* supported the effort and also supported faculty willing to conduct classes somewhere other than the usual classroom. Such a break from the norm would keep the university from falling back into the status quo of the days before the takeover, it claimed.[116] The next day, the editorial was again pointing fingers at the administration as it lauded a police report that showed the administration's claims of fewer students and a large number of outsiders involved in the takeovers were false. This was more proof that the administration was out of touch with what was going on around campus.[117]

## WRITING ABOUT THE PROTEST

The takeovers and protest were about the only news subjects the newspaper covered for several weeks. Some days the paper's eight pages contained nothing but protest-related stories. Reporters tried to cover every aspect of the protests, interviewing students in and outside the buildings, trying to talk to administration, police, and faculty. When protesters blocked the entrances to the occupied buildings, the only way in was through windows, so reporters crawled in and out of the windows to get their stories. With the exception of one *Village Voice* reporter, the protesters only let student journalists join them inside.[118] Many of the professionals trying to cover the story had to rely on reports from the student reporters who could get inside. "We became the primary news source for everybody," Friedman said. Reporting about what was happening in Hamilton Hall became difficult, though, because the staff had no black reporters and only blacks were being allowed into the building. Friedman wishes he could have had more diversity on staff and been able to cover the Hamilton Hall front better. Then his staff would have had a better understanding of the important role the black students really played in the protest.[119]

The protests of that spring spoiled the staff with news that was easy to find. No scrounging was necessary to fill the space. "The news was just handed to us on a plate," Stern said. "All we had to do was be there, be honest, and keep our eyes and ears open. We didn't have to do anything. We didn't have to work. We didn't have to dig. . . . I thought we did a really good job as kids reporting on a story that was bigger than we knew."[120] Stulberg recalled the energy of the time. "There was a constant surge of excitement is the other thing that stays with me," he said. "You'd get up in the mornings and go down to the office, and you didn't know what the day held in store and that was very exciting, to feel you were going to be involved in unpredictable and emerging events, moment to moment. It was infectious."[121]

The editors and reporters still have vivid memories of the major events, such as watching white protesters file out of Hamilton Hall as already noted, but also other events that never made the news. Stulberg recalled standing shoulder-to-shoulder with Tom Hayden, one of the SDS leaders, on the south side of the pedestrian bridge over Amsterdam Avenue that connected the law school with the main campus. Hayden was addressing a large assembly of high school students on the street below, trying to energize the youths who had come up Amsterdam to show their support for the college student strike. Hayden was explaining how important it was to focus on the issues behind all the protests. "Then he turned to me, and he whispered, 'what's the first demand?'" Stulberg said. "So I gave it to him. Then he asked me for the next one." The exchange continued as Stulberg reminded Hayden of all the student demands. Telling the story still makes Stulberg laugh. "I never reported on that," he said. "It would have been a wonderful little piece for the newspaper."[122] Stern recalled how difficult the administration could be when reporters, both students and professionals, were trying to get information. After the buildings had been emptied by the police, Stern and a *Washington Post* reporter, Nicholas von Hoffman were at Low Library. The frustrated *Post* reporter kicked open the door and stormed in. "It was great," Stern said. "You couldn't do that as a student."[123]

Friedman found an unexpected job he had to do when the takeovers happened: handle the professional press. "I had to entertain and educate the entire national press corps," he said. "The first thing they said when they got to my office is 'what the hell is going on here?' *The New York Times* reporter and the *Washington Post* reporter were filing their stories from our office, so I was holding their hands. [The national reporters] were parachuting into a campus that they knew nothing about. They knew none of the people. They were learning on the job. They were asking the right questions, but they were starting from a position of ignorance. It's a position I have often found myself in later on [as a reporter and editor]. You reach out to whoever you think are the most trustworthy people to give you guidance and advice." Protesters would not let the professional press into the buildings, so the reporters had to rely on the student reporters for information.[124] Root remembers *Times* reporter John Kifner, who was only a few years older than the students, hanging out in the *Spectator* office, talking and listening to the students, something other professional reporters never did.[125] The editors had less positive interactions with other *Times* reporters. "They really missed the story," Stern said. "Eventually we put a sign up saying none of them were welcome in the office because they were such assholes."

Stern ran into a unique problem with the *Times*: another man named Michael Sterne, with an "e" on the end of his name, was a *Times* reporter. Many people did not realize there were two with such similar names reporting the same event. "They kept asking why I could write such crap in the *Times* when I seemed to get it right in the *Spectator*," Stern said. When student Michael Stern later went to Cambridge University in England on an English fellowship, he discovered the other Michael Sterne had been transferred to the London news bureau, so the confusion continued.[126]

Some of the editors and reporters remember the violence that occurred when the police removed the protesters because they were assaulted as well. Part of Root's experience was documented on film and appeared in the *Spectator* without his knowledge or approval—he found it embarrassing. Student photographer Alan Epstein had snapped a picture of Root being helped to his feet after being battered by police, a grimace of pain on his face. "It was unbelievable because I knew everything that went into the paper every day," Root said. "The fact they got it into the paper without my even knowing about it was quite a little trick." He had been standing with the crowd of bystanders outside one of the occupied buildings, Avery Hall, when the police started to clear the campus in the early morning hours of April 30. "I was just there observing what was going on," said Root, who was wearing a coat and tie as the reporters always did at the time to look professional. "All of a sudden, some cop hit me from behind and knocked me down. I caught a glimpse of him. He was a plainclothes cop. The plainclothes cops were some of the most brutal. I fell down and while I was on the ground, was hit or kicked a number of times. I was just standing there with my notepad and my pen."

Later that night, as police arrested about 700 protesters, one grabbed Root, who was standing on the steps of Low Library taking notes. He told the officer he was a reporter for the *Spectator* and was just doing his job and even pulled out his light blue press card to prove his story, but the officer ignored it and put him in a line with other students who were being arrested. "Every cop I passed, I'd say, 'I was arrested for exercising my First Amendment right, the right of the press to cover events,'" he said. He was loaded into a paddy wagon and then taken off again to wait for a bus. Once again he tried to tell the officers he was a journalist and not a protester. When an officer finally asked him if he had wanted to get arrested, Root told him no, so the officer said he was allowed to leave. Another officer who saw him leave the line tried to force him back, but the first officer intervened, and Root was allowed to leave.

Meanwhile, Friedman, thinking Root had been carted off to jail, called Root's father, an attorney, who had telephoned his law partner at about 2 a.m. to have him deal with the situation. Root learned what happened when he got back to the newspaper office and called his parents to straighten things out. Root said through it all, the only real casualty was his favorite corduroy jacket. The left sleeve was ripped. "I got it sewed up," Root said. "You could always see that it [had been ripped], sort of like a scar. I wore it for a number of years."[127]

Root saw more violence a few weeks later during the second wave of protests and police action. "I certainly remember the out-of-control brutality by the police in public was even more pronounced at the second big bust," he said of the police as they charged across the south part of the campus bisected by College Walk. "They were just beating the hell out of some people. It was pretty scary to watch them with their night sticks and blackjacks, just beating people up. Some people received some pretty bad beatings in that." He saw Sanford Garelik, the chief inspector of the New York Police Department. "He was there witnessing his cops going completely wild and did nothing to stop them," he said. It was class resentment turned to violence. "There were a lot of larger issues that were playing out between the police and the students," Root said, noting that an officer had been injured by protesters so there were some police who were out for revenge.[128] Stern, who suffered a black eye and even was arrested and charged with trespass at one of the off-campus protests, explained the class issue: "These were lower middle class Irish cops who just hated everything that we were—and with good reason. Their kids were in the Army and going to Vietnam, and there we were at college."[129]

After the main protests were over, Friedman and some of the others started to realize that they had a great story that needed to be marketed. First, they decided to reprint all the issues from the takeovers in a booklet they titled *Crisis at Columbia: An Inside Report on the Rebellion at Columbia from the Pages of the Columbia Daily Spectator.* It contained eighty pages of the *Spectator*, from the morning after the Hamilton Hall takeover, April 24, through May 10 and the publication of *Connection*, a magazine-style insert that reporters produced with in-depth stories about what had happened. Friedman said the business manager had refused to fund the project so the other editors scrounged financing to do it themselves and then sold the copies for $1 each. Later, he spearheaded the project to write the book about the protests and had a book contract in hand by June 1. Building on the reporting they had done, the students researched even more, re-interviewed many people, and had *Up Against the Ivy Wall* completed by the end of August.[130]

For Friedman, who is now an editor at *Bloomberg News*, the experience at the *Spectator* was the beginning of his journalism career. He was able to learn storytelling skills there that have served him throughout his career in journalism.[131] The other four dabbled in journalism some after graduation, and all learned a great deal from their experience on the newspaper. "I learned more about how things work writing and later editing than anything else I learned in college, really," said Rothfeld, who spent three years writing for *Fortune* magazine and then two as assistant to Time Inc.'s chair and CEO before turning his interest to Wall Street and then Broadway as a play producer.[132] Stulberg, who was a reporter and editor in Miami for five years before attending law school, is now an attorney in New York. He said he still uses the investigative skills that he learned at the *Spectator* in his law practice. "We also gained a huge amount of experience in working as a team under an enormous amount of time pressure to produce a product," he said. He likes to hire employees who worked for a student newspaper because he knows first-hand the skills they have gained.[133] Root also spent time as a journalist for a summer in Philadelphia and then nights at another paper but "I didn't type fast enough," so he too became a New York lawyer. He traces his ability to write up against a court deadline back to the *Spectator* publishing deadlines. "To be able to write decently and communicate well and not have people be totally distracted by bad or sloppy writing comes in useful no matter what one does," he said.[134] Stern had a brief stint at the *Washington Post* and *The Wall Street Journal* before teaching English for 10 years then also becoming an attorney. He remains proud of the job the *Spectator* did in covering the protests. "We got the facts and the context of the demonstrations themselves and what that meant right, I think. It wasn't just a police story. It was about the university's role in society. That was the real story, and that was the right time for it. That, I think, we did get right."[135]

## CONCLUSION

As already noted, Howard and Columbia universities shared many commonalities. Their student newspapers, even with dissimilar views on journalism, also shared some important values that actually made their approaches to similar stories more alike than one might realize.

First, accuracy was critical to both. Advocacy and objective journalism both have factual, accurate reporting at the core. Indeed, the validity of any kind of journalism rests on the journalist's credibility for producing accurate reports. Even the smallest infraction can seriously damage the reputation of a newspaper, so accuracy is held in high esteem. Every individual interviewed expressed the importance of accuracy in the reporting and editing they did.

Secondly, students of both staffs were completely devoted to their work on the student newspaper. The differing publication schedule—weekly at Howard and daily at Columbia—seemed to have little impact on the amount of time students spent at the newspaper office in what should have been basically part-time jobs. All of those interviewed talked about a work schedule of longer hours than even a regular full-time job. And they all reported struggling to do their best academically because the newspaper demanded so much of their time.

The challenges of doing the best job were similar for both staffs. Even though neither administration tried to muzzle the student newspaper, administrators did not always make themselves available for comment, which frustrated reporters at both schools. Both staffs also tried to go deeper in the issues and provide a clear understanding of what the issues really were instead of the "police story" approach the professional media gave student protests of the era. Crushing press deadlines were also a problem at both newspapers, certainly a common problem at most student newspapers throughout the country at any point in history.

The political stances of the members of each staff also ran the gamut, yet all those interviewed reported good relations among the staff and few disagreements that could not be resolved. As Oren Root explained, the newspaper participants were self-selecting because they had to be willing to spend sixty to seventy hours, six and half days a week working on the *Spectator*. "To a certain extent, if you didn't get along with the people, it just wasn't a place that you wanted to spend that much time."[136] Most of the former staffers at *The Hilltop* have not kept in touch. *Spectator* staffers from that year still contact each other a few times a year, and all expressed that they continue to be friends. Of course, they also formed a different kind of bond because they had the chance to work closely on the book about the events, and some of them lived together during the summer while they did it.

The kind of journalism each staff practiced is a reflection of the professional influence each had as neither school offered a journalism degree at the time. (Columbia's School of Journalism was for graduate degrees only.) Most had worked on their high school papers, so they had a notion about how a reporter goes about writing a story in the form they read in the professional newspapers. At Howard, Manns, who had often read an advocacy publication, decided early on that she wanted to emulate what she saw there. Other students at Howard were also familiar with the Afro-American publications, many of which also published in an advocacy style, and would be influenced by those newspapers in the writing they did for the student newspaper. Staffers also did not think it seemed out of line when at least two of the staff members, Manns and Stewart, became participant journalists, which is a subcategory of advocacy journalism.

At Columbia, student editors and reporters aspired to be *The New York Times* in their approach to the news, with objectivity as one of the key goals. However, as Robert Stulberg pointed out, the *Times,* like all newspapers, has reporters and editors who bring their own life experiences, opinions, and biases to their work. When a *Times* reporter was asked about the *Spectator's* coverage of the protests, the reporter had responded, "'They've done a very good job for a newspaper with a point of view.' That has always stayed with me, as if to say that the good, gray *New York Times* did not have a point of view," Stulberg said chuckling.[137] Complete objectivity, then, can be an elusive place to reach, even for professionals.

Only Robert Friedman and Pearl Stewart made journalism their main adult careers. The others found different passions that fulfilled them. Yet their time at college had done just what colleges have done for centuries and continue to do today: help young adults define who they are, develop some of their beliefs, and shape their future. The time on the newspaper also provided the laboratory for them to experiment with writing styles, management styles, and leadership styles. It provided the opportunity to hone more than their writing skills but to master friendship, perseverance, and team work as well.

*          *          *

Adrienne Manns Israel teaches African and African-American history in Greensboro, North Carolina, where she is the past vice president of Academic Affairs at Guilford College. She laughs when she thinks about how much trouble she caused as a student at Howard with her sarcastic jabs at the administration. "When the students do it to me now, I feel like it's payback," she said with a chuckle. She said the *Guilfordian* student newspaper has more of her respect because she understands what they are trying to do and how hard it is to do it.

Pearl Stewart went on to earn a master's degree in communication and have a career in various types of print journalism, including some public relations. She was the first African-American woman to serve as an editor at a major daily newspaper, *Oakland Tribune*. She has also taught college journalism and now does freelance writing and editing from her home in Jackson, Mississippi.

Clyde Waite never intended to practice journalism as a career. "My career has always been one of serendipity," he said. "Opportunities present themselves and I sort of fall into them." After law school at Yale, he was an attorney until becoming the first black common pleas court judge in Doylestown, Bucks County, Pennsylvania, in 2003.

Robert Friedman taught high school for a year before earning a master's degree in English from Columbia and heading back to professional journalism where he has spent the rest of his career. He worked for many publications, all based in New York City, including *The Wall Street Journal*, the *Village Voice*, New York *Newsday*, *Life* magazine, and *Fortune* magazine. He also freelanced for *Esquire*, *Rolling Stone*, and other publications. He has been with *Bloomberg* since 2008.

Oren Root spent time as a public defender and then a private criminal defense attorney after finishing Fordham Law School. His interests in immigration detention have brought him to the nonprofit Vera Institute of Justice where he works on providing counsel and legal information to people in immigration-detention and police-immigrant community relations.

Michael Stern earned a PhD from Yale and his law degree from Berkeley. His California law practice deals with technology law, intellectual property, and licensing issues.

Robert Stulberg became an Emmy-award winner for his investigative work on a documentary he wrote in Miami about the Florida citrus industry. He then attended Antioch School of Law and now is a labor attorney in New York City.

Michael Rothfeld has been a journalist and private equity investor, has devoted time to nonprofit organizations, and serves as a member of the Board of Trustees at Columbia University.

## NOTES

1. Adrienne Manns, telephone interview by author, August 11, 2012.
2. Robert Friedman, telephone interview by author, August 14, 2012.
3. James L. Moses, "Journalistic Impartiality on the Eve of a Revolution: *The Boston Evening Post*, 1770–1775," *Journalism History* 20, no. 3/4 (Winter 1994): 125.
4. Harlan S. Stensacis, "Development of the Objectivity Ethic in U.S. Daily Newspapers," *Journal of Mass Media Ethics* 2, no. 1 (1986): 50–60.

5. Lambert A. Wilmer, *Our Press Gang: A Complete Exposition of the Corruptions and Crimes of the American Newspapers* (Philadelphia: J. T. Lloyd, 1859).

6. Stensacis, "Development of the Objectivity," 51.

7. John W. C. Johnstone, Edward J. Slawski, and William W. Bowman, "The Professional Values of American Newsmen," *Public Opinion Quarterly* 36, no. 4 (Winter 1972–1973): 522–540.

8. "What is *Mother Jones?*" *Mother Jones*online, accessed November 13, 2012, http://www.motherjones.com/about#13.

9. Tony Gittens, "More Trouble Expected at S.C.: Three Students Murdered in Cold Blood in Peaceful Desegregation March," *The Hilltop* (Washington, D.C.), February 16, 1968, 1.

10. Manns interview.

11. Mark Kurlansky, *1968: The Year That Rocked the World* (New York: Ballantine Books, 2004), 82.

12. Ibid., 192–208.

13. Tom Myles, *Centennial Plus 1: A Photographic and Narrative Account of the Black Student Revolution: Howard University 1965–1968* (Washington, D.C.: Black-Light Graphics, 1969).

14. Jerry Avorn et. al., *Up Against the Ivy Wall* (New York: Atheneum, 1968).

15. Howard University Annual Report 2015–2016, accessed May 24, 2017, https://www2.howard.edu/sites/ default/files/pdf/2.01.1_HU_Annual_Report_FY2016.pdf.

16. "Howard University Facts," March 31, 2017, accessed May 24, 2017, https://www2.howard.edu/about/ president/statements/howard-facts.

17. "James Madison Nabrit, Jr. Biography," Howard University School of Law, accessed October 17, 2012, http://www.law.howard.edu/1113.

18. Kurlansky, *1968*, 82.

19. Tom Myles, *Centennial,* 7.

20. Manns interview.

21. Tom Myles, *Centennial.*, 9, 22, 25.

22. Ibid., 36.

23. Myles, *Centennial Plus 1.*

24. Clyde W. Waite, telephone interview by author, August 10, 2012.

25. John Turner, "Chuck Stone Challenges Howard to be Black," *The Hilltop* (Washington, D.C.), February 9, 1968, 1.

26. Gayleatha Brown, "Rap Brown Endorses D.C. Black Front," *The Hilltop*(Washington, D.C.), February 9, 1968, 6.

27. Sanders Bebura, "Student Government: 'We Need to Have a Mild Revolution,'" *The Hilltop* (Washington, D.C.), February 9, 1968, 1.

28. "Editorial: What We Want," *The Hilltop* (Washington, D.C.), March 8, 1968, 1.

29. Manns, interview.

30. "About *The Hilltop*," *The Hilltop*: The student voice at Howard University, accessed May 24, 2017, http://www.thehilltoponline.com/editorial-office/about.

31. Manns interview.

32. Pearl Stewart, telephone interview by author, August 9, 2012.

33. Manns interview.

34. Ibid.

35. Ibid.

36. Ibid.

37. Ibid.

38. Ibid.

39. Ibid.

40. Stewart interview.

41. Waite interview.

42. Stewart interview.

43. Waite interview.

44. Ibid.

45. Ibid.

46. Clyde Waite, "Students Take Over the University's Administration Building; Over 1000 Stage Indefinite Days of Vigil until Their Demands Are Met; President Absent for Unprecedented Student Action," *The Hilltop* (Washington, D.C.), March 22, 1968, 1.

47. Waite interview.

48. Stewart interview.

49. Ibid.

50. Pearl Stewart, "Together, Most Students Say after Seizure," *The Hilltop* (Washington, D.C.), March 22, 1968, 1.

51. "The Motley Crowd," *The Hilltop* (Washington, D.C.), March 22, 1968, 4.

52. Stewart interview.

53. Waite interview.

54. Cindee Marshall, "Sit-In Proves to be Effective," *The Hilltop* (Washington, D.C.), March 29, 1968, 2.

55. Cindee Marshall, "Roving Reporter: Sit-Inners Surveyed," *The Hilltop* (Washington, D.C.), March 29, 1968, 3.

56. Clyde W. Waite, "HU Aids Bowie Demonstration," *The Hilltop* (Washington, D.C.), >March 29, 1968, 1.

57. Brenda Adams, "Students Struggle for Black University," *The Hilltop* (Washington, D.C.), March 29, 1968, 1.

58. "'Do Nothing' Administration," *The Hilltop* (Washington, D.C.), March 29, 1968, 4.

59. Manns interview.

60. "'Do Nothing' Administration."

61. Manns interview.

62. Ibid.

63. "Patricia Harris," *The Hilltop* (Washington, D.C.), March 1, 1968, 6.

64. "Harris' Reply to HILLTOP," *The Hilltop* (Washington, D.C.), March 8, 1968, 6.

65. Manns interview.

66. Robert Stulberg, telephone interview by author, September 27 and October 7, 2012.

67. Jerry Avorn, "Disclose Affiliation Between Columbia, Defense Institute: Individual Professors Do Weapons Research," *Columbia Daily Spectator* (New York), March 31, 1967, 1.

68. Avorn, et al., *Up Against the Ivy Wall.*

69. Friedman interview.

70. P. Alan Green, "Friedman, Garaufis Named to Head Spectator Staffs: Editorial and Business Managing Boards Merged for First Time Since 1939," *Columbia Daily Spectator* (New York), March 15, 1968, 1.

71. A. Stuyvestant Van Nes, "Spectator Promotes Staff Members," *Columbia Daily Spectator* (New York), March 15, 1968, 3.

72. Michael Stern, telephone interview by author, August 17, 2012.

73. Michael B. Rothfeld, telephone interview by author, September 11, 2012.

74. Stulberg interview, September 27, 2012.

75. Oren Root, telephone interview by author, August 28, 2012.

76. Stulberg interview, September 27, 2012.

77. Friedman interview.

78. Root interview.

79. Rothfeld interview.

80. Friedman interview.

81. Stulberg interview, September 27, 2012.

82. Friedman interview.

83. Root interview.

84. Stulberg interview, September 27, 2012.

85. Friedman interview.

86. Stulberg interview, September 27, 2012.

87. Root interview.

88. Rothfeld interview.

89. Stern interview.

90. Root interview.

91. Stern interview.
92. Stulberg interview, September 27, 2012.
93. Friedman interview.
94. Stulberg interview.
95. Rothfeld interview.
96. Stulberg interview.
97. Root interview.
98. Rothfeld interview.
99. Michael Rothfeld, email to author, September 12, 2012.
100. Rothfeld interview.
101. "What are the goals?" *Columbia Daily Spectator* (New York), April 26, 1968, 4.
102. Rothfeld interview and email.
103. "An Editorial," *Columbia Daily Spectator* (New York), April 28, 1968, 1.
104. "Cops Out," *Columbia Daily Spectator* (New York), May 2, 1968, 4.
105. Friedman interview.
106. Ibid.
107. "A Day of Warning," *Columbia Daily Spectator* (New York), April 24, 1968, 4.
108. "The Final Alternative," *Columbia Daily Spectator* (New York), April 25, 1968, 4.
109. "The Way Out," *Columbia Daily Spectator* (New York), April 26, 1968, 4.
110. "A Glimmer of Hope," *Columbia Daily Spectator* (New York), April 27, 1968, 2.
111. "An Editorial."
112. "What are the Goals?" *Columbia Daily Spectator* (New York), April 29, 1968, 4.
113. Friedman interview.
114. "The Reconstruction," *Columbia Daily Spectator* (New York), May 1, 1968, 2.
115. "Cops Out."
116. "The Strike," *Columbia Daily Spectator* (New York), May 6, 1968, 2.
117. "Misrepresentations," *Columbia Daily Spectator* (New York), May 7, 1968, 2.
118. Stern interview.
119. Friedman interview.
120. Stern interview.
121. Stulberg interview.
122. Ibid.
123. Stern interview.
124. Friedman interview.
125. Root interview.
126. Stern interview.
127. Root interview.
128. Ibid.
129. Stern interview.
130. Friedman interview.
131. Ibid.
132. Rothfeld interview.
133. Stulberg interview.
134. Root interview.
135. Stern interview.
136. Root interview.
137. Stulberg interview.

## Chapter Five

# Lessons from Reporting Crisis

A story about four students gunned down by national guardsmen at Kent State the day before, probably the most significant event of the entire protest era, was one of the smaller stories on the front page of *The Daily Collegian* at Pennsylvania State University on May 5, 1970. After all, the University Park campus had plenty of its own troubles to fill almost the entire front page that day. The same action that had students at Kent State protesting the previous day—President Nixon's announcement of expanding the war in Southeast Asia by sending troops into Cambodia——had sparked reactions at Penn State as well. A student committee had called for a two-day strike, according to the lead story on page 1, while another Collegian story explained that a panel was reviewing the cases of forty students charged with disrupting the campus in previous weeks. In all, six of the eight stories on the broadsheet's front page were centered on campus unrest.

It was the same story being told in campus newspapers across the country that day and the days that followed. Many of the campuses, such as Ohio State University (OSU), had already been embroiled in protest before the Kent State shootings occurred. For several days the Ohio State *Lantern* had been plastered with stories of student strikes and protests. National guardsmen also had been called in to quell unrest at OSU, about 130 miles southwest of Kent. The guardsmen faced conflicts with protesting students almost daily. Then the Kent State shootings happened and students were dead. The protests throughout the spring of 1970 were the finale for almost an entire decade of violence that had rocked U.S. campuses as students played activist roles on issues of race, free speech, and finally the Vietnam War.

Five former student editors now tell their stories of what happened at their student newspapers after the Kent State shooting.

*    *    *

*Daily Kent Stater* editor William "Bill" Armstrong was in the student newspaper office in Taylor Hall on May 4, 1970, when he heard what sounded like muffled firecrackers going off nearby. Then one of his freshmen reporters ran into the busy newsroom, tears streaming down her face, to report that the National Guardsmen who had been called to campus to maintain order had opened fire on students. After a quick call to the university public relations office to alert them to what he had heard and to try to verify the story, Armstrong ran outside to see for himself. He saw the troops retreating and students running. "My sister was on campus, and she came out of her dormitory to cry in horror with her roommate," he recalled. "I put my arms around both of them as I watched [victim] Jeffrey Miller, the blood pouring out of his head on the pavement in our parking lot." He watched as *Stater* photographer John Filo snapped what became the Pulitzer Prize-winning, iconic picture of student protest: a sobbing young girl, later identified as a fourteen-year-old runaway, screaming over Miller's body.[1]

Within two hours, the Kent State University campus in northeast Ohio was closed by a court order. Buses were brought in to take dormitory residents away. The phone system collapsed. Guardsmen were posted at every entrance to keep people from entering. By that afternoon, the campus was cleared and the university was closed for the remainder of the term. Armstrong and his newspaper staff never got to report about what was probably the most famous event to occur on a college campus during the protest years. The shooting deaths of four Kent State students and the critical wounds to nine others were reported nationally by two reporters who were on the scene that morning: *CBS News* television correspondent Ike Pappas and reporter John Kifner of *The New York Times*. The wide reporting immediately sparked increased violence across the country that led to protests, demonstrations, student strikes, two more deaths ten days later at Jackson State College in Mississippi, and the closing of more than 500 universities and colleges across the country.[2] Even though the *Kent Stater* staff did not get to report on the most serious violence that happened there, hundreds of other student newspapers did write about the violence that was sparked on their own campuses. This chapter looks at five campuses where various levels of protests followed the Kent shootings, as well as comparing how student newspapers in Ohio and Mississippi framed the tragedies at Kent State and later Jackson State that gripped campuses in each state in May 1970. The events put young journalists through a *baptism by fire* experience—learning to do their jobs in a crisis. This chapter also considers how college students handled the challenges of reporting in a crisis, thus adding a small piece to the picture of twentieth-century journalism.

## SHOOTINGS AT KENT STATE—MAY 4, 1970

Few major protests of any kind during the protest years were spontaneous events. It was no different at Kent State University, located about forty miles southeast of Cleveland. The deaths on Monday, May 4, were the culmination of several days of protest that was initially spawned by the announcement from U.S. President Richard Nixon the previous Thursday that the United States would be sending troops across the Vietnam border into Cambodia to wipe out Viet Cong staging areas. This was widely interpreted as expanding the Vietnam War. Many student protests about the war at the time also included what they saw as the complicity of their college or university in the war through the Reserve Officers Training Corps (ROTC) on campus and research that the Department of Defense used in combat. At Kent State, Armstrong recalled, that research included the Liquid Crystal Institute, whose technology was pioneering uses in various instruments used by soldiers.[3]

Other issues had also spurred Kent students to protest for the previous few years. In the fall of 1968, police recruiters were on campus from Oakland, California. It was the birthplace of the Black Panthers organization, which had many confrontations with the Oakland Police Department, including Panther co-founder Huey P. Newton, who killed a police officer during a traffic stop. Black students at Kent State saw the recruiters as an insult and staged a five-hour sit-in to prevent the job interviews. Then in April 1969, members of the Students for a Democratic Society (SDS) physically assaulted campus police who were stopping them from entering and taking over the administration building. The protesters were arrested, suspended, and barred by a temporary restraining order from setting foot on campus. Later, a group of students who were trying to attend the suspension hearings and block any action found themselves locked into the building; fifty-eight were arrested. A huge rally planned for the following Monday was supposed to shut down the university, but it fizzled, in part because the student newspaper editorialized against it in a special edition that morning. The action of the student newspaper was applauded by an investigatory panel of the Ohio General Assembly that summer; the University's response was praised by the U.S. House of Representatives Committee on Internal Security (the old House Un-American Activities Committee) in Washington, D.C., in the summer of 1969. Kent State was in the news, and it remained a target for the SDS although the four students who had been arrested and suspended would serve a jail term until April 30, 1970.[4] That was the night that Nixon went on television to announce he was sending troops into Cambodia.

Protesters held a rally the next day near the Victory Bell where they buried a copy of the U.S. Constitution. That night, as happened on many Friday nights, young adults from all over northeast Ohio descended on Kent to enjoy the night life. Someone lit a bonfire in the middle of an intersection, and people spilled out of the bars to see what was going on. The mayor declared a state of emergency and ordered the bars closed. Using tear gas, police started pushing the revelers back toward campus through the business district where the young people began throwing rocks through store windows. By Saturday night, the newly elected mayor requested that the governor dispatch to Kent some of the National Guard troops that had already been mobilized to protect roads and bridges during a Teamsters Union strike. The mayor did not tell university officials of his request. The National Guard already had units at Ohio State University in Columbus to also keep order. By the time the guardsmen arrived in Kent that night, however, they had to watch helplessly as the Kent State ROTC building, set ablaze by protesters, burned to the ground. The protesters also pelted fire fighters with rocks and chopped up their hoses.[5]

Students planned another rally at noon on Monday to protest the war and the National Guard that was now encamped on their campus. The guard tried to clear the students from the commons area, and then the shooting began. No one has been able to definitively say why the guardsmen fired though there were reports that someone fired a gun at or near the troops, who then returned fire for about thirteen seconds. In all, four students died, and nine suffered injuries.

Bill Armstrong had witnessed many of the events that preceded the shootings on May 4, 1970, and as the activism reporter had written about most of them. "I was on the floor with the black students," he said of the 1968 protest that stopped the police recruiting. He heard the university vice president of student affairs use a bull horn to address the protesting black students as "you people," which only exacerbated the problems between the blacks and the administration. He covered the speeches of the SDS leaders and was one of the few student journalists on campus in 1969 when the SDS planned that Monday rally, hoping to take over the administration building and close down the university. Almost all the other *Kent Stater* staff members were in Cincinnati at a journalism conference. Armstrong, who was a political science major, and a few other staffers did not attend the conference. When he heard about the coming protest, Armstrong approached Journalism Department Chairman Murvin Perry about putting out a special edition on Monday. (The newspaper typically published Tuesday through Friday.) With Perry's blessing, Armstrong and a few others put out a four-page newspaper on Monday morning that exposed the SDS tactics and then editorially urged students to stay away from the rally. Few students ended up attending, and the SDS plan to shut down the university failed.[6]

Armstrong watched the ROTC building burn that Saturday night in 1970. Several student reporters and photographers were covering the event. "Three of my photographers were approached by people we did not know and told 'don't take any fucking pictures here or we'll bust your cameras. If you're going to be here, put your cameras away. We don't want any record of this,'" Armstrong said. "That was very unusual for our photographers to be told not to cover an event but to be threatened directly and personally. Obviously, some of them did take pictures because there are pictures of the building being burned." Armstrong had heard the National Guard was coming, so he was not too surprised to find himself surrounded by military uniforms as he walked away from the burning ROTC building. He acted quickly, identified himself as the editor of the campus newspaper and requested press credentials. He was referred to a public information officer and was the first journalist to get the credentials that would allow him freer access to the campus when it was closed.

Armstrong had only been the editor for about five weeks—a new editor was named each term. Since Nixon's announcement about escalating the war, he had been receiving numerous phone calls from other universities around the country, asking him to join in a petition to the president to stop the Vietnam War. Armstrong said: "I'm getting these calls from everywhere. I said, 'look, we've got our own situation here. I can't deal with the big perspective right now. Our campus is occupied. Helicopters are flying overhead, dropping tear gas, searchlights on our students, dormitories being surrounded by guardsmen. I can't deal with this now.'" Although many students were frightened by what was happening at Kent State, Armstrong was not. "I always felt protected by my credentials," he explained. "I personally felt I was not at risk because I'm a reporter, and I can use that shield to defend myself. I was not afraid at all."

He was also trying to figure out how the newspaper would cover all the action. "I flirted with the idea of trying to create another special edition [like the previous year]. Here's Bill Armstrong trying to do this, who did it the previous year, and was successful in editorializing against a mass assembly that could lead to violence. Did I still have that magic? Is there anything we could have said or done that might have changed the outcome?" Instead, he decided to wait until the regularly scheduled Tuesday paper. He expected one of his top reporters, John Hayes, to come back from Columbus with a long story and pictures of the National Guard occupation of the Ohio State University campus. He had his other reporters busily writing reports of the Friday night bonfire and subsequent violence in downtown Kent as well as the Saturday night burning of the ROTC building. Tuesday's paper would be a blockbuster. And it would have been filled with reports by some very talented journalists. "We had great people on that staff. In all, four of the people who worked for me would go on to win Pulitzer Prizes: two for reporting, one for photography, and one for political cartooning," Armstrong reflected.

But after the shootings Monday, campus closed and the students never published that paper. "I didn't have a staff," Armstrong explained. "And more importantly, everybody in my circulation area had been sent away. There were no students to see what I would have produced. They were sent home. There were no classes. There were no faculty."

Some of the student work did get out, though. Student photographer John Filo took his photos with him to his hometown newspaper in Pennsylvania where the picture of fourteen-year-old Mary Ann Vecchio screaming over Jeffrey Miller's body was picked up by the Associated Press (AP) wire service and sent to newspapers across the country. Howard Rufner's picture of a wounded student being attended by others was on the cover of *Life* magazine on May 15. That July, Armstrong wrote a 35,000-word piece that appeared in a twenty-page supplement to the *Record-Courier,* the local newspaper in Kent where he had been a stringer while he was attending the university. Titled "Forging a New Community," the article examined town-university relations that had become strained during this period. He also co-wrote a book titled *Behind the Ivy Curtain* with a Kent instructor, Barclay McMillen. The book analyzed the administration's handling of the events. It was never published though it was the topic of a symposium in 2000.[7]

## SHOOTINGS AT JACKSON STATE—MAY 14, 1970

The staff of the Jackson State *Blue and White Flash* also never got to write about the two deaths on their campus ten days later. The shootings there left two dead and twelve wounded when police and highway patrolmen fired on students. Again, the campus closed and the newspaper did not publish again until fall. Like hundreds of other protests around the country in the days and weeks after the Kent State shootings, the protesting at Jackson State on May 14 was partially in response to the shootings at Kent State. However, the protest that day was mainly fueled by "historical racial intimidation and harassment by white motorists traveling Lynch Street, a major thoroughfare that divided the campus and linked west Jackson to downtown."[8] Then a rumor started that a black mayor, who was the brother of slain Civil Rights activist Medgar Evers, had been killed. A small group of Jackson State students began rioting about 9:30 p.m. Around midnight, police and highway patrolmen opened fire on the crowd.[9]

Though neither of the two schools where the shootings occurred got to report on what happened on their campus, other campus newspapers certainly did. By the time many got to report on Kent State, they were also reporting campus violence that had erupted all over the country and often on their own campuses. As on most issues, the newspapers' reactions varied depending on the liberalness of the school and the amount of activism on campus. For instance, two days after the Kent State shooting, *The Daily Universe* at Brigham Young University, a conservative church-owned school in Provo, Utah, finally ran an Associated Press story about the outbreak of violence that followed Kent State at other colleges and universities, noting the decidedly nonresponse in Provo.[10] Such a mild response was to be expected in the newspaper and on campus, however, because Brigham Young University (BYU) President Ernest Wilkinson kept a tight rein on students, particularly when it came to activism of any kind.[11] Yet, fifty miles to the north, on a campus populated by many similarly conservative students, the University of Utah student newspaper, *The Daily Chronicle,* was reporting on rallies, a possible student strike, and sit-ins on its own campus.

## FRAMING TRAGEDY

The student newspapers at other universities closest to the two shooting tragedies—those in Ohio and Mississippi—would be expected to write more about the shooting events than other student newspapers. However, that was not always the case. Many factors affected what student journalists were able to do, factors that framed the way the story was played. Framing is one of the ways researchers attempt to understand how journalists, both print and broadcast, organize their work to make sense of the world. Erving Goffman, who first introduced the idea of framing in 1974, maintained that everyone practices framing; it is how people understand and manage the complex social world in which they live.[12]

Extensive use of framing in communication has only been going on for about fifteen years when it became a distinct communication theory.[13] Reese provides a working definition of frames that incorporates the many pieces that are part of this idea: "Frames are organizing principles that are socially shared and persistent over time, that work symbolically to meaningfully structure the social world." The organizing varies in completeness. The principles are abstract. The frame must be shared and durable through routine use. The frame is seen in symbolic expression and has a pattern or structure.[14]

Any discussion of framing can be somewhat confusing because it sounds like agenda setting. McCombs, Shaw, and Weaver see frames as second-level agenda setting. Agenda setting is often defined as not telling people *what* to think, but what to think about; frames, then, tell people *how* to think about it.[15] Thus, framing moves beyond agenda setting. Entman explains framing as selection and salience. "To frame is to select some aspects of a perceived reality and make them more salient in a communicating text, in such a way as to promote a particular problem definition, causal interpretation, moral evaluation, and/or treatment recommendation for the item de-

scribed."[16] The process of selection also means the exclusion of some information, which is a key component of framing as well. Gitlin describes the
selection as "little tacit theories about what exists, what happens, and what
matters,"[17] and what is left out. The framing process also provides a quick
way to assign and package news for audiences.

Watkins points to two important aspects of frame analysis that must be
examined in order to understand framing: (1) specific media technologies
and processes as well as internal factors such as budgets and external factors
such as access to events and sources; (2) selection of specific wording and
images.[18] Also, one must understand that frames are created by media professionals in an active process, employing news values that determine what
makes events newsworthy, such as proximity and timeliness.[19] The students
making the news judgments in this study are not professionals. Still, professors and advisers work to impart news values to the student journalists who,
in turn, make these same news value judgments for student newspapers.

Several components are often included in the framing discussion and are
applicable here. First is size. The amount of space a newspaper or media
outlet devotes to the topic indicates how much significance the journalists
placed on the story. More important stories are given more space and more
prominent positions.[20] Size also refers to another aspect here. The size, physically or psychologically, of the incident also plays a role. Some journalists
equate size of the event with importance.[21] The deaths of six students on two
campuses in May 1970, while not huge in physical numbers, would be expected to be treated with importance because of the psychological enormity
of the loss of any lives at the hands of U.S. troops and police firing on
unarmed American citizens.

The media attention cycle plays a role in the framing as well. This cycle
"refers to the sudden ascendance of an issue from previous obscurity to a
sustained prominence . . . that dominates the news for a period of time before
once again fading from media attention."[22] Gamson and Modigliani found
some of these cycles are not linked to a trend while others are tied to major
events.[23] Certainly the shootings at Kent State and Jackson State qualify as
major events.

Framing of the tragedies at both Kent State and Jackson State in the
media is unique from other kinds of stories because race becomes a factor as
well. Kent State was predominantly white and Jackson State was predominantly black. According to Gandy (1996), framing can influence the way
non-blacks perceive equality, fair play, and affirmative action. Thus, the role
of framing can be critical to audience understanding of issues and events.[24]

## REPORTING THE SHOOTINGS

On Tuesday, May 5, all three Ohio newspapers considered here (*Lantern,* Ohio University (OU)*Post,* and the Bowling Green University *BG News*) played the Kent State shootings as the main story on the front page, with the *Lantern* and *The Post* placing the story (an identical version from United Press International [UPI] news wire) above the nameplate. *The BG News* splashed a two-line, six-column head across the front to address its two biggest stories at once: the Kent State shootings (an AP story) and the cancellation of classes that morning at Bowling Green.

Both the *Lantern* and *The Post* included stories on their front page that day about other campus unrest. Ohio State had been rocked by protests for several days already as a strike that began the previous week lingered on, building up steam because of the Kent State shootings. The *Lantern* had two stories about the continuing strike and a third story about students suspended because of actions that had started the strike the week before. *The Post* reported that 2,500 students had rallied the night before and voted to strike. The paper offered its support by adding "***STRIKE***" to each side of its nameplate.[25]

Racial issues were also a high priority at both OSU and OU as reflected on the front page of both that day. The *Lantern* used a story about funding for a Black Studies program, which was a key piece of the demands black students had brought forward as part of the protesting that had begun the week before. In one story, *The Post* reported that two black professors were leaving and, in a second story, explained about the six student-run committees created by the Black Studies Institute to address racial issues that had been presented in a petition.

Both *The Post* and *Lantern* tried to create a business-as-usual feel, however, by including other campus news on the front page. *The Post* featured a report of a speech by public relations pioneer Edward Bernays for Communication Week and a small story about a coed pleading not guilty to defiling an American flag. The *Lantern* added a short preview of the Corps Day Review scheduled for Thursday. Both newspapers included regular inside pages filled with typical campus news such as sports, entertainment, and even community news.

*The BG News*, however, was all about the current crisis. After learning about Kent State on Monday, a group of Bowling Green students staged a sit-in outside the university president's office, demanding a meeting. The protest did not last long, and the only page 1 photo was of officers trying to get students to leave. The president promised to meet with students Tuesday morning and canceled morning classes. A front-page editorial encouraged all students to attend that meeting on the steps of Williams Hall.

That one day's coverage was reflective of the kind of focus each newspaper would have for the next few weeks. A majority of the stories in *The BG News* each day would be about the continuing unrest, either on their own campus or other college campuses, about the aftermath and investigations at Kent State, about the continuing Indochina war that moved into Cambodia and Laos, and about congressional action in Washington, D.C. trying to deal with it all. *The Post* and the *Lantern* published many of the same kinds of stories but used more space than *The BG News* would devote for campus issues as well as sports, entertainment, and features.

Besides stories scattered throughout other pages of the eight-page paper, two full pages inside *The BG News* on May 5 indicated the kind of coverage they would be doing throughout the month. Four AP stories discussed protests, or the lack of protests, at other campuses. Two AP stories discussed Cambodia and air attacks on North Vietnam, and a third detailed the stock market response to both events. Two more stories, one from AP and another by one by the *News* editors, were eyewitness accounts of the Kent shootings. One story discussed student reaction at Bowling Green and another the school president's "state of urgency." An editorial on page 2 indicated that racial issues were also weighing on the minds of students at Bowling Green, an issue that would continue to be covered in the next few weeks. The editorial supported the demands black students had presented to the president the previous week, noting that their requests were fair. One almost ironic report on the sports page was of the BG Falcons beating the Kent State Flash at baseball the previous Friday.

*The Post* had already made up its mind on May 5 about the editorial stance it would take on what was happening on campus and across the nation. The words "***STRIKE***" on either side of the nameplate might as well have included arrows pointing to the page 2 editorial where editors urged students, faculty, administrators, and staff to join the nationwide college strike to protest the escalating war in Southeast Asia. The lengthy piece, which ran down about two-thirds of the page in a two-on-three-column format, carefully outlined the students' positions and rational for supporting the strike.

When editors at the *Lantern* selected a UPI story for page 5 on May 5, they must have been shaking their heads in amazement. The story, which was designed by UPI to run in professional newspapers the Sunday before the shootings at Kent, had predicted that major campus disorder would occur that spring. It had certainly been true on the OSU campus where an Ad Hoc Committee, which was formed by a group of students that included some *Lantern* staffers, had called a strike the previous week. The committee was demanding that the administration address a number of issues in three general areas: granting students more say in their education, dealing with concerns of the Afro-American black student group, and finding ways to stop indirectly supporting the Vietnam War. Much of the campus news reporting for the next several days was related to these three issues and the results of students protesting in support of them.

Most of the letters to the *Lantern* on May 5 dealt with the issues of the strike the previous week. One lengthy story inside included students reporting their tales of spending time in jail after being arrested at the strike the previous week.

In contrast to the Ohio student newspapers, the Mississippi student journalists were virtually silent about reporting the protesting and the Kent State shootings. *The Daily Mississippian* at Ole Miss did not publish a single news story about the shootings though a story on the Friday, May 8, front page detailed the plans of fifteen Ole Miss students to attend the weekend protest march in Washington, D.C., that would also mourn the death of students killed at Kent State. The following Monday, the newspaper reported the death of one of those students in a traffic accident on the way home from the march. *The Daily Mississippian* instead filled its eight pages each day that May with all locally written articles because it apparently did not subscribe to a wire service such as UPI or AP. On May 12, editors reprinted an editorial that had appeared during the previous week in the Memphis *Commercial-Appeal* about the Kent State tragedy. The editorial encouraged Americans to settle problems "with mind-power rather than brash, brutal force."

Like their counterparts at other colleges and universities, *The Mississippian* editors and reporters were grappling with racial issues. A May 6 front-page story discussed the Student Senate's approval of a bill that condemned the burning of the Rebel flag, noting that "fuel was added to [the] fire of campus racial unrest" when the bill passed.[26]

*The Mississippian* was the only one of the three Mississippi newspapers to report the Jackson State shootings that occurred on the night of Thursday, May 14. A short piece was tucked into the bottom left hand corner of page 1 the next morning, Friday. *The Daily Mississippian* only published two more issues after that before the term was over and publication ceased. Nothing appeared in the May 18 paper. The final paper of the year included a two-page spread of stories and photos of local reaction to campus unrest around the country. Kent State was specifically referenced but Jackson State was never mentioned. The stories spread across the double-truck (the two center pages of the newspaper) were written by a campus reporting class. One was an interview with a professor who insisted the lack of protest at Ole Miss was not an indication of apathy. Instead, students there had never developed a tradition of demonstration. Though exposed to the same news as other college students, the professor said, Ole Miss students had chosen to react differently. A spokesman for the Black Student Union said in another story that the 200–300 black students on campus was the reason there was no violence. He noted that the black students had concerns that still needed to be addressed. Other stories included various student views on protest, another professor claiming the lack of protest was the result of a lack of awareness, and the chancellor saying the unrest at other schools was a rebellion against authority. A financial aid administrator said Ole Miss students were more willing to work through problems in traditional ways because they realized they could lose their federal financial aid by being disruptive.

*The Reflector* at Mississippi State University published two issues that month, May 1 and May 5. Of course, the May 1 issue was before either of the shooting incidents. The May 5 issue did not include any information about Kent (the newspaper did not subscribe to any wire services) though it featured a report of racial violence for two days in Starkville, the city where the university is located. The newspaper staff did not publish another edition until September 18 when the fall semester began.

*The Student Printz* at the University of Southern Mississippi (USM) reported on an "Indochina reaction" rally sponsored by the Progressive Students Association three days after the Kent State shootings[27] but did not include any news reports of the shootings, probably because like all the other university newspapers in the state, it did not subscribe to wire services. The paper also reported on four USM students who traveled to Washington, D.C., for the national Emergency Demonstration the weekend following the Kent shootings.[28] Though it never reported the Jackson State shooting as a news story, the *Printz* did spend most of the summer following up on the suspensions, hearings, and appeals for three USM students accused of spreading erroneous leaflets around campus announcing that classes would be canceled for two days to honor the students killed at Jackson State College; indeed, campus officials had not canceled classes.

The Jackson State shootings occurred on the night of Thursday, May 14. As noted, only one Mississippi student newspaper wrote about the event. A check of two other smaller college papers—the *Alcorn Herald* and Delta State *Miss Delta*—found no references there as well. The OU *Post* picked up a small story in its May 15 edition, burying the piece on the bottom of page 4. No UPI initials are included at the beginning of the story as was the usual practice at the paper, but it is still likely that the story came from UPI. The student editors of *The Post* were more concerned with a bigger story that hit squarely at OU—the violence had finally convinced officials to close the campus. The story explaining the closure covered most of the front page, with a doomsday-size headline "School closed" blaring across the top of the page. Students would not resume production of the newspaper until late June when the university reopened.

OSU had shut its door days after the Kent State shooting and did not resume classes until Tuesday after the Jackson State shootings, so the *Lantern* did not cover the shootings as a news event. The entire front page of the paper that first day back was devoted to the strike crisis on the OSU campus and stories surrounding that issue (such as how to handle grades for the interrupted term) or the Kent State probe. A mention of Jackson State came on page 13 in a story about other campus closings around the state, including the University of Toledo, which closed for three days to honor the dead at Jackson State.

*The BG News* did not run anything about the shootings at Jackson State in its Friday, May 15, edition. It is likely that deadlines kept the editors from being able to include any report of the event that occurred about midnight Central Time, 1 a.m. in Ohio. The *News* editors, however, did not wait until the regular Tuesday issue to report the event. A four-page tabloid-sized special edition hit the stands on Monday. The cover story was about the cancellation of the ROTC review, noting that the Jackson State shooting was one of the reasons for doing so. University President William T. Jerome III was quoted as saying he hoped the Jackson State slaying would not be pushed into the background, thus "piling of tragedy upon tragedy." A picture of black students marching silently around the campus on Friday stretched across the bottom of the front page. The second-day news story about Jackson State appeared on page 4.

The remainder of the special section was filled with other news: OU's closing; comments from OU's baseball team, who were at Bowling Green for a three game series; an editorial calling for nonviolent protest, noting that "the energy has waned"; criticism and support for the New University concept, a program on campus that allowed students a forum to discuss the current questions and problems of society; the speaker of the Ohio house praising Bowling Green for being one of two state schools that did not have to close its doors; the U.S. Senate discussing plans to halt war spending; a reprint of the campus codes about what constitutes misconduct.

The story of Jackson State stayed in the headlines for the next few weeks at the *News*. The next day, Tuesday, May 19, *The BG News* ran a small announcement on page 1 about a memorial service planned for the Jackson State dead. A picture from that memorial service appeared on the front page the next day, and an AP story on page 5 told of Jackson State students trying to keep workers from repairing the damage to buildings although campus officials said the workers were collecting evidence. A story on page 3 on Thursday, May 21, told of a judge ordering that workers be allowed to remove parts of the scene at Jackson State as needed for evidence. A front page AP story on Tuesday, May 26, announced the formation of a presidential commission to investigate the shootings at both Kent State and Jackson State. On May 27, the newspaper reported in a small story on page 3 that Bowling Green students had raised $500 to send to the relatives of the two students killed at Jackson State. The money had been raised at a rally that only brought out 700 students, compared to the 3,000 who attended a memorial for the Kent students. Without quoting anyone, the story said the disparity had brought charges of racism against the Bowling Green campus for being "less concerned about the deaths of blacks than of Whites."

## AFTER THE SHOOTINGS

The shootings at Kent State and then Jackson State galvanized a response on college campuses like no other protest, demonstration, or action throughout the turbulent 1960s. By some estimations, a million to 4.3 million college students left classes when colleges shut down to either mourn the dead or stave off potential conflicts on their own campuses. About 500,000 students participated in demonstrations of some kind. During the first week of May, thirty ROTC buildings were burned. National Guard units were sent to twenty campuses in sixteen states.[29] "All in all, it was by far the largest number of students ever to demonstrate in a single spasm."[30]

As noted above, Bowling Green University, located twenty-five miles south of Toledo in Northwest Ohio, saw milder protests than some campuses and along with the University of Toledo did not close during the aftermath of Kent State though morning classes at Bowling Green were canceled for one day. Lee Stephenson was managing editor of *The BG News* at the time, and though he does not remember sending reporters to Kent State or putting out the special edition following the Jackson State shootings, he does recall the work students were doing to cover all the events going on. Many discussions occurred in the newsroom, "practical turning of the gears about what was happening," he explained. "How to deploy staff, what was coming up, what we might be missing, keeping a date book of things that should be on our radar screen. Beyond that, I think there was a lot of just sort of creative group grope. How the heck do we try to do something with this, with limited resources and limited access to information as students? During that time there was an enormous sense of excitement that it was almost difficult to remain in the office because there were so many things happening. It was hard to keep enough eyes and ears out there to feel like you really could capture it all."[31]

Stephenson's job as managing editor was to get each day's newspaper out and make sure people were available to do the work. The editor, Bruce Larrick, who died in 2007, was responsible for the editorials as well as handling the politics of the administration and demands of student groups like the Black Student Union, so Stephenson has little memory of those activities. Still, the issues the black students raised were "an equally important front in the things that were happening." Stephenson also recalled the challenges that inexperience presented for student reporters. "Of course, we thought we were brilliant, but inexperience was huge. I think there was a lot of grappling with what really is the professional approach to this, maybe given our youth and skill. Not only how would other professionals do it but how could we do it better?"

The pressures from the administration presented challenges as well. "We felt like we were pushing the limits a lot of the time," he said, explaining that Larrick was called into the president's office a few times because the administration questioned what the newspaper was doing, what priorities they had, and to remind them the freedom they had to publish also carried great responsibility. Occasionally, student groups or the administration questioned the newspaper's story choices of news around the world instead of covering some campus issues like fraternity social events. He praised the newspaper adviser, Ralph Johnson, who provided daily critiques of the newspaper but never tried to censor their work. "He never said 'don't do that again.' It was more 'Did you miss something in this story? Did you really give every side of this issue a voice?'"[32]

Carl Schwartz had just been named editor-in-chief of *The Daily Illini* about two weeks before the Kent State shootings occurred, but he was already a seasoned student journalist. He had worked for his hometown paper during high school and then worked as a reporter, city editor, news editor, and now editor-in-chief of the student newspaper at the University of Illinois. In fact, on his first day on campus as a freshman he got an assignment that ended in a front page story. "I was hooked," he said.

In May, 1970, Schwartz was just wrapping up his junior year. "Illinois was a very active campus and saw quite a bit of protest," he recalled. "There were major, major demonstrations. . . . There was no loss of life and there was no huge property damage like you saw at [University of] Wisconsin. There was a rejection of violence at that level. But if you talked to the administrators on campus, there was significant student unrest. It really did shut down the campus for a short time."

*The Daily Illini* saw a difference in tone between Schwartz and his predecessor, John Hundley, a conscientious objector to the war who brought a more militant feel to the newspaper. "I strongly believed in the protest," Schwartz said. "We sent people out to cover all the major demonstrations in Washington [D.C.] I think I was out there twice, maybe three times, for the anti-war marches in Washington. We were very aggressive in encouraging students to protest and demonstrate, but we were nonviolent. We were objective in our news columns but very progressive and anti-war on our editorial pages." The editorial he wrote two days after the Kent State shootings is a good example of what Schwartz referred to here. The piece criticized President Nixon for his comments after Kent State and urged the University of Illinois president to join other university presidents in condemning the war and urging the faculty senate to take a stand. It ended with a call to students to support a nonviolent strike of classes.[33] The editorials reflected the majority opinion of the editorial board "although the editor was first among equals in shaping that policy," Schwartz explained.[34]

The Illinois campus was becoming more radical but generally was never as strong as the University of Wisconsin, which was one of the most radical at the time. Before spring 1970, the *Illini* staff was interested in learning from their counterparts in Wisconsin at a staff retreat an hour away at Lake Bloomington. "We invited a couple of editors from *The Daily Cardinal* [at the University of Wisconsin] down to talk to us about what was going on at their campus. We had a sense that the Illinois campus was moving in that direction. They started their program by setting fire to the American flag indoors and tossing it in the fireplace. We kicked them out. We said, 'Get out of here. This is not what we're about.' We still thought of ourselves first as journalists trying to cope with this very difficult anti-war time, where indeed the war was the dominant issue for students."[35]

Schwartz made it clear that the student reporters were not to be involved in the protest activities as long as they were reporting for the student newspaper. "It was our job to remain objective in what we reported," he said. Some of his reporters and photographers ended up getting arrested during the protests while they were trying to do their job. The National Guard that was called in to maintain order would round up all the students at the protest, including the press. At one point, camera film shot by an *Illini* photographer was subpoenaed because authorities thought they could use it to identify more protesters. "I took possession of the film and resisted the subpoena and with the help of legal counsel prevailed in that. I still have those negatives to this day," Schwartz said.[36]

Many lessons came from covering the protests. "The most jarring memory of all of this is actually from the Jackson State incident," he said, explaining that because the shootings happened about midnight on a Thursday night, the staff was able to only get in sketchy details before they had to go to press. "It was very short and it wasn't the banner story of the day like Kent State," Schwartz recalled. "I awoke the next morning to face a very large, angry crowd of black students—the Black Student Association and a lot of their supporters. They were incensed that we had paid so little attention to this story. The public doesn't really understand deadlines and production exigencies or anything like that. All I could do was say, 'We made the best effort we could to get as much information in the paper as we had time to do and still get the paper printed,' but that was a very tough sell. We were accused of racism. We were accused of not treating the deaths of black kids as seriously as we did the deaths of white kids at Kent State."

The paper covered the issue more in-depth in the following days and editorialized about it, but it was an experience that stuck with Schwartz. Later, as news editor at the *Milwaukee Journal*, he would push to do as much as possible when covering late breaking news because "people won't understand the next morning if we underplay this story simply because it was difficult. We need to make the play commensurate with the importance of the news if at all possible because it is so difficult for people to understand why you couldn't do more. If I learned any lesson from anything it was that lesson."[37]

He also learned an important lesson about the value of objectivity. "By maintaining your objectivity, your reporting built your credibility with your news sources," he said. That opened doors with administrators who might have otherwise not wanted to talk to the student reporters. "We always tried not to be personal about anything. We didn't try to demonize. We tried to be professional and adult about what we were doing." Because of that, the student staff was also able to maintain an independence that kept them from being pressured by the administration to write stories a certain way or ignore stories.[38]

As noted previously, other issues besides the Vietnam War riled students at many colleges and universities. *Daily Texan* editor Mark Morrison remembers at least two incidents earlier in the school year at University of Texas at Austin that had ramped up the protest mood for students. First was the Waller Creek protest, which occurred October 2, 1969. At issue was a plan to expand the football stadium that required the removal of a number of old oak trees. Architecture students presented an alternative plan that would have saved the trees, but administrators ignored it. "Students were trying all kinds of legal ways to block that development and preserve the natural habitat there," Morrison said.[39] When bulldozers arrived to take down the trees, more than 200 students were there to block the way. Students and the dean of architecture chained themselves up in the branches of the trees and refused to get down. UT Board of Regents Chair Frank C. Erwin Jr., who Morrison called "kind of a tyrant" and who was the chief supporter of the expansion plan, told police to "arrest all the people you have to. Once these trees are down there won't be anything to protest." Eventually, twenty-seven students were arrested and the trees removed.[40] "It was quite a showdown," Morrison said.[41] The second incident occurred November 10, 1969, when students and nonstudents scuffled with police at the Chuckwagon coffee house at the student union. The administration and some student government leaders had been attempting to curtail radicalism on campus by making the coffee house off limits to nonstudents. Eight were arrested, including five students.[42]

UT-Austin students participated in several war protests throughout the year. The day after the Kent State shootings, a student rally of about 8,000 left campus and finally ended up at the Capitol Building, where officers fired tear gas at students who ran through the halls of the building. Students successfully conducted a strike of classes on Thursday and Friday. The biggest protest occurred the Friday after the Kent State shootings when about 25,000 students conducted a march from campus, thirteen blocks long that lasted for more than three hours.[43] *The Daily Texan* student newspaper, usually a sixteen-page broadsheet that published Sunday and Tuesday through Friday, put out a special edition on Saturday to report almost exclusively on the event.

In preparing for the interview for this chapter, Morrison looked back at the *Texan* newspapers from that time. He said he was just as impressed today with the professional quality of the work the students had produced as he was at the time he was directing the work as the editor. "I think everyone just did a wonderful job of being journalists, covering things, both sides of the story, and just basically finding the facts and getting them in the newspaper," he said. "Our good journalism training and instincts came through. I'm just amazed, when I look back, at the quality of work that a lot of colleagues did back in those days. There's nothing I see or remember that I would change. I think we were responsible in covering what was happening." The newspaper operated much like its professional counterparts and covered more than just campus events. With access to Associated Press wire service, the students were able to report major stories from all over the world. "We did try to make sure we weren't hyping these issues. We felt that students should be focused on these issues and that they should be certainly informed about not only the issues but on how some students were opposing certain policies and how they were demonstrating and so forth."[44]

The students worked to remain objective in the news sections, but on the editorial page, which was Morrison's responsibility, the newspaper favored the nonviolent, law-abiding protests. That irked the radicals on campus who hoped for more support. "I and most of my colleagues at the *Texan* were not radicals by any means," Morrison explained. "We were for the most part sort of traditional liberals, but we were very anti-establishment and anti-war in terms of our opinions. We expressed those in the paper." In the days preceding the largest march, the *Texan* editorialized in favor of the city granting the permits necessary for the march because it was a free speech issue. Shortly before the Kent State shootings, the newspaper had editorialized in support of having national activist Abbie Hoffman, co-founder of the Youth International Party (known as the "Yippies"), speak on campus after Rice University had canceled his speech there. Nearly 11,000 students attended the speech in Austin.

Morrison was not afraid to tackle almost any issue or person, including Frank Erwin, the chairman of the Board of Trustees, who was very involved in the management of the Austin campus and had little sympathy for protesters. "We took out after him regularly and had an ongoing war with him," Morrison said. "He would call up and be very irritated about our editorials. But he was influenced by them, and of course that just made it all the more fun for us or the more satisfying that we were having that kind of impact. What really bugged him is we would not let go of an issue. We would start writing about something and then there would be another editorial a few days later and another a few days later. He understood, and that was a lesson I learned as well, that you don't just take your position in a single editorial and then move on to other issues. What really has impact is to follow an issue or a story day after day after day, and that's the power you have to communicate with readers and get them to focus on a particular issue. Maybe they agree with you and maybe they don't but at least they understand the issue."[45]

Student editors in more conservative areas also faced challenges. Angelyn Nelson, editor of *The Daily Utah Chronicle* at the University of Utah in Salt Lake City, said the newspaper would be criticized for being too liberal by one group and then too conservative by another. One of the "too liberal" critiques came after activist Jerry Rubin, a co-founder of the Youth International Party and one of the infamous Chicago 8 defendants in a riot that occurred at the 1968 Democrat National Convention, spoke on campus. "We had this huge debate in the office about whether to write it verbatim or not," Nelson said. "So we did. He used the 'F' word as a synonym for the war, and we printed it on the front page of the *Chronicle*. I thought I was going to get kicked out on my ear." The university received complaining phone calls afterward, and the head of the Publication Council came to visit her and asked why she had allowed it. "It's kind of hard to cover the speech and not put in the word that he's using as a synonym for the war. I said, 'We were just trying to be honest in covering the speech.' It was a big deal."[46]

The newspaper also got heat from protesters who wanted it to be more liberal in supporting what they were doing. One of Nelson's editorial writers was ex-military, who wrote about young soldiers "sloshing through the [Mekong] Delta in Vietnam," but that only riled protesters who wanted the newspaper to come out strongly against the war. "Instead, we wrote about the soldiers. I was in the middle of it all the time and kind of ambivalent, going back and forth, and wanted to give everybody their fair share or say," she said. Editorially, the newspaper tried to support what the majority of students wanted, which was usually a more conservative position than other universities across the country. "I didn't support the protesters per se because it was a small group that was trying to cram down everybody's throat what they wanted," Nelson said. "I supported what the [majority of] students wanted to do. If they wanted to go on strike, fine. If not, then that was the will of the students."[47]

The night following the Kent State shootings, a few hundred protesters were rallying on the lawn of the union building to get support for a student strike, and they had had enough. "They decided the *Chronicle* hasn't been forceful enough in calling for strikes and an end of the war, so they're going to come and take it over and put it out themselves and kick us out," Nelson recalled a staffer covering the rally dashed up to the newspaper office in the union building to report the plan. Nelson and managing editor Heidi Soren-

sen grabbed all the copy for the next day's eight-page paper and headed to
the University Press building where the newspaper was typeset on linotype
machines. They contacted the campus police and reported the threat. About
150–200 protesters went to the newspaper office but found no one there.
Some walked up to the press building but were not allowed in. They demanded to meet with Nelson to make her put out a newspaper that supported
the strike, but she refused. She maintained that the students should be allowed to vote on a strike and not have a small group of radicals force one.

Nelson was not about to let the radicals win. When the typesetting was
completed, she and Sorensen took the paper to the printing plant located in
the next county to the north and later personally delivered the copies around
campus. Then they went underground. For three days they worked out of the
medical offices of Sorenson's grandfather in downtown Salt Lake City, using
the phones and typewriters there to write stories. A story on the front page of
the May 7, 1970, paper reported only that the campus newspaper office was
closed although student editors and reporters were working off-campus. "We
were young and idealistic and believed in freedom of the press. Nobody was
going to take it over. It was our responsibility and we weren't going to give
up control. It's not that we disagreed with them [radicals] about the war. It's
that we disagreed with their tactics to get what they wanted. . . . We knew if
we went back to the *Chronicle* office, we'd have three days of fights and
disagreements with this group of students who were just waiting for us to go
back, so we didn't go back. We also didn't sleep for three days. We didn't do
anything for three days except get the *Chronicle* out."[48] An editorial on May
7 reconfirmed the editors' commitment to continue to publish many different
viewpoints in spite of the takeover attempt, noting the irony of a group of
students who were demanding freedom of expression for themselves were at
the same time trying to deny the student journalists their right to a free
press.[49]

That Thursday, more than eighty University of Utah students were arrested in a sit-in at the Park Building to protest the president's failure to give
in to student demands. Then Friday morning, students voted against a strike
though they condemned the Vietnam War. On Saturday, Nelson joined a
delegation of students who traveled to Washington, D.C., to meet with Utah
Senator Frank Moss and discuss what had been happening on campus. They
also attended the anti-war rally there. She then wrote about the trip.[50]

Looking back, Nelson said she felt a great responsibility in what she was
doing. "You look at what happened at Kent State and think, 'I don't want this
to happen here.' I felt a responsibility to let the students' voices be heard and
not to escalate the situation. We did cover the rallies, and we did cover the
speeches. We did talk to the radical students, the student officers, the average
students, the administrators, the faculty. I was a journalism major, and I had
the ideal about freedom of the press, which I still have 42 years later, that we

should be allowed to cover and let people know what's going on. That was my responsibility."[51]

## DISCUSSION: COMPARING OHIO AND MISSISSIPPI SCHOOLS

Each of the student newspapers considered here framed the protests of May 1970 in different ways. The three Ohio newspapers and the three Mississippi newspapers based their decisions on how to cover the Kent State and Jackson State shootings on many of the same criteria but with different results. In a nutshell, the three OU newspapers covered both events more extensively than the three Mississippi university newspapers, including the shooting that occurred in Mississippi. Obviously, the issue of access to material was critical for all six of these newspapers. None of the Mississippi college newspapers subscribed to wire services in 1970, so obtaining information for stories about either event was limited. Instead, they chose to write local stories and included pieces of information about the shootings as it related to campus events: students at Ole Miss and USM attending the Washington, D.C., march and the leaflet scandal that attempted to stop classes at USM after the Jackson State shootings. All three Ohio universities had access to wire services and thus were able to include news stories about the events and follow-up stories about the investigations.

As Watkins pointed out, production issues play a role in the framing issue.[52] The production schedule, which follows the school calendar at most colleges and universities, interfered with any serious coverage students might have thought about at some of the schools. At Mississippi State, the production schedule for *The Reflector*, which did not publish in the summer, halted the paper for the term the day after the Kent State shootings, making it impossible to even consider covering Jackson State. *The Daily Mississippian* at Ole Miss was able to insert one small news story about Jackson State the day after the shootings. This was probably quite a breaking news coup for the production staff because the shootings occurred about midnight, which would have been near the press deadline. The article likely replaced another front page story that had originally been dummied for that space or the story above it was cut a few inches to accommodate it. Campus closures interfered with the publication of the student newspaper at both Ohio State and OU. OU closed its doors on May 15 until June 22, so *The Post* only had the opportunity to report the initial news story. OSU was already closed when the Jackson State shootings occurred.

The element of timeliness then became an issue for many of the newspapers. By the time OSU had reopened on May 19, the Jackson State incident was old news from four days ago. Bowling Green's special edition, which also dealt more with other issues than Jackson State, appeared three days after the shootings. *The Daily Mississippian's* double-truck spread on campus violence on May 19 had likely been planned and written before Jackson State occurred as there was no mention of that incident.

Proximity also played a role in how the student newspapers framed their coverage of violence. OSU had its own unrest boiling over before Kent State happened. *Lantern* staffers had plenty of stories to cover on their own campus without planning extensive space for unrest elsewhere. Not surprisingly, the Ohio schools all covered the Kent State issues and the investigations that followed at their sister institution. From some of the reporting about Kent, it is clear that reporters from at least Bowling Green rushed to the northeast Ohio campus in Kent to report firsthand because they were located close enough to do so.

The three Ohio universities shared a cultural proximity as well because they were all part of the same higher education system and governed by the same higher education boards. Both Bowling Green and OSU were struggling with similar issues of trying to get student representation on the board of trustees that made decisions for their campuses. That issue was one of the keys in the protests that had been occurring at OSU even before the Kent State shootings. Both Bowling Green and OSU newspapers had stories about the issue both before and after the Kent shootings occurred.

When it came to covering Jackson State, proximity played a significant role as well. With less physical proximity to Jackson State, coupled with conflicts on their own campuses, the OSU and OU newspapers either chose to ignore it or were unable to cover it because of campus closures. The Bowling Green newspaper, however, which was less embroiled in an atmosphere of violence on its campus, did cover Jackson State but certainly less than it had Kent State, which is only about 150 miles away compared to 925 miles to Jackson, Mississippi.

Were the two shooting incidents—one of white students and the other of black—treated differently? When speaking about the student newspapers in Mississippi, one would have to conclude that both incidents were treated identically—they were almost completely ignored, with just one small news story reporting the Jackson State shooting appearing in the Ole Miss newspaper. In Ohio, only one of the three newspapers considered in this study gave the Jackson shooting much ink, though as mentioned earlier, the other two Ohio universities were closed.

Still, one should not consider that these responses are any indication that these colleges were not dealing with racial issues. Indeed, most of these six student newspapers ran stories during May 1970 that had connections to the issue in one way or another. In Mississippi, black students suspended at Ole Miss was the top story on May 4. In the final issue of the term, a black student quoted in a story about campus unrest predicted that violence would come to the campus if black student demands there were not addressed.

Racial violence was the top story in the last issue of *The Reflector* at Mississippi State University on May 5. A detailed report of two days of violence in Starkville, where the university is located, started on the front page and included a photo then jumped inside.

At Ohio State, the Black Student Union was one of the integral groups involved in the strike that had begun the week before the Kent State shooting. The demands of the Black Student Institute at Ohio University was the top story in *The Post* on May 1, and it was still making the front page the day after the Kent shootings. At Bowling Green, the top story in the edition just before the Kent story broke was about the Black Student Union negotiating with the president's advisory council on a number of demands such as recruiting more black students and creating a Black Studies program.

Also, *Lantern* editors and reporters recognized that racial issues were at the core of the protests on the OSU campus. Despite the contention that student newspapers historically do not do adequate in-depth coverage of the serious causes of events, [53] the *Lantern* published two analyses that traced the buildup of unrest on the OSU campus to an event earlier that year when black students had presented administrators with a list of demands. The students were seeking such changes as the development of a Black Studies program, the hiring of more black security officers, and the recruitment of more black students. The black students had given administrators five days to address their concerns, but when they arrived at the Administration Building on March 13 to hear the answer, the 200 protestors were met by 100 police officers in front of the locked doors. Both of the in-depth articles detail the development of the strikes in May from that point in March, starting with the first a month later when the School of Social Work showed its support of the black students by walking out of classes. One troubling point in the analysis, however, was that thirteen *Lantern* staff members, who were never named, were indicated as being part of the Ad Hoc Committee for Student Rights that was the main force behind the strikes. Without being able to track those individuals and the input they had on the stories written about the strike, it is impossible to gauge the level of bias in the reporting of the strikes and unrest that the strikes sparked.

Still, the analysis is an indication that the budding journalists were trying to be responsible and do a thorough, fair job, including admitting their potential biases. Students at OSU and Bowling Green were obviously trying to do the best job possible in covering as many aspects of the events surrounding the protests. It is likely that editors brainstormed daily about various angles to cover. At OSU, for instance, *Lantern* staffers interviewed professors about their positions on the escalating war, talked to area merchants about the impact the unrest had on their businesses, tracked down names of students arrested in the protests, and followed their hearings.

## DISCUSSION: ILLINOIS, TEXAS, AND UTAH

The student newspapers at the University of Illinois, UT-Austin, and University of Utah used wire stories to write about Kent State and then were immediately hammered with the work of writing about protests on their own campuses, much like Ohio State and Ohio University. Still, editors at these three universities used many of the same framing principles as the Ohio and Mississippi schools in writing about their own demonstrations.

Just as the production schedule played a role in Ohio and Mississippi, Carl Schwartz noted the tight production schedule that kept his staff at the *Illini* from doing a thorough job of reporting the Jackson State shooting until days later. Production requirements kept the *Chronicle* from running any story until Monday, May 18, four days after the Jackson State incident. Stories that happen near or on deadline have to be left to the next day's paper. In the case of the student newspapers that typically do not publish on the weekends, a late Thursday night story such as the Jackson shootings does not make it into print until Monday morning. Also, the staffs must rely on a part-time workforce. It is a common problem that has always hampered student newspapers because students' first jobs are supposed to be successfully completing classes and not working for the student newspaper. In reality, the reverse is more often the case.

Proximity was the key framing principle in how the student newspapers wrote about the protests on their own campuses. Not only were the protests physically close, they were emotionally close to the reporters and editors. Though none of the staffs allowed their reporters to be a part of the protest as long as they were reporting, editors noted that they did not know if staff members participated on their own time. Most staffers had strong feelings about the intent of the protests and those feelings came out on the editorial pages. The *Illini* and the *Texan* editors supported the protest movement in their editorials, while the *Chronicle* tried to reflect more of the majority campus opinion that favored nonviolent protest.

Unlike the Mississippi and Ohio schools, issues raised by black students on campus did not have the same intensity on the Utah and Texas campuses, and neither had black students on the newspaper staff.

## CONCLUSION

All of the editors interviewed for this chapter had one goal in common: objective, professional reporting. "It was a challenge because we were in unchartered territory for most of us as student journalists," Mark Morrison said,[54] sentiments that reflect how all the student editors felt at this time. They all tried to do their best to meet that goal, even given the challenges all newspapers, both professional and student, face—challenges like time and space constraints as well as not having enough staff to do all the things they wanted to do.

The student editors all learned valuable lessons from their crisis reporting experiences during that school year, lessons they used throughout their professional careers in various areas of journalism. Bill Armstrong did not get to tell the story of the Kent State tragedy in his college newspaper, but the ideals he learned as a student reporter have stuck with him: "From the beginning I was a reporter. I'm still a reporter no matter what I do. I'll tell you what happened. I'll give you the facts, and I'll give you my analysis. But I'm not going to try to spin it for you politically, left or right. I'll tell you what happened and you can come up with your own analysis of how you feel about it."[55] Carl Schwartz learned that same lesson, noting that remaining objective gave the student reporters and editors credibility and earned them the trust of their sources. He also pointed to the imperative that reporters must work harder to get more complete information on tough stories, even on deadline.[56] Nelson learned lessons at the student newspaper that translated over to her professional life immediately: "How am I going to get everything done? It's the challenge that every journalist has no matter what they're doing, that I had for the next forty years of my job." Also, "it doesn't matter if it's a student newspaper or the biggest paper in the state, you never have enough people."[57]

Mark Morrison learned a lesson that did not come through covering crisis, but its implications could have reached into it. During football season, he accepted an airline ticket to go to a game in California. The ticket was courtesy of Frank Erwin, the Board of Trustees chair who was often butting heads with the student newspaper. Morrison said he had rationalized that as the editor of the newspaper he deserved that ticket to the game. He immediately regretted it. "The Chairman, as we used to call him [Erwin], clearly thought I owed him something for that. He even said at one time that he was considering running an ad in *The Daily Texan* to advertise the fact that I had gotten that ticket. That [accepting the ticket] was certainly a mistake. I was naïve and did not make the right ethical decision and never did anything like that in my journalism career. But it was a lesson I learned the hard way."[58] Though Morrison said the editorial stances and news coverage did not change after the incident, such ethical lapses can affect how reporters and editors write about any event, including protests and other campus crises.

*        *        *

William Armstrong graduated from Kent State and worked for the AP for one year. He went on to have a varied communications career that included such jobs as editing an employee newsletter, working for two chairmen of the Republican National Committee, serving as assistant dean of the NYU Graduate School of Business, writing speeches, working as a Wall Street broker, working as a New York-based public relations executive, writing books, and serving thirty years in the Navy Reserve. He is an adjunct professor of public relations at Fairfield University and serves on several nonprofit boards.

Angelyn Nelson Hutchinson graduated from the University of Utah in journalism and completed a master's in print journalism at Northwestern. She did some public relations work, but spent thirty-five years of her career working for two newspapers in Salt Lake City, Utah (*Salt Lake Tribune* and *Deseret News*), retiring as the assistant managing editor of the *Deseret News*.

Carl Schwartz graduated from the University of Illinois and worked for the *Milwaukee Journal* and its successor, *Journal Sentinel*, for thirty-eight years, retiring as senior editor for national and world news. He continues to work with Wisconsin communities in urban bird conservation through Bird City Wisconsin, is past president of the state Ornithological Society and serves as editor of *The Badger Birder* newsletter.

Mark Morrison graduated from University of Texas-Austin and then went on to work at the *Houston Post* before moving to *Business Week* magazine where he was a reporter and editor for more than thirty years. He taught at his alma mater and now serves as executive committee chair of the Headliners Foundation of Texas, which promotes journalism in Texas.

Lee Stephenson graduated from Bowling Green, worked for the *Dayton Journal Herald*, and then migrated to Washington, D.C., where he has been involved in public interest work, and freelance writing and editing. His work in the environmental movement included becoming an environmental educator and parks professional.

## NOTES

1. William Armstrong, telephone interview by author, November 27, 2012.

2. R. E. Peterson and J. A. Bilorusky, *May 1970: The Campus Aftermath of Cambodia and Kent State* (Berkley, CA: The Carnegie Commission on Higher Education, 1971), 17.

3. Armstrong interview.

4. Ibid.

5. Ibid.

6. Ibid.

7. Ibid.

8. M. Susan Orr-Klopher, *Where Rebels Roost: Mississippi Civil Rights Revisited* (Lulu.com, 2005), 563.

9. Tim Spofford, *Lynch Street: The May 1970 Slayings at Jackson State* (Kent, OH: Kent State University Press, 1988).

10. "After Kent State Incident, Nation's Campuses Erupt," *The Daily Universe* (Provo, UT), May 6, 1970, 1.

11. Tracey Dean Smith, "Agitators in the Land of Zion: The Anti-Vietnam War Movements at Brigham Young University, University of Utah, and Utah State University" (Thesis, Utah State U., 1995), accessed July 6, 2011, http://lynx.lib.usm.edu/docview/304229020?accountid=13946.

12. Erving Goffman, *Frame Analysis: An Essay on the Organization of Experience* (Boston: Northeastern University Press, 1974).

13. Paula M. Poindexter, Laura Smith, and Don Heider. (2003). "Race and Ethnicity in Local Television News: Framing, Story Assignments, and Source Selections," *Journal of Broadcasting & Electronic Media,* 47 (2003): 524–536.

14. Stephen D. Reese, "Prologue – Framing Public Life: A Bridging Model for Media Research," in *Framing Public Life: A Bridging Model for Media Research,* ed. Stephen D. Reese, Oscar H. Gandy, & August E. Grant (Mahwah, NJ: Lawrence Erlbaum Associates, 2001), 11.

15. Maxwell McCombs, Donald Shaw and David Weaver, *Communication and Democracy: Exploring the Intellectual Frontiers in Agenda-Setting* (Mahwah, NJ: Lawrence Erlbaum Associates, 1997).

16. Robert M. Entman, "Framing Toward Clarification of a Fractured Paradigm," *Journal of Communication,* 43 (1993): 52.

17. Todd Gitlin, *The Whole World Is Watching: Mass Media in the Making and Unmaking of the New Left* (Berkeley: University of California Press, 1980), 6.

18. S. Craig Watkins. "Framing Protest: News Media Frames of the Million Man March," *Critical Studies in Media Communications,* 18 (2001): 83–101.

19. Zhongdang Pan and Gerald M. Kosicki, "Framing Analysis: An Approach to News Discourse," *Political Communication,* 10 (1993): 55–75.

20. Entman, "Framing Toward Clarification."

21. Watkins, "Framing Protest."

22. John McCarthy, Clark McPhail, and Jackie Smith, "Images of Protest: Dimensions of Selection Bias in Media Coverage of Washington Demonstrations, 1982 and 1991," *American Sociological Review,* 61 (1996): 481.

23. William A. Gamson and Andre Modigliani, "Media Discourse and Public Opinion on Nuclear Power," *American Journal of Sociology,* 95 (1989): 1–37.

24. Oscar H. Gandy, "If It Weren't for Bad Luck: Framing Stories of Racially Comparative Risk," in *Mediated Messages and African-American Culture,* eds. Venise T. Berry & Carmen L. Manning-Miller (Thousand Oaks, CA: Sage, 1996): 55–75.

25. The *Lantern,* May 5, 1970.

26. Patsy Brumfield, "Senate Hits a Flag Burner," *The Mississippian* (Oxford, MS), May 6, 1970, 1.

27. "Progressives Sponsor Indochina Reaction: Estimated 700 Students Gather, Hear Students, Faculty Members," *The Student Printz* (Hattiesburg, MS), May 12, 1970, 1.

28. "USM Students Attend Protest," *The Student Printz* (Hattiesburg, MS), May 14, 1970, 1.

29. Charles Chatfield and Robert Kleidman, *The American Peace Movement: Ideals and Activism* (New York: Twayne Publishers, 1992); Todd Gitlin, *The Sixties: Years of Hope, Days of Rage* (New York: Bantam Books, 1987); Kenneth J. Hieneman, *Campus Wars: The Peace Movement at American State Universities in the Vietnam Era* (New York: New York University Press, 1993).

30. Gitlin, *The Whole World Is Watching,* 410.

31. Lee Stephenson, telephone interview by author, December 27, 2012.

32. Ibid.

33. "Kent Massacre: The Domino Theory," *The Daily Illini* (Champaign, IL), May 6, 1970, 8.

34. Stephenson interview.

35. Carl Schwartz, telephone interview by author, December 5, 2012.

36. Ibid.

37. Ibid.

38. Ibid.

39. Mark Morrison, telephone interview by author, December 7, 2012.

40. Leah Caldwell, "1969: Waller Creek Riot," *Issue* 3 (2003), 12.

41. Morrison interview.

42. "Chuckwagon Incident," Briscoe Center for American History, accessed January 7, 2013, http://www.cah.utexas.edu/ db/dmr/image_lg.php?variable=di_06989.

43. Beverly Burr, "History of Student Activism at University of Texas at Austin: 1960–1988," (Thesis, U. of Texas at Austin, 1988), accessed December 6, 2012, http://www.campusactivism.org/server-new/uploads/burrthesis.pdf.

44. Morrison interview.

45. Ibid.

46. Angelyn Nelson, telephone interview by author, November 27, 2012.

47. Ibid.

48. Ibid.

49. "Strike Decision Rests with All the Students," *The Daily Utah Chronicle* (Salt Lake City, UT), May 7, 1970, 2.

50. Nelson interview.

51. Ibid.

52. Watkins, "Framing protest."

53. Clifford Wilcox, "Antiwar Dissent in the College Press: The Universities of Illinois and Michigan," in *Sights on the Sixties* ed. Barbara L. Tischler (New Brunswick, NJ: Rutgers University Press, 1992).

54. Morrison interview.

55. Armstrong interview.

56. Schwartz interview.

57. Nelson interview.

58. Morrison interview.

*Chapter Six*

# Different Decade, Same Challenges

For several days in November 2015, the staff of *The Maneater* student newspaper at the University of Missouri-Columbia (MU) stopped what they were doing and gathered around the television in the newspaper office at the top of the CNN newscast every half hour. For several minutes they were almost mesmerized by the images of their campus and the tent city they all walked by to get to class. They listened as national media journalists interviewed students and other campus faces they knew. They shook their heads in disbelief that their beloved campus was the scene of historic protests over racism—including a hunger strike and football boycott—that ended with the resignation of the University of Missouri System president and the Mizzou chancellor.

Finally, as the broadcast turned to other stories, the staff of mostly freshmen and sophomore college students returned to the daunting task of providing the best coverage possible of those same events in their weekly publication and daily online. It was a task the editors and reporters had been doing throughout the entire semester, a semester filled with many controversial issues and numerous protests: graduate students demands, Planned Parenthood and abortions, undocumented alien tuition hikes, sexual assaults and campus safety, and, most notably, racism. From the first issue of the newspaper on August 26, *The Maneater* weekly print edition was reporting on the rallies, debates, protests, marches, and sit-ins that followed. Indeed, every one of the fifteen front pages that fall semester sported a story about one of the controversies. Additional stories and sometimes stand-alone photos were included inside. Some stories appeared only online at themaneater.com.

With all the controversy mounting on campus, the reporters and editors of the Mizzou student newspaper found themselves doing just what student journalists in the 1960s also struggled to do: report on what happened with as much professionalism as they could. During the week in November when the protests came to a head with the resignation of the president and chancellor, *The Maneater* staff accomplished something professional journalists might call a small miracle: they reported, wrote, and edited sixty stories about what had just happened—without having to publish a single correction. [1]

Their experiences mirrored those of the student journalists of the 1960s in several other ways. They faced many of the same challenges of being a good student while also being a good journalist, of reporting accurately and thoroughly on the fast-paced events engulfing the campus, of competing with the national media that also covered the protests. They pulled all-nighters at times to get the print version out on time. They dealt with young, inexperienced writers, worked long hours for little or no pay, published even when rumors of threats swirled around campus, picked up the slack when one editor had to be replaced, and still published every week without fail.

"I'm proud that our staff survived," editor-in-chief Elizabeth Loutfi said. "It was such an emotionally taxing time for everyone." [2]

This chapter considers how the editors and reporters of *The Maneater* covered the protests throughout the school year, 2015–2016. Six editors, a reporter, and a columnist provided their memories and observations about what happened as the staff worked to provide what journalism has famously been described as being—"the "first rough draft of history." [3]

## A SEMESTER OF PROTEST: UNIVERSITY OF MISSOURI, COLUMBIA — 2015

The first days of fall semester 2015 began with graduate student protests. A threatened walkout by graduate students appeared on the bottom of page 1 of *The Maneater's* first issue on August 26. [4] The graduate students made several demands: raise graduate student pay; give all graduate student employees full tuition waivers; reinstate a subsidized health care plan that had been dropped just before school started; provide more graduate student housing; return affordable, on-campus daycare; and waive supplemental fees for graduate students.

In the second issue a week later, the editors, again on the bottom of page 1, tackled the controversy surrounding Planned Parenthood and abortions as the Missouri Senate Interim Committee on the Sanctity of Life investigated abortion services conducted through Planned Parenthood. The committee was particularly interested in MU's involvement in bringing abortion services back to the city of Columbia, where Mizzou is located. State law at the time forbade public funding, such as tax dollars the legislature allocated to the university, for abortions. MU Chancellor R. Bowen Loftin was called to testify at the committee hearings. [5] The university went on to rescind contracts with Planned Parenthood, spawning student rallies,[6] though new contracts later in the semester reinstated the relationship.[7]

A month into the semester, the core protest issue arose: racism on campus. It began with a Facebook post from Missouri Students Association President Payton Head, a gay black student, who reported being called racial slurs as he walked through campus. He called for awareness and discussion about the problem. *The Maneater* wrote about the incident as the lead story on page 1 of the fourth issue, noting that Head "wanted to focus on creating a dialogue instead of making the post about his own personal hurt."[8]

Racism at MU is not a new issue. A search of *The Maneater* stories online found at least one story dating to 1996 that discussed racism. Racist-oriented events have made news through the years since then, including a notable incident in 2010 when two white students were arrested for dropping cotton balls on the front lawn of the Gaines/Oldham Black Culture Center.[9] After that, the administration began the One Mizzou diversity initiative, but it soon became an athletic slogan, and the university discontinued its use in spring 2015 because it had lost its diversity emphasis.[10]

Diversity issues were not confined to just Missouri during the 2015–2016 school year. As of December 8, 2015, more than seventy-five universities around the country, including such institutions as Dartmouth College and Yale University, had students making demands related to race and gender.[11]

The current racial issues at Mizzou didn't just start surfacing in fall 2015, either. Taylor Blatchford, as a freshman reporter in spring semester 2015, wrote about race relations and students demanding a call to action because of the hostile racial environment on campus.[12] Throughout the fall 2015 protests, black students reported many incidents of being "called out of your name"—a phrase that describes being referred to by insulting words rather than one's name.[13]

*The Maneater* continued to follow several other controversial issues throughout the semester. The results of a Campus Climate Survey on Sexual Assault found "38.8 percent of senior undergraduate women had experienced some form of nonconsensual sexual contact during their time at MU."[14] When a law professor filed a lawsuit against the university, calling a policy that prohibits guns on campus unconstitutional, students voiced their opinion about the policy.[15] The university's decision to discontinue "refer and follow" privileges that effectively stopped abortions in Columbia was followed by more rallies[16] before contracts with Planned Parenthood were reinstated.[17] Graduate students continued to pursue their demands and announced plans to unionize.[18] Recent legislation aimed at undocumented immigrants on campus and other national and international events related to immigration sparked at least five stories, one column and one editorial throughout the semester.[19] In late October, the newspaper reported a second anti-Semitic vandalism incident in the past year when a swastika was found drawn on a residence hall wall with feces.[20]

Despite these controversial issues, racism took the forefront through most of the semester. On September 24, almost two weeks after Payton Head first posted on social media about being called racial slurs, the first Racism Lives Here rally took place with participants criticizing Chancellor Loftin for taking six days to respond to the racism that Head suffered.[21] Other Racism Lives Here rallies followed.[22] The group Student Coalition for Critical Action encouraged students to cover a campus statue of Thomas Jefferson with notes that describe another side of the famous third president of the United States: slave owner.[23] Another student started a petition to have the statue removed while the College Republicans countered by organizing a "Stand with Jefferson" movement.[24]

More racial slurs made the headlines when a drunk man talking on a cell phone interrupted the play practice of the Legion of Black Collegians on Monday, October 5, as students prepared for their Homecoming week performance. When ordered to leave the practice, the man reportedly told the person to whom he was speaking on the phone that "these niggers are getting aggressive with me." A sit-in to protest the lack of administration action followed the next day in the lobby of Jesse Hall, the main administration building at MU.[25] Chancellor Loftin then responded with an announcement of campus-wide diversity and inclusion training beginning in January.[26] Graduate student Jonathan Butler criticized Loftin's plan as needing more than just training.[27] Butler was one of the founders of the protest group Concerned Student 1950[28] that created a chain to block MU President Tim Wolfe's car in the Homecoming parade later that week. He said he was hit by Wolfe's car when campus police finally forced the protesters back so the parade could continue.[29]

Ten days later, on October 20, the Concerned Student 1950 group had a list of demands for the administration that included the resignation of the president of the University of Missouri system, Tim Wolfe, and a 10 percent increase in the number of black faculty and staff by fall 2017.[30] The next day, the UM System Board of Curators held a four-hour closed session and rumors began to fly on social media that the curators would fire Chancellor Loftin.[31] Members of Concerned Student 1950 met with President Wolfe on October 26, but the group reported that Wolfe had not agreed to any of their demands.[32]

Finally, on Sunday, November 1, a weeklong climax of the semester's racial tension began. Jonathan Butler announced a hunger strike that he intended to continue as a protest of unaddressed racism issues until Wolfe resigned. He joined other Concerned Student 1950 organizers who had pitched tents on Carnahan Quad.[33]

On Tuesday, the Concerned Student 1950 group called for a boycott of campus food services and buying of apparel in the student center as a further protest.[34] That same day, the English department announced a "no confidence" vote for Chancellor Loftin.[35]

On Wednesday, Loftin expressed his support for Butler's hunger strike as a "peaceful protest" although he said he did not want to see the student put his health at risk.[36]

On Thursday, CS1950 led a walkout of hundreds of students, faculty, and staff through some campus buildings and finally to the camp site on Carnahan Quad.[37] The Faculty Council met and afterward released a statement of concern about the leadership of the MU system.[38]

Campus support for the protest continued to swell. Some faculty canceled classes in favor of a "teach-in" at the camp site.[39] Several campus departments announced their support as well.[40] On Friday, President Wolfe issued an apology for his reaction to the Homecoming parade protest that occurred almost four weeks earlier, fulfilling one of the demands Concerned Student 1950 had issued.[41] Hours later, Wolfe was at a fundraiser in Kansas City, and faced protesters at UM-Kansas City.[42] Later Friday night, two black students reported being called racial slurs by four white men while walking near the campus rec center.[43]

Mizzou protesters took their cause to prospective students attending Meet Mizzou Day on Saturday with a march around campus that included chants about the protest and the claim that they were showing prospective students "the real MU."[44] That night, black Mizzou football players announced a boycott of any further practice or games as a show of solidarity for Butler's hunger strike. They vowed to boycott until Wolfe resigned.[45] The rest of the team joined the boycott Sunday morning.[46] Also Sunday morning, Governor Jay Nixon released a statement denouncing racism in the state's colleges and universities.[47]

President Tim Wolfe said Sunday that he would not resign.[48] Then early Monday morning, just as Butler's hunger strike reached its one-week mark, the Missouri Student Association Executive Cabinet, led by President Payton Head, released a letter they had sent to the Board of Curators, demanding Wolfe's firing.[49] A couple of hours later, Wolfe resigned.[50] Then a few hours after that, Chancellor R. Bowen Loftin announced his resignation, effective January 1.[51] Concerned Student 1950 said Wolfe's resignation was just the beginning and issued new demands that included meeting with the Board of Curators and the governor.[52]

A video taken at the camp site on Monday ended up going viral on the internet, further pushing the Mizzou conflict into the national spotlight. Communications assistant professor Melissa Click was videoed ordering student photojournalists to leave the area and calling for other students to help remove them from the premises.[53] Click ended up being criminally charged with assault for the incident[54] and fired from Mizzou in February of the next semester.[55]

As the protesters disbanded the camp site on Carnahan Quad and the protest appeared to be over, a new issue arose. On Tuesday, anonymous threats appeared on Yik Yak, another social media site, causing many students to fear for their safety on campus.[56] Police arrested a student on Wednesday for making the threats.[57] Then, sometime that same night, a vandal spray painted over the word "Black" on the sign in front of the Gaines-Oldham Black Culture Center.[58]

Thursday, the Board of Curators announced an interim president.[59] Later they scheduled a listening session for November 20 where they heard students' concerns about what it would take to make Mizzou the school it ought to be.[60]

The university ended the semester with the creation of a special office to investigate all reports of discrimination on campus.[61]

Although the protest atmosphere on campus was considerably calmer in the spring semester of 2016, controversial issues continued to be part of the discussion across campus, including graduate students voting for unionization[62] and student government election problems that forced the newly elected president to resign.[63] One new issue raised its head: a lack of diversity on the board of curators who would be selecting the new UM president and the new chancellor at Mizzou.[64] *The Maneater,* in an editorial, endorsed a move to make the board more diverse.[65] Following the fall protests, the UM System officials decided to create a position of chief diversity, equity and inclusion officer to deal with racism issues.[66]

## THE MANEATER

*The Maneater* first appeared at the University of Missouri-Columbia campus on February 18, 1955.[67] The printed version of the student paper during the 2015–2016 school year sported volume number 82, indicating that *The Maneater* had adopted the twenty-plus-year lineage of the *Missouri Student,* which it supplanted—a common practice of newspapers throughout history.

Just as the editor in 1955 reported that the newspaper would be an independent student voice—"a tiger with fangs bared and claws sharpened ready to analyze the facts and then to pounce"[68]—so the publication remains today. The university administration has little authority over the newspaper. The chancellor selects members of the student publication board that serves in an advisory capacity. That committee can recommend to the vice chancellor if the editor-in-chief needs to be removed but has no power to do so itself. The newspaper is funded entirely by advertising dollars, including paying for printing costs, providing small stipends for editors per issue, and paying the salary of a full-time adviser who helps manage the budget but has no control over the editorial product. The university supplies space in the student center, but the newspaper has to pay for its phones, data ports, office supplies, and anything else necessary to operate. The newspaper also runs its funding through the university's accounting system, but the students control how the money is spent within the university's guidelines.[69]

The 6,000-circulation, weekly print publication, which appears on newsstands between noon and 2 p.m. on Wednesdays during the regular school year, is produced by undergraduate students, mostly freshmen and sophomores. Before they ever come to campus, incoming freshmen apply for writing positions as did assistant sports editor Alec Lewis, reporter Thomas Oide, and diversity columnist Kennedy Jones, who all worked on the paper throughout the 2015–2016 school year. The three were among the writers who wrote about some of the protests during the year. Other students who had been at the paper for at least a year and were mostly sophomores held editor positions, including Taylor Blatchford, who was projects editor and later university news editor, opinion editor Jack Herrick, and copy chief George Roberson.

After their sophomore year, most print journalism students leave *The Maneater* and expand their experience with at least one semester at *The Columbia Missourian,* another campus-based newspaper but with an off-campus focus. The *Missourian* began in 1908 when the Missouri School of Journalism opened and is "a community news organization managed by professional editors and staffed by Missouri School of Journalism students who do the reporting, design, copy editing, information graphics, photography and multimedia."[70] However, *Maneater* managing editor Katherine Knott, a senior, and editor-in-chief Elizabeth Loutfi, a junior, had chosen to continue at the student newspaper during the 2015–2016 school year. During fall semester 2014, Knott had fulfilled a print journalism requirement to work at least one semester at the *Missourian,* but returned to *The Maneater* to finish out her college career and graduate in May 2016.[71] Loutfi went to *The Missourian* after her stint as editor-in-chief ended in May 2016.[72]

As is typical at student newspapers, the editors of *The Maneater* reorganize and delineate duties for various editors, often every year. Loutfi and Knott had separate titles but chose to manage the newspaper more as partners, almost like co-editors-in-chief. Knott redefined the managing editor role to be a support structure for the editor-in-chief. Initially, she managed the three news editors so Loutfi could concentrate on relations with other campus groups. However, when the November protest began, the two worked in tandem to assign stories and photos, to write and edit stories, to basically do whatever needed to be done at the time—irrespective of their job titles. The two directly supervised about twenty-five other student editors and managers who worked on various aspects of the newspaper, including the

MOVE feature section, sports, editorial, projects, photography, production, graphics, copy editing, social media, and the newspaper's web page. Many of these student editors found themselves filling roles other than the ones they were assigned because any available, willing staffers were needed at times to cover the protests. Throughout the year, the newspaper had about fifty students involved.

## CHALLENGES OF REPORTING

The student staff faced many challenges during fall semester 2015, including overcoming a poor reputation, a lack of diversity on the staff, difficult access to information, and attending classes.

The bad reputation hurdle was one the newspaper had garnered when a previous staff published an April Fools' edition in 2012 where they changed the name of the paper to "The Carpeteater." In 2011, the April Fools' issue was named "The Manbuzz." "We're not a well-respected publication on our own campus, much to our own chagrin," Knott explained. In the past, the newspaper staff appeared to be more "tone deaf" and columnists were given more free reign. That can be a problem, she said, because readers don't always distinguish between columns and news. "When we publish something that makes a lot of people angry, we take responsibility for that," Knott said, "even if it's our columnists, not us."

*The Maneater* was not the only student newspaper dealing with reputation issues during that fall. Protesters also boycotted the *Brown Daily Herald* at Brown University after two racists opinion pieces appeared. The *Argus* at Wesleyan University came under fire for not covering a Black Lives Matter protest and then saw funding cut in half after a controversial opinion piece appeared. The *Argus* staff made changes and tried to improve coverage of minorities but ran into a wall that many student newspapers, including the *Brown Daily Herald*, have hit on campus: the protesters who demand more representation in the newspaper refused to talk to them. Some of those who want to talk do so only when the newspaper promises to agree to their demands to report the story the way the protesters want it told.[73]

The editors worked diligently during the 2015–2016 year to try to improve *The Maneater's* tarnished reputation. Making sure the editorial editor had at least twenty-four hours to craft the editorial position each week was one of the processes they instituted to become more respectable. In the past, the editorial was written at the last minute, with editing late in the evening of production. "Missteps cost us a lot," Knott said. "We don't live on a forgiving campus that lets us make a mistake that is an honest mistake. We're not trying to offend people, but an honest mistake results in people asking why we're allowed on campus." Staffers also diligently enforced a requirement for all reporters to verify all quotes. Every story then went through several reads—the section editor, the copy editors, the copy chief, and finally the managing editor and editor-in-chief. Any story could be flagged along the way and sent back to the reporter for more work. This attention to detail meant fewer corrections and a more professional product. "I'd like to think that we made some inroads on that reputation," Knott said, "and at least let people know that we know we've been problematic in the past, but we are trying to change."[74]

The editors realized early in the semester that they needed to have a plan. Finally, they sat down to talk about it after the hunger strike began. Managing editor Katherine Knott, who spearheaded most of the coverage planning throughout the semester, said they discussed two ways they could handle the stories: write about every little thing as it happened or take a step back and provide more context. They decided the bigger picture was the focus they would like to work on, but quickly they got swept up in the breaking news and weren't able to really do the stories with context that they had hoped to do. Instead, as the hunger strike and the associated protest built up, the weekly printed newspaper added stories daily to the online newspaper site. Most of the sixty stories written during that week appeared only online.[75] Poynter Institute, an organization focused on journalism, lauded the newspaper's work to move from a weekly print mentality to digital first. Knott discussed the staff's work in an article published on the institute's website.[76] The newspaper churned out regular updates online and discovered readers were heading to the website to find out the latest because "they learned to trust us, and they learned that we'll keep them informed," Knott said in an interview for this chapter.

The Poynter article also pointed out an online feature—an interactive timeline—that broke *The Maneater's* record for the most page views with about 180,000 in one week. The timeline idea arose in late October when Knott and Projects editor Taylor Blatchford talked about how to give readers an easy way to view all the different controversies—with racism at the core—that had rocked their college campus throughout the fall. Blatchford then worked with Tessa Weinberg, assistant Outlook editor, and Carlie Procell, online development editor, to create the timeline using the Timeline JS program. They posted it on November 5, a few days before the national media descended on the campus.[77] The timeline (see http://www.themaneater.com/ special-sections/mu-fall-2015/), titled "A Historic Fall at MU," featured pictures with almost every brief that was created for each of the events chronicled there. Most of the briefs linked to longer stories the newspaper had published online; many stories also appeared in the printed version of the weekly newspaper.

Blatchford continued to update the timeline throughout the semester.[78] Eventually the thirty-three items entered by November 5 became fifty-three when the semester ended. *The New York Times,*[79] as well as the *Washington Post,*[80] linked to the timeline in at least one of their stories. The three time-line creators won first place in the multimedia package category at the Missouri College Media Association conference in April 2016. It was one of the twenty-four awards *The Maneater* took home, including best overall newspaper; fourteen of the winning individual entries had appeared during perhaps the most tumultuous semester the campus had ever seen—fall 2015.

Every day the editors thought about how to best cover the protests. "We were thinking very, very critically as coverage came up," Editor-in-Chief Elizabeth Loutfi said. "We needed to think about 'how can we package this to make sure that people see it and that people understand that it is a follow up to this story?' A lot of the discussions in the fall were 'how do we package this and how do we make sure that people are staying up to date? Where do people get the information the easiest?'"[81]

Another critical challenge was something the staff could do little about at the moment—a serious lack in diversity among the staff members. Only two black students consistently worked for the paper during the fall semester 2015: Kennedy Jones, the diversity columnist, and Alicia Washington, a social justice beat writer—both unpaid positions. Recruiting minority students has been difficult, Knott said, mostly because of the poor reputation the newspaper has suffered the last few years. She said the improvements in the last year will help in the future with recruitment but "the culture change will take time."[82]

The university itself has few black students. In fall 2015, the campus had 2,544 black or African-American students, which was about 7.2 percent of the 35,448 undergrad and graduate students. Another 951 students identified themselves as two or more races, non-Hispanic.[83] The number of blacks among the School of Journalism students was even lower; 4.8 percent of the 2,097 undergrads (98 students) and graduate students (4) identified as black or African-American.[84] Because almost all *The Maneater* staff members are journalism undergraduate majors, the pool for possible black writers and editors is small.

The editors recognized that having few blacks on the staff hampered their coverage in some ways. "It was something we knew, but we just had to go out into the community and try and report and try to understand," Loutfi said.[85] Knott said the lack of diversity didn't make much of a difference in the reporting "because we were playing by the rules everyone else was and we got the same stories." However, in hindsight, things could have been different, she said. "I wish all the editors had taken more time to be in certain spaces like the Black Cultural Center beforehand so that we weren't coming up and playing catch up and be like, 'hey, we're here to cover your story,'" she said. "No, we should have been there two months before; we should have been listening; we should have been engaging. That's what would have made the difference. . . . What hampered us more than anything was not doing the proactive leg work we needed to do."[86]

As noted before, Kennedy Jones, a freshman from Las Vegas, was one of two active black writers on the staff. She got involved with the newspaper before her freshman year began through the newspaper's incoming freshman Facebook page. When editors posted a position as a diversity columnist, she applied and got the job because, she said, she was the least militant of all the black women who submitted work. "They were ecstatic that I was somebody who wasn't angry when I was writing," Jones explained. "But that was because I had nothing to be angry about yet." Her work appeared almost every week under the logo The Kaleidoscope View, a name her mother helped her select. The two had discussed how the column would be looking at different viewpoints and blending those ideas just as a kaleidoscope creates changing symmetrical patterns as it is rotated. Jones assumed that she would talk to students of various ethnicities and write stories about them in a way that would inform the student body about different cultures. She didn't know racism would be the key topic for almost every column.[87]

Jones's father warned her that Mizzou had racism issues and she would have to pick a side: either be friends with white students or with black students because the two don't really mix. That suggestion surprised her because, growing up in Las Vegas, she socialized with other teens of all backgrounds and didn't confront racism or feel personally attacked because of her skin color. Once at Mizzou, though, she found her father was right about how it worked. And she had to figure out how to deal with it. "I showed up at the Black Culture Center like everyone else [who was black]," she said. "I went to the parties like everyone else. I tried to get groups of friends like everyone else. I just picked my side because I'm black so I obviously was going to go somewhere where I felt like I could automatically have an in." And at the end of the day, every day, she felt as if her race had played a role in how people treated her. "I felt personally attacked all the time," she said. "I think a lot of it was because it was a trigger so every time someone would look at me in a rude way, I automatically thought it was because I was black."[88]

Before coming to MU, she had wanted to join a sorority, and she wrote about that desire in the sample column she submitted that got her the job. Her research, however, changed her mind. As she searched social media about the various sororities available at MU, she realized only two of the groups posted pictures that included black girls. She then looked up the same sororities at other university campuses and found they were not exclusively white elsewhere. "But at Mizzou," she said, "it was like nobody had escaped 1958." MU does have some black fraternities and sororities, but Jones decided not to join them either. She said people told her about racial incidents that happened that they asked her not to report, like stories of white guys being kicked out of fraternities because they brought black girls into a fraternity party.[89] *Maneater* Opinion Editor Jack Herrick said he quit a fraternity when he found that was the unwritten rule.[90]

Whatever diversity issue or point of view Kennedy wanted to explore in her column was fair game. Some columns were inspired by national events such as black pop singer Beyonce's tribute to the Black Panthers during the 2016 Super Bowl half-time show. Jones supported the performance and encouraged students to watch the *Saturday Night Live* skit, "The Day Beyonce Turned Black."[91] A public speaking class discussion sparked a column about how perceptions define individual definitions of diversity, noting that some definitions are probably not even feasible to consider.[92] Name calling incidents on campus spawned columns, such as one explaining that only blacks can use the word "nigga" to each other, not whites.[93] The chancellor's slow response to the student body president's report of being called racial slurs prompted a column that described the first Racism Lives Here rally and then urged students to speak against racism because silence encourages it.[94] Another column urged the black community to make some changes to improve their lives.[95] Her work earned her the top columnist of the year award from the Missouri College Media Association conference in April 2016.

The blacks on campus had a problem with *The Maneater* to start with, Jones found out. Black students didn't want to talk about racial issues with a *Maneater* reporter because "they felt *The Maneater* would write about it in a way that made it look like it was the black student's fault." Even when the black students were protesting about being called names, they thought the newspaper would make it sound like they were wrong for protesting at all. When the protests began in earnest, the organizers would organize what they called "town hall meetings" and allowed any interested student to attend though it wasn't really a public meeting. They would allow no recordings, no cameras, and no reporters—fearing the event would be reported in a racist way, Jones said. She was allowed in but only on the condition she did not report on the event.

Another *Maneater* staffer, freshman Thomas Oide, who hailed from the Sacramento, California, area and is of Japanese descent, was also allowed inside the town hall meetings, again on the condition he did not report the meeting. Oide, a general assignment reporter, had become the newspaper's primary contact with the Concerned Student 1950 group. He and another reporter covered the Racism Lives Here protest on September 24 as an assignment,[96] and then Oide decided to follow up with an in-depth interview with one of the participants and a CS1950 founder, Reuben Faloughi. Oide had been warned about the poor relationship the newspaper had with various racial groups because of past misquoting, so he let Faloughi read his story before it was published to make sure it was factual. Faloughi like the piece,[97] and the two began to build a relationship that lasted throughout the semester and made *The Maneater* one of the few local news outlets the protesters would talk with. The newspaper had other reporters who were assigned to cover race and social justice issues, "but I just became the Concerned Student 1950 guy," Oide said. His relationship with Faloughi and other CS1950 students made it possible for him to write a piece on the group as a whole that ran after the final protest ended.[98]

He learned important lessons from these experiences about the positive results of building relationships: "As long as you're a reporter and you just do good work, and you ask the right questions, and you fact check and you quote check, and you make sure that everything you're doing is right, the [bad] reputation can go away a little bit." Those trusting relationships made it possible for him at the end of the school year to interview Jonathan Butler, the grad student who went on the hunger strike, for one of the six profiles of the most influential students on campus featured in the Year in Review publication the newspaper put out.[99]

The editors had hoped that Oide could report on the town meetings he attended, but ultimately Knott was not concerned that he attended but did not report. "We were playing the long term when it comes to covering the situation," she explained. She recognized that having him just attend the meetings would give him a better understanding of what was going on and would make him better prepared to write other stories about the protests.[100]

When the tent city sprang up on Carnahan Quad, Oide walked by it every day but other than visiting it the first day, he did not enter. "I didn't want to put myself in a position to intrude on their privacy," he explained. Besides, he didn't really need to visit the site to gather information; he had phone numbers for Faloughi and another CS1950 organizer, Max Little, and could call or text either to get the latest information. Unlike the national media, he decided sitting outside the campsite, waiting for something to happen, was not a productive use of his time. He said: "I went with the mindset that 'hey, I have these relationships with these people and I have the opportunity to tell the story of the group,' and that's what I set out to do during that time. I wanted to tell their story from their perspective as much as I possibly could."[101]

Opinion Editor Jack Herrick visited the campsite on several occasions and was kicked out twice. He tried to spend a few hours almost every day listening to many people's perspectives to really understand the issues. The protesters at the campsite often had issues with the news media covering their activities and speeches, claiming their privacy rights were being trampled when the media tried to cover these events. Herrick was in the newsroom when one reporter assigned to cover the protest came in crying because the protesters confronted her, took her phone, and erased all her messages. "They made her feel awful for being in journalism," he said. "I won't stand for it." So he went to the camp and tried to talk to the protesters, telling them they had few expectations of privacy when talking to 250 people in an open air public space. His words fell on deaf ears. "It was as if they thought that we were in the '60s, and that people were getting lynched, and separate but equal was still a thing."[102]

As often as her schedule allowed, Jones went to the tent city on Carnahan Quad. One editor asked her to try to find someone for an interview but she never did. At first she had hoped to talk to protesters about her column and then become a voice for them, but it never went that way. Instead, when she was at the campsite, she was participating not reporting. "I was very into it," she said. She walked in the marches, she sat with the sit-ins. "We went down and prayed every day at 10 o'clock while they had the campsite up," she said. "It became a big part of my life, to be honest." She even had the African word "ase" tattooed on the inside of her right wrist. The word was part of a chant the protesters often repeated. The leaders would call out "ase" and the protesters would respond with "power!" She explained that ase "means whatever is said next is indisputable. So it is indisputable that black people have power. That's essentially what the chant means."[103]

Jones did not participate in the activities because she had been called racial slurs like others who attended—she avoided Greek town where she said most of the incidents reportedly occurred. Instead, "I felt like it was my thing to protest about because there was always a chance that I could be called out of my name," she said. "My friends were being called out of their name. It was a hostile environment. You'd go to class and they're talking about it. And you could tell that all the Caucasian kids thought it [the protest] was stupid. 'They're ruining my school's reputation. They're acting like children. They're toddlers. They're just throwing a tantrum.' They didn't understand that it wasn't a tantrum. It was basic life. If felt that every black student had a reason to be out there, whether they were called out of their name or not, because it's an attack on you as well."

In some ways, having the national media camped out around campus also presented problems. Protesters, like the central figure Jonathan Butler, were more likely to speak to the more famous journalists than the student reporters at *The Maneater* or other local media. "That was challenging because it felt in a way like people [national reporters] were coming in without as much background on the situation compared to what we had because we had been covering the buildup all semester, but they were getting easier access," Projects editor Taylor Blatchford said, noting that the larger outlets might be getting more access, but they weren't doing as thorough a job as the students. "It was frustrating, also, to see [national] stories that that didn't include very much context or [did include] incorrect context to the resignations and the protests because we had not only been covering it, we had lived everything as students. It's very frustrating to see people portray campus incorrectly."

When the football team joined the protests by boycotting practice and games until the hunger strike ended, *Maneater* assistant sports editor and writer Alec Lewis found access became a big issue. Like many college and university campuses, Mizzou athletes were expected to follow a strict media access policy. Reporters were supposed to go through the sports information director to interview any student athletes. If that couldn't be arranged, within the guidelines of the policy, reporters were forced to try to catch the players at dorms or somewhere around campus. That could cause problems, though, and the student newspaper could lose its access privileges, Lewis said. So it was frustrating to read the tweets from some of the more outspoken players and not be able to get access to interview them about what they said.[104]

Getting it right was also a constant concern, especially with a young inexperienced staff. "We have to hope that two months into their college career they are as prepared as they can be," Knott said, "but we also didn't have the ability to check everything they were doing."[105]

George Roberson found his job of copy chief challenging because so much information that needed careful editing was pouring in. Often about fifty people circulated through the newsroom, writing, editing, taking photos, and designing. Coupled with the fact that a staff of mostly freshmen and sophomores were dealing with powerful ethical issues and trying to do the same job professionals were doing, getting the story right became a big challenge. "None of us had ever reported on something that big before," he explained. "I think I edited virtually every single story that week. We suspended the rules a bit of what got a story ready to publish because there was just no way we could go through the usual four reads." Students who didn't normally edit copy, had to read stories. However, the most important stories might have eight reads. "Everyone wanted to make sure that we were on the same page, that we were getting the story right," he said.[106]

One of the greatest challenges during the final weeks of the protest had nothing to do with working for the newspaper and everything to do with the students' first priority: attending class and doing schoolwork. Many of the staff never attended classes or missed most of them that week. Knott decided she'd better call one of her professors about missing class rather than email because she was so distracted with everything she might forget what she was doing if she sat down at her computer to type. On the Wednesday after the resignations, with many students staying away because of the Yik Yak threats, she did make it to class, "when campus was dead. That was weird. That felt very weird to be in class."[107] Blatchford, like many of the editors, spent at least fifty hours in the newsroom the week of the resignations. She skipped most of her classes, though some were canceled anyway. "Ultimately, the biggest challenge was having all the pressure of being a journalist competing with professional journalists but also living the life of a student and having those responsibilities as well," she said.[108]

The strain of all the work also became difficult. Physically, the staff was stressed, working on little sleep (Knott and others slept in the newsroom at least one night), and struggling to keep up on what was happening to make sure reporters went out to cover it all. [109]

Blatchford found she had a lot of adrenaline after a long day. "Coming home at the end of the day and thinking another student could potentially die for this cause," she explained, "that's a really heavy thing to think about." Also having friends on different sides of the issues could be stressful. [110]

A few weeks after the hunger strike ended, the staff box on page 2 changed. The university news editor's name disappeared from the list. The week of the protests, Loutfi and Knott had given him his two-weeks' notice. It was not a decision made lightly. "*The Maneater* is not a paper that kicks people out," Knott said in a follow-up interview. "We are a teaching paper. That is a part of our core. . . . I was invested heavily in helping [him] to succeed as an editor. We had been having chats since September about different ways to overcome challenges." He stayed through the final protest coverage to help out as much as possible at the end. [111]

Taylor Blatchford had also applied for the position of university news editor in the spring. The editor-in-chief and managing editor positions are filled in early April. Individuals interested in those positions apply, go through a debate and then an election by the outgoing staff. Loutfi and Knott ran unopposed. After their election, they accepted lengthy applications from interested students for all the editor positions, interviewed the candidates for all the section editor positions, and then named Blatchford as projects editor and the other candidate for the news editor position. The new editors then spent one week shadowing the editors they would replace and the next week putting out the paper by themselves. Then the semester was over. Students published two issues during the summer but spent most of the time recruiting writers, working other jobs, and preparing individually to run their section in the fall. [112]

It was clear by mid-September that the demands of the university news editor position was not a good fit for the editor they had selected. Knott pulled him aside in August and the two talked about what could be coming that semester. It was the first day and he was already faced with covering a big issue—the grad student protest—and his reporters weren't even in place yet. "I told him, 'I feel for you. This is going to be a [difficult] year,'" Knott said. [113]

Knott cited newspaper policy of not discussing personnel issues for not wanting to discuss particulars about what happened with the news editor. In general terms, though, she explained that *The Maneater*, like student newspapers everywhere, requires a commitment that the staff members' make the newspaper their highest priority after school work. "If that's not your mentality, you're not going to be successful," she said. "You don't get good grades working for *The Maneater*. If you do, that's incredible. It is hard to excel academically and excel at the paper. . . . It's not kind to your GPA."[114]

Throughout the semester, Blatchford helped out on the news desk a lot and transitioned into the university news editor position after the hunger strike ended. Her title changed in the staff box for the next semester. A new sports editor came on board at that time as well as two projects editors. "It felt like a different year," Knott said of the spring semester.[115] Loutfi also noticed the tension and frustration had decreased among other editors who had worked to pick up the slack. "For some people, it just wasn't what they signed up for," she said.[116] The university news editor was not interviewed for this chapter.[117]

## COVERING THE PROTEST

Although the newspaper had various protests throughout the semester to write about, the largest race-based protest that drew national attention lasted a little over a week, from Monday, November 2, when Jonathan Butler began his hunger strike through Monday, November 9, when the UM president and Mizzou chancellor resigned. The newspaper staff continued after the resignations to cover the protest aftermath and the Yik Yak threats that arose the next day.

On Tuesday night, November 3, the staff was busy in production for the regular Wednesday print edition. The newspaper carried only a small story on the front page about the hunger strike.[118] "No one at that point anticipated what it was going to turn into," Taylor Blatchford explained. But she and the other editors and reporters kept following the activities at the campsite and watched the tensions building on campus. "At that point we didn't sit down and have one planning meeting or anything like that. We were just covering things as they came up." Blatchford was helping with the coverage because the university news editor was transitioning out and she was transitioning into the job. She was especially valuable to the team because she had covered higher education for the last year, which gave her the needed background knowledge about the administration and the University of Missouri system.[119]

Loutfi and Knott adopted a plan to prepare for the worst and expect the best. "And our worst meter kept changing," Knott said. "We were preparing for the reality that there might be riots on campus. That was the kind of vibe we were getting, that something was going to happen that would set a lot of people off." They hoped that preparation would keep them from being blindsided by it.[120] On Thursday, the editors sat down and created a spreadsheet to keep track of stories and used the white board to brainstorm ideas and keep track of things.[121]

On Sunday, *The Maneater* went into overdrive—on Saturday night, the football team had called a boycott of practice and games until the hunger strike was over. Loutfi had been out of town for the weekend and came back Sunday. She had to rely on Knott to catch her up and then "jump in head first" to help with the coverage.[122]

Knott had spent Saturday afternoon in the newsroom, editing stories about the Meet Mizzou Day protests. She found out about the football boycott at the end of the day and called various members of the sports team to cover it. Her byline appeared on the story. Afterward, she went to a bar to unwind with friends. She left her car at the bar and returned to her apartment to sleep it off. At about 8 a.m. Sunday, she woke and checked the news, learning that the national news had jumped on the boycott story. She knew she needed to get to campus and start coordinating coverage, but she didn't have her car and couldn't rouse her roommate to get a lift. So she walked the three miles to campus, fielding calls—including one from MSNBC—and responding to emails on her smart phone. Once at the campus, she sat in the newsroom trying to monitor the social media messages on Twitter—and her phone was dying. She discovered people were staking out University Hall where UM President Tim Wolfe was at the time. She found a staffer to give her a ride there and then later a friend to help her retrieve her own car from the bar. Finally, at about 10 p.m., she returned home to shower and do some homework.[123]

Twitter was reporting that people were staking out University Hall, so Knott returned to campus and stayed with the other reporters until about 1 a.m., following up on just one of many rumors that something might be happening. That night she went to the newsroom to sleep. "I cannot be away from campus right now," she recalled thinking at the time. Others also slept in the newsroom some of the nights during this time.[124]

Assistant sports editor and writer Alec Lewis went to bed early on Saturday and woke up later Sunday morning to find 10–20 texts and calls from Knott and the sports editor, Bruno Vernaschi, alerting him to the football boycott. He hopped on Twitter and learned reporters and others were gathering at the Missouri training complex, so he headed there to join them, waiting for something to happen. A few football players walked out of the facility but refused to comment. Some of the reporters decided to move to another spot but found a gate surrounding the area locked, so they all hopped over the fence. Lewis recognized CBS Sports Senior Columnist Dennis Dodd from Kansas City among the group, the only national media representative he recognized that day.[125]

Lewis's assignment that Sunday was to reach out to players and try to find out firsthand why they had decided to boycott practice and games. With players not talking, his effort was futile. The next day, Monday, November 9, he hoped his luck would be better at the weekly press conference scheduled with Gary Pinkel, head football coach, and Athletic Director Mack Rhoades, who didn't normally attend the press conference but did that week. The routine press conferences usually included some of the football players as well so Lewis thought he should be able to get some quotes. Sports editor Bruno Vernaschi, Lewis, and reporter Will Jarvis went to the press conference, but soon learned that no players would be talking to reporters. Someone in the crowd said the players were going to speak at Carnahan Quad where the hunger strike was ending now that the president had resigned, so Vernaschi and Jarvis went there, hoping to get a story, and Lewis stayed at the press conference.[126] Later that day the three pooled their work to write about the boycott.[127]

The three sports writers also recognized that this was a much bigger story than what they had been able to tell so far. Many people speculated that the football boycott was the straw that broke the proverbial camel's back, forcing the UM system president and the Columbia campus chancellor to resign. It was certainly the aspect of the story that drew most of the national attention to the campus. This story needed more telling, they reasoned. "It said a lot that the student-athlete could generate the kind of buzz that they did," Lewis said. So they got busy. Many of the quotes they garnered Sunday and Monday ended up in the piece. Inspired by the work of Wright Thompson, a writer for *ESPN the Magazine*, the three produced "A Sideline Stand: Proving the power of student-athletes." It started on the front page of the December 2 issue (less than a month after the hunger strike ended) and, along with pictures, filled four pages inside the paper, the longest story the newspaper had published that semester.[128]

On Monday morning, November 9, the staff waited to see what would happen. "After Wolfe had resigned that morning, we made a list on the board of people to try to get reactions from and Loftin was one of them," Blatchford recalled. "And then after Loftin resigned, I remember either Katherine [Knott] or I going over to the board and just crossing Loftin's name off." Before Loftin resigned, though, someone using a fake Twitter account attributed to the *Columbia Missourian* tweeted that Loftin had resigned, and *The Maneater* editors started scurrying around, thinking they had missed it. Knott sent people to various points on campus trying to get the story then called them back in when she learned it was a fake. However, about an hour later, Loftin did announce his resignation and by then the staff was ready to cover it.[129]

Monday and Tuesday, the news staff was struggling to get information online as fast as possible. But the editors recognized that the resignation of two key administrators Monday called for an official print edition. Getting it printed at the Sedalia, Missouri, *Democrat* sixty-five miles southwest of Columbia where they usually printed the paper wasn't what they wanted to do: they wanted something new. The production staff got busy Monday night and designed a four-page E-edition using the usual InDesign program just as they would for the print edition, and then posted the completed PDFs to Issuu.com. Using social media, the editors alerted the campus on Tuesday that although they wouldn't find the paper on the stand, they could still read it online just as if they were reading the printed edition. The E-edition, as they called it, was something the editors wanted to try, and the resignations provided the perfect opportunity.[130]

When it was completed, the E-edition featured two stories on the front page, one for each of the two resigning officials, including large photos, all under a banner headline: "ADMIN DEPARTURE: Wolfe, Loftin resign."[131] The stories continued to page 2, where another story with a photo discussed a new diversity initiative the Board of Curators announced in the wake of the resignations.[132] Page 3 featured four photos of celebrating members of Concerned Student 1950 and a story with their reaction that Wolfe's resignation, which was one of their demands, was a start to making changes at Mizzou.[133] The football boycott, which really only lasted about two days, filled page 4, along with two photos.[134] In all, nine students had worked quickly to write the copy for the E-edition while a number of others were involved in editing and production. "I'm so glad we did it because it gave us some time to pause and appreciate the moment of what had happened that day," Knott said.[135]

With the E-edition finished Monday night, the staff turned to the next printed edition, which they would produce Tuesday night to appear on stands Wednesday, November 11. Staffers wrote more stories. The editors realized they had enough copy to do a twenty-four-page paper. They opted to run three-pages of the weekly arts and entertainment section, MOVE, but filled most of the rest of the paper with stories and photos about the protest, including a small story about the interim chancellor, Hank Foley, who would take over January 1.[136] The double truck in the middle of the paper was turned into a printed version of the online timeline Blatchford and others had worked to create the week before. The issue also featured stories on the continuing grad student protests[137] and a preview of the student body elections,[138] both topics that would turn into more controversy in the spring semester. Even sports had two boycott-related stories that filled two of its five pages. A tight page 2, which usually sported a feature photo next to the staff box, instead included a list of forty-four staffers, naming them all staffers of the week for their work covering the protests. Knott and Loutfi left themselves off, however.

One unexpected story in the November 11 paper was about the anonymous threats the previous day on the social media platform Yik Yak. One threat warned students not to go to campus on Wednesday because it might not be safe. Rumors began to fly that the Ku Klux Klan might be on campus, a rumor student body President Payton Head confirmed in a social media post and then deleted and apologized for posting.[139] The threats frightened many students, including the newspaper staff that was deep into production Tuesday night. The newsroom, located on the bottom floor of the student center in G210, seemed too open to the editors. It had windows in the door and a large window on the south wall. They all grabbed their laptops and headed down the hall to MUTV studio, which is behind two locked doors that required a card for access. They hunkered down there for about an hour. "The MUTV studio really is like a bunker," Knott explained in a follow-up email. "The added protection made us feel less like sitting ducks."[140]

They didn't work much on the next day's paper, however. They monitored Twitter and other social media to find out what was happening. "At that time, any tweet we sent out was getting like 100 retweets," Knott said. "It was ridiculous." After the panic subsided, the editors decided to return to the newsroom and finish the night's production, although that too became a challenge because the photo editor was out sick, so the editors didn't have all the cutline information they needed.[141]

Through all the panic of the threats, the editors were trying to confirm rumors. Knott sent photographer Jordan Kodner, Sports editor Bruno Vernaschi, and the outgoing university news editor to chase down the rumors.[142] Some reporters were listening to the police scanner and then posting to Twitter, which caused more panic on campus. Editors made sure that only verified information was tweeted from the main *Maneater* account. One error slipped by, though, and the editors tried to correct it but no one retweeted the correction.[143] Mostly the editors would post a rumor to an internal group for just the staff and ask for conformation. Reporters were being sent all over campus, sometimes on a wild goose chase such as trying to confirm a report of a counter protest after Wolfe resigned on Monday. At one point on Tuesday, Roberson recalled, a rumor went out to the internal group for verification. "Someone posted in all caps: SNIPERS ON TOP OF CORNELL HALL, which is of course a horrifying notification to get on your phone," he said. "You think, 'oh, my God, it must be true.' But the idea was that people were supposed to verify it, debunk it. . . . The next day I was walking on campus and I noticed Cornell Hall has a slanted roof. Where would a sniper be on the roof of Cornell? There are a lot of things we look at now that are outrageous. There was so much to process and so much to make sense of that we didn't think of that."[144]

The mounds of stories that could go in the print edition on Wednesday, November 11, became a challenge. Blatchford was trying to help deal with the work and had skipped all her classes. When Knott and Roberson realized Blatchford had been in the newsroom for about nine hours and hadn't eaten or left the room, they insisted she take a break. "We definitely watched out for each other as far as making sure people were taking care of themselves," she said. "Obviously, no one got a lot of sleep that week, but people also would keep an eye out for each other, too."[145] Others also spent untold hours in the newsroom without breaks. Roberson pointed to just such a staffer, a new copy editor, Nancy Coleman, who had only been on the job for about two weeks. She stayed in the newsroom most of the time for 24–36 hours and ended up writing some stories as well as copy editing. "Everyone wrote stories that week," he said. "It showed how dedicated some people were."[146]

That Tuesday night, Knott ended up sending copy chief George Roberson back to his dorm where he was a resident assistant. The Yik Yak threats had been unclear as to who might be targeted with violence. Roberson said that raised his concerns for the 350 freshmen and sophomore students he and other resident assistants (RAs) were responsible for in the dorm where he lived. Once at the dorm, he and other RAs locked the doors and walked the halls all night. Most of the residents were sitting in the halls and lounges throughout the night, and everyone was talking about the threats. "It brought people out into the community like I had never seen," Roberson said, attributing it to "a combination of fear and a need for community during a turbulent time."[147]

## THE EDITORIAL POSITION

*The Maneater* has a reputation of taking editorial positions on just about everything. The fall semester of 2015 was no different. The editorials focused on many of the controversies the campus had faced, such as calling for graduate student unity,[148] telling state officials to worry about something else rather than abortion services,[149] asking for undocumented immigrant students to get a break.[150] Four days after the student body president posted to Facebook about being called a racial slur, the editorial discussed the problem and demanded that the chancellor or other administrator issue a formal response.[151] A month before the hunger strike, after someone used racial slurs toward the Legion of Black Collegians while practicing a Homecoming performance, the lengthy editorial called on everyone at the university to engage in a discussion about the problem and finally break the cycle of racism on campus.[152]

Some alums waited eagerly to hear what editorial stance the newspaper would then take about the hunger strike and football protest on the November 11 opinion page two days after the resignations of President Wolfe and Chancellor Loftin. None came. "Dear readers," the editor's note read at the top of the page. "Given everything that has taken place this week regarding Concerned Student 1950 and the resignations of UM System President Tim Wolfe and Chancellor R. Bowen Loftin, you might have expected an editorial in our issue this week. However, this week, there will be no editorial. We are still primarily focused on the coverage of these issues and believe it is too immediate to develop an opinion as a majority of the *The Maneater* editorial board. In the coming weeks, we ask that you look to our editorial page for the student voice regarding everything that has taken place."[153] The newspaper never did go back and address what had happened during that momentous protest week. And the silence was intentional.

Opinion editor Jack Herrick wrote all the editorials. The opinions he wrote were developed following a meeting with the editorial board made up of the other editors where a consensus would be sought on whatever issue the board thought the opinion should address. Typically, the board would meet Monday to discuss the topic and Herrick would spend the next twenty-four hours writing the opinion. "I was better at writing about just about anything else than social justice in terms of our editorials because with social justice I would have trouble getting the language right," he said. "There's just a way you have to write and talk about things, the vernacular that I wasn't really good with." When it came time to tackle the hunger strike protest and the football boycott, the editorial board decided to leave it alone. "Doing nothing is a decision, too, and that was the decision we made," Herrick said. He didn't want to write an opinion piece about the protest no matter what the stance would be because "it would have been perceived as white students taking up too much space and trying to either hijack or take credit or be a part of what you shouldn't be, of the whole movement, kind of diluting it." Even if the editorial totally supported the protesters, it would have angered readers, he said.[154]

All the editors agreed with not taking a position on the protests. Knott said any editorial position could have compromised the reporting. "We needed to be the trustful source," she explained. "Students needed to feel they could come to us and get what was going on. . . . We call ourselves the voice of the students and we needed to be the voice of the students. That doesn't mean we had to be the voice through our editorials. We had to do that throughout our reporting. We had to make sure that we could get the stories that we needed to get. We also didn't want people to think our coverage was slanted either way. I think that was ultimately the biggest factor in our decision. Also, anything we would have said would have had zero impact on the situation." When Melissa Click's firing hit the news pages in the spring semester, the editorial board also decided not to take stand on that either. "We chose to let our reporting speak for itself," Knott said. "We needed to let our reporters be reporters because even though our freshmen out in the field had no say in editorials, they would still feel the repercussions."[155]

The editors were also concerned the national media would pick up any editorials and make the newspaper the story. To some extent, that happened without an editorial. Blatchford recalled being in the newsroom on Sunday, the day before the resignations, and answering the editor-in-chief's phone because Loutfi wasn't there. It was the PBS News Hour wanting to ask questions.[156] The next day, Loutfi started getting phone calls from other national media, seeking to interview her about the newspaper's coverage of the events. National Public Radio did an interview, and CNN requested an interview, but had to preempt it for another story. She also interviewed with other student newspapers around the country. [157]

The editors may have decided to not tackle the protest issue in the editorials, but several letters to the editor did, as well as diversity columnist Kennedy Jones. Her final column for the year in 2016 was a call for the Greek community to take responsibility for the racist climate on campus, but it never appeared in the paper or online. She feared editors had squashed the column because of possible connections they had with the Greek fraternities and sororities. [158] Knott and Herrick both denied that any such action occurred. Knott said the column was kicked back to Herrick from the copy desk for more editing, [159] and Herrick said he just hadn't had the time to work with Jones to fix some of the problems. [160]

## REFLECTIONS

Almost a year after the protests, most of the editors and reporters interviewed were still processing what happened. Many of their feelings were summed up in something most people didn't even know appeared in *The Maneater*. For many years, the staff has written a short note in the page 2 staff box in each issue that only those looking for will probably notice. That note is meant to be a comment on the week or some event that usually only the staff really understands. The comment printed in the November 11 staff box reflected the intense news environment created by the protests, the boycott, the resignations, and the anonymous threats and then the newspaper's response to the reporting challenge: "Campus didn't want us to put out a paper. We did it anyway. Get at us." It summed up the editor's pride in seeing about sixty stories appear either in print, online or both, in having a young, inexperienced staff come through with award-winning work, in just surviving it all as a staff. Loutfi praised the staff who stayed true to the masthead—"the student voice of MU"—and the freshmen reporters who "hit the ground running from day one and impressed me every single day and never quit." [161]

When the next semester began, the newspaper made major changes in its format. Loutfi said she and Knott realized *"The Maneater* can't survive another crazy semester like we did this past semester and be able to get the news out [in print] on time." The two of them worked over Thanksgiving break and came up with "substantial and drastic changes," a long document about how to make the paper more online-oriented. One of the changes to the print edition would be to add the name of the first editing reader to the bottom of every story, to create an accountability process so people could trace mistakes back to the editors who had read the story first and contact them about problems. [162]

The editors started a daily newsletter sent free via email to administrators and students who subscribed. The newsletter, consisting basically of briefs, linked to longer stories found on the newspaper's website. That left the editors with the ability to plan for more in-depth reporting in a news magazine style in the weekly print edition, something Knott had hoped the newspaper would have been able to do during the protests. "I wish we could have done more bigger-picture coverage that really would have delved into these issues, more to show that racism really is a problem on campus," she said. "There's a lot of people who thought it wasn't and still do. I wish we could have been able to give a voice to people who just did not like what happened in November, but give them a fair voice so we don't come off like ignorant racists." The national coverage made it seem as if the entire campus supported the protest, but that was not true. However, because that side of the issue did not have an organized group, it was difficult to show that side. [163]

She also said the newspaper could have played another role. "I wish we would have held the institutions that were responsible for healing campus more accountable," she said. "There's a lot of groups on campus and administrators that should have played more of a role last semester in hosting forums and fostering dialogue among different groups."[164]

## WRITING THE FIRST DRAFT OF HISTORY

Did these student journalists know they were, just as the phrase goes, writing the first draft of history? Most of them realized it at one point or another during that momentous week. For sports writer Alec Lewis, that moment was during a sports press conference on Friday after the administrators resigned. At the press conference he learned that long-time head football coach Gary Pinkel, who was suffering with lymphoma, was leaving at the end of the season. "I remember being at the press conference, and it being, like, 'Wow, this week couldn't be scripted.' I think that was the moment it kind of hit me," he said. "It wasn't just a story, this wasn't just a few events at Mizzou. This probably was something that will resonate for a long time."[165]

Editor-in-chief Elizabeth Loutfi realized she was involved in a historic event on Monday, after Wolfe's and Loftin's resignations. "It hit the evening of November 9 that we were somehow contributing to recorded history," she said. "It hit me super hard. This is going to be talked about for years to come. People are going to read and research it."[166] Managing editor Katherine Knott realized from the student body president's social media post in September and then the Homecoming protests that "it had all the makings of a year that none of us were ready for."[167]

Many of the staff, like reporter Thomas Oide, found the entire experience to be surreal but also incredible. "It's so surreal that I got to do something like that," Oide said. "I just think of it as a stroke of luck. I knew it was going to be historically significant, but I never stopped and thought, 'oh, man, I'm writing history.'"[168] Projects editor Taylor Blatchford recalled the editors discussing the once-in-a-lifetime opportunity they had as student journalists to write about the protests and being grateful for it. "I wouldn't trade it for anything," she said. Having their campus as the top news was also a surreal experience. "Watching Mizzou on national news constantly on our TV [in the newsroom] was very bizarre," Blatchford said, noting that the story first appeared on CNN when the football boycott began. "Eventually we were on NBC Nightly News, like we were the top story for three or four days in a row. It was just really crazy. You never expect that your school will be the one on national news. Then it happens."[169]

## CONCLUSION

The experiences of *The Maneater* staff in covering the protests during the 2015–2016 school year in many ways shows that the challenges of putting out a student newspaper has not changed in the forty-five years since the protest years of the 1960s. The students continued to face perhaps their biggest hurdle: being a good student while getting the paper out on time. *The Maneater* staff reported skipping classes during the heart of the protest and almost exclusively doing newspaper work for that week. They pulled all-nighters, sometimes slept in the newsroom, and worked as many as fifty hours each week, all for little pay. Their counterparts in the 1960s reported doing the same thing then.

The Mizzou students had other challenges also faced by the students in the 1960s. Like the *Spectator* staff at Columbia in 1968 when the managing editor quit in the middle of the protest, *The Maneater* staff had to pick up the slack when an editor couldn't handle all the work the newspaper required. They eventually fired him.

The staff also faced problems in access to information, especially when the protesters refused to talk to the reporters, didn't allow reporters to cover town meetings, and when football players boycotting practice and games didn't want to talk to the press about it later. Most of the students in the 1960s also had problems getting all the information they needed in a timely fashion as well. *The Mississippian* editors weren't always invited to participate in the press conferences and some of the parts of their stories were happening hundreds of miles away in an era without internet and immediate access to information.

*The Maneater* editors were justly proud of the work their staffs did. Just as their counterparts in the 1960s, they thought their staff worked hard and produced a good professional product, often getting information more accurate than the professional presses. *Spectator* staff at Columbia and *The Mississippian* staff at Ole Miss were both critical of the accuracy in the professional media.

And just like student journalists everywhere, *The Maneater* staff was young and inexperienced. Even those who had been at the newspaper for a couple of years were not really prepared to handle the crush of covering all the different protests. It was for them, just as it was for the staffs of the 1960s, a baptism by fire—and an experience they were all grateful they got to have.

\*          \*          \*

Katherine Knott graduated from Mizzou in May 2016 with a degree in journalism and a magazine writing emphasis. She went off to do internships and look for a permanent job.

Elizabeth Loutfi, a senior in the fall of 2016, continued at Mizzou and though she was no longer actively writing or editing for *The Maneater,* she worked with alumni relations for the newspaper. She hoped to become an investigative journalist.

George Roberson, a junior in the fall of 2016, took over the role of managing editor at *The Maneater.* However, he was planning to leave journalism and major in political science and geography so he could pursue an interest in urban planning.

Alec Lewis, a sophomore in the fall of 2016, became the sports editor for *The Maneater,* and was unsure of what area of journalism he would eventually specialize in.

Taylor Blatchford, a junior in the fall of 2016, worked as *The Maneater* university news editor through spring 2016. She began working at the *Columbia Missourian* in the summer and continued there for the fall semester. She plans to work full time as a newspaper reporter when she graduates.

Kennedy Jones left Mizzou after her freshman year and returned to her hometown of Las Vegas, Nevada. She was planning to finish a bachelor's degree at University of Nevada-Las Vegas as an English major.

Thomas Oide returned home to California to do a ten-week internship at *The Sacramento Bee* during the summer of 2016. Back at Mizzou in the fall as a sophomore, he did not work for *The Maneater.* Instead, he delved into the computer science and statistics classes he will need as a data journalist when he graduates.

Jack Herrick, who also hosted a radio talk show *The Student Voice* on the student radio station KCOU FM at Mizzou, left the *The Maneater* after the 2015–2016 school year. A junior in fall 2016, he plans to do convergence business reporting after graduation.

## NOTES

1. Katharine Knott, telephone interview by author, June 6, 2016.

2. Elizabeth Loutfi, telephone interview by author, June 13, 2016.

3. This phrase has been attributed to *Washington Post* President and Publisher Philip L. Graham and widely reported to have first been used in the 1960s. However, it has also been traced to 1943 and attributed to journalist Alan Barth in a book review in the *New Republic*. For a discussion on the origin of the phrase, see the *Slate* article by Jack Shafer, "Who Said It First? Journalism is the 'first rough draft of history." Retrieved from http://www.slate.com/articles/news_and_politics/press_box/2010/08/who_said_it_first.html. Another source says it appeared as early at 1905. See http://www.barrypopik.com/index.php/new_york_city/entry/first_draft_of_history_journalism/ for another discussion.

4. Emily Brehe, "The start of a movement: Graduate students walk out," *The Maneater*, 26 August 2015, 1.

5. Tessa Weinberg, "University hospital investigated for facilitating abortions," *The Maneater*, September 2, 2015, 1.

6. Waverly Colville, "MU Health Care unanimously votes to discontinue 'refer and follow'," *The Maneater*, 25 September 2015, accessed May 2016, http://www.themaneater.com/stories/2015/9/25/mu-health-care-unanimously-votes-discontinue-refer/.

7. Hailey Stoltze, "Two months after canceling agreement, MU enters new contract with Planned Parenthood," *The Maneater*, 21 October 2015, accessed May 2016, http://www.themaneater.com/blogs/city-state-and-nation/2015/10/21/two-months-after-canceling-agreement-mu-enters-new/.

8. Allyson Sherwin, Lucille Sherman and Emily Gallion, "MSA president combats campus discrimination," *The Maneater*, 16 September 2015, 1.

9. Janese Heavin, "Two arrested in cotton ball incident," *Columbia Daily Tribune*, 3 March 2010, accessed from http://www.columbiatribune.com/news/crime/two-arrested-in-cotton-ball-incident/article_d9781cd7–52ee-5f18–801b-a66de6d6720c.html.

10. Sarah Wynn, "Administrators discontinue One Mizzou, developing new marketing campaign this summer," *The Maneater*, accessed May 2016, http://www.themaneater.com/stories/2015/6/3/administrators-developing-new-marketing-campaign-s/.

11. See http://www.thedemands.org/.

12. Blatchford, "Administrators give race relations update, answer student questions," *The Maneater*, accessed May 2016 http://www.themaneater.com/stories/2015/4/30/administrators-give-race-relations-update-answer-s/.

13. Kennedy Jones, telephone interview by author, 31 May 2016.

14. Morgan Magid, "Campus Culture: Low reporting numbers highlighted in AAU climate survey," *The Maneater*, 30 September 2015, 3.

15. Elane Edwards, "Associate law professor questions gun policy at MU; The MU concealed carry policy may be considered unconstitutional," *The Maneater*, 7 October 2015, 7.

16. Tessa Weinberg, "Women's Health: MU rallies after Planned Parenthood investigations," *The Maneater*, 30 September 2015, 3.

17. Hailey Stoltz, "Two months after canceling agreement, MU enters new contract with Planned Parenthood," *The Maneater*, 21 October 2015, accessed May 2016, http://www.themaneater.com/blogs/city-state-and-nation/2015/10/21/two-months-after-canceling-agreement-mu-enters-new/.

18. Emily O'Connor, "Grad Rights: MU graduate workers look to unionize," *The Maneater*, 28 October 2015, 3.

19. See the following *Maneater* articles: Bryanna Leach, "Tuition: Undocumented immigrants facing tuition hike," 26 August 2015, Page 1; Tessa Weinberg, "A+ Scholarship: Undocumented immigrants face barriers to college," 30 September 2015, Page 1; Editorial, "DACA students deserve a fair shot at an affordable education, 30 September 2015, Page 9; Lily Cusack, columnist, "The Millennial: The pope's inspiring message on immigration," 30 September 2015, Page 10; John Richmond Herrick, "Immigrants sue MU over in-state tuition," 14 October 2015, Page 9; "Candidates get flak on Twitter for DACA misstep," 28 October 2015,

Page 7; Madison Plaster, "Human Rights: SEED is voice for undocumented immigrants," 4 November 2015, Page 3.

20. Allyson Sherwin, Elane Edwards and Lauren Wortman, "Swastika drawn in residence hall with feces," *The Maneater*, 29 October, 2015, accessed May 2016, http://www.themaneater.com/stories/2015/10/29/swastika-drawn-residence-hall-feces/.

21. Emily Gallion and Thomas Oide, "Protest reminds students, faculty that 'Racism Lives Here'," *The Maneater*, 25 September 2015, accessed from http://www.themaneater.com/stories/2015/9/25/protest-reminds-students-faculty-racism-lives-here/; Madison Plaster, "Protesters raise awareness of campus racism during third Racism Lives Here event," *The Maneater*, 11 October 2015, accessed May 2016, http://www.themaneater.com/stories/2015/10/11/protesters-raise-awareness-campus-racism-during-th/.

22. Madison Plaster, "Second 'Racism Lives Here' event calls for administration to act on social injustices," *The Maneater*, 1 October 2015, accessed May 2016, http://www.themaneater.com/stories/2015/10/1/second-racism-lives-here-event-calls-administratio/.

23. Thomas Oide, "Social Justice: SCCA takes action on social change," *The Maneater*, 21 October 2015, 1.

24. Thomas Oide, "Jefferson statue remains center of latest campus debate," *The Maneater*, 28 October, 2015, 1.

25. Elizabeth Loutfi and Lauren Wortman, "Racism: MU jolted by LBC discrimination," *The Maneater*, 7 October 2015, 1.

26. Elizabeth Loutfi, "Chancellor announced campus-wide diversity and inclusion training," *The Maneater*, 8 October 2015, accessed May 2016, http://www.themaneater.com/stories/2015/10/8/chancellor-announces-campus-wide-diversity-and-inc/.

27. Jonathan Butler, "Guest Column: Dear Chancellor Loftin: Diversity training isn't enough," *The Maneater*, 14 October 2015, 12.

28. The protest group's name includes the year that black students were first allowed to enroll at MU – 1950. In a list of demands presented on October 20, 2015, the group leaders said the group "represents every Black student admitted to the University of Missouri since then and their sentiments regarding race-related affairs affecting their lives at a predominantly white institution."

29. Elane Edwards, Katherine Knott, Marilyn Haigh, "LBC supports Homecoming protesters, administration silent," *The Maneater*, 16 October 2015, accessed May 2016, http://www.themaneater.com/stories/2015/10/16/lbc-supports-homecoming-protesters-administrators-/.

30. "List of demands from Concerned Students 1950 group," *Columbia Daily Tribune*, 23 October 2015, accessed May 2016, http://www.columbiatribune.com/list-of-demands-from-concerned-student-group/pdf_345ad844–9f05–5479–9b64-e4b362b4e155.html.

31. Hailey Stoltze, "Bow untied: Rumors rampant around Curators' special meeting," *The Maneater*, 21 October 2015, accessed May 2016, http://www.themaneater.com/stories/2015/10/21/bow-untied-rumors-rampant-around-curators-special-/.

32. Kasia Kovacs, "Protesters say talks with Wolfe did not achieve resolution," *The Columbia Missourian*, 27 October 2015, accessed May 2016, http://www.columbiamissourian.com/news/higher_education/protesters-say-talks-with-president-wolfe-did-not-achieve-resolution/article_d142295e-7ce2–11e5–96a2–7b5a0b8b51c3.html.

33. Thomas Oide and Katherine Knott, "Student's hunger strike aims to take Wolfe down," *The Maneater*, 4 November 2015, 1.

34. Thomas Oide, "Concerned Student 1950 and others plan to boycott Student Center," *The Maneater*, 3 November 2015, accessed May 2016, http://www.themaneater.com/stories/2015/11/3/concerned-student-1950-and-others-plan-boycott-stu/.

35. Katherine Knott, "English department vote highlights faculty dissatisfaction," *The Maneater*, 5 November 2015, http://www.themaneater.com/stories/2015/11/5/english-department-vote-highlights-faculty-dissati/.

36. Taylor Blatchford, "Loftin responds to student's hunger strike," *The Maneater*, 4 November 2015, accessed May 2016, http://www.themaneater.com/stories/2015/11/4/loftin-responds-students-hunger-strike/.

37. Peter Baugh and Tessa Weinberg, "Concerned Student 1950 organizers and supporters trek across campus in walkout," *The Maneater*, 5 November 2015, accessed May 2016, http://www.themaneater.com/stories/ 2015/11/5/concerned-student-1950-organizers-and-supporters-t/.

38. Quinn Malloy and Taylor Blatchford, "Faculty Council releases statement of concern regarding university leadership," *The Maneater*, 5 November 2015, accessed May 2016, http://www.themaneater.com/stories/2015/11/5/faculty-council-discusses-hunger-strike-library-fe/.

39. Hailey Stoltze, "Concerned faculty cancels class," *The Maneater*, 9 November 2015, accessed May 2016, http://www.themaneater.com/stories/2015/11/9/concerned-faculty-cancels-class/.

40. Katherine Knott, "Faculty show support for Concerned Student 1950," *The Maneater*, 6 November 2015, accessed May 2016, http://www.themaneater.com/stories/2015/11/6/faculty-show-support-concerned-student-1950/.

41. Quinn Malloy, "Wolfe issues apology to Concerned Student 1950," *The Maneater*, 6 November 2015, accessed May 2016, http://www.themaneater.com/stories/2015/11/6/faculty-show-support-concerned-student-1950/.

42. Jennifer Prohov and Katherine Knott, "Tim Wolfe, student protesters meet in Kansas City," *The Maneater*, 7 November 2015, accessed May 2016, http://www.themaneater.com/stories/2015/11/7/wolfe-student-protesters-meet-kansas-city/.

43. Hailey Stoltze, Katherine Knott and Waverly Colville, "Students called racial slur near MizzouRec," *The Maneater*, 7 November 2015, accessed May 2016, http://www.themaneater.com/stories/2015/11/7/students-called-racial-slur-near-mizzourec/.

44. Madison Plaster and Tess Vrbin, "Demonstration urges to prospective students to meet 'the real MU'," *The Maneater*, 7 November 2015, accessed May 2016, http://www.themaneater.com/stories/2015/11/7/demonstration-urges-student-meet-real-mu/.

45. Katherine Knott, Peter Baugh and Tyler Kraft, "Missouri players plan to boycott until Wolfe resigns," *The Maneater*, 7 November 2015, accessed May 2016, http://www.themaneater.com/stories/2015/11/7/missouri-football-players-plan-boycott-until-wolfe/.

46. George Roberson and Peter Baugh, "Missouri football cancels practice amid boycott," *The Maneater*, 8 November 2015, accessed May 2016, http://www.themaneater.com/stories/2015/11/8/missouri-football-cancels-practice-amid-boycott/.

47. "Gov. Nixon statement regarding student protests at the University of Missouri," 8 November 2015, accessed May 2016, http://governor.mo.gov/news/archive/gov-nixon-statement-regarding-student-protests-university-missouri.

48. Taylor Blatchford, "Wolfe released statement, will not resign," *The Maneater*, 8 November 2015, accessed May 2016, http://www.themaneater.com/stories/2015/11/8/wolfe-releases-statement-will-not-resign/.

49. Emily Gallion and Nancy Coleman, "MSA letter to curators calls for Wolfe's removal," *The Maneater*, 9 November 2015, accessed May 2016, http://www.themaneater.com/stories/2015/11/9/msa-letter-curators-calls-wolfes-removal/.

50. Hailey Stoltze, Nancy Coleman, Taylor Blatchford and Waverly Colville, "Wolfe announces resignation as UM System president," *The Maneater*, 9 November 2015, accessed May 2016, http://www.themaneater.com/stories /2015/11/9/wolfe-announces-resignation-um-system-president/.

51. Quinn Malloy and Taylor Blatchford, "Loftin announces resignation effective Jan. 1," *The Maneater*, 9 November 2015, accessed May 2016, http://www.themaneater.com/stories/2015/11/9/loftin-announces-resignation-effective-jan-1/.

52. George Roberson, "Concerned Student 1950 reacts to Wolfe's resignation in new conference," *The Maneater*, 9 November 2015, accessed May 2016, http://www.themaneater.com/stories/2015/11/9/concerned-student-1950-reacts-wolfes-resignation-n/.

53. Claire Mitzel, "Petitions started to remove two MU employees after incident with journalists," *The Maneater*, 10 November 2015, accessed May 2016, http://www.themaneater.com/stories/2015/11/10/petitions-started-remove-two-mu-employees-after-in/.

54. Alyssa Bessaparis, "Melissa Click reaches deal with city prosecutor," *The Maneater*, 30 January 2016, accessed May 2016, http://www.themaneater.com/stories/2016/1/30/melissa-click-reaches-deal-city-prosecutor/.

55. Nancy Coleman and Taylor Blatchford, "Melissa click fired by Board of Curators," *The Maneater*, 25 February 2016, accessed May 2016, http://www.themaneater.com/stories/2016/2/25/melissa-click-fired-board-curators/.

56. Hailey Stoltze, "MUPD increased security following YikYak threats," *The Maneater*, 10 November 2015, accessed May 2016, http://www.themaneater.com/stories/2015/11/10/mupd-increases-security-following-yik-yak-threats/.

57. Mary Helen Stoltz, "Student arrested for social media threats," Missouri University of Science and Technology News, 11 November 2015, accessed May 2016, http://news.mst.edu/2015/11/student-arrested-for-social-media-threats/.

58. Bruno Vernaschi and Hailey Stoltz, "UPDATE: Black Culture Center sign vandalized," *The Maneater*, 12 November 2015, accessed May 2016, http://www.themaneater.com/stories/2015/11/12/black-culture-center-sign-vandalized/.

59. Nancy Coleman and Taylor Blatchford, "Mike Middleton named interim UM System President," *The Maneater*, 12 November 2015, accessed May 2016, http://www.themaneater.com/stories/2015/11/12/mike-middleton-named-interim-um-system-president/.

60. Taylor Blatchford, "Students bring hopes for campus improvement to curators' listening session," *the Maneater*, 20 November 2015, accessed May 2016, http://www.themaneater.com/stories/2015/11/20/students-bring-hopes-campus-improvement-curators-l/.

61. Taylor Blatchford, "Eardley to lead new Office for Civil Rights and Title IX," *The Maneater*, 1 December 2015, accessed May 2016, http://www.themaneater.com/stories/2015/12/1/eardley-lead-new-office-civil-rights-and-title-ix.

62. Kyra Haas, "Graduate Union: Grad workers vote for unionization," *The Maneater*, 20 April 2016, 1

63. Emily Gallion, "MSA Meltdown: How MSA Senate toppled their president-elect," *The Maneater*, 3 February 2016, 1.

64. Claire Mitzel, "Representation: Curators enter presidential search with a diversity problem," *The Maneater*, 17 February 2016, 1.

65. "UM Board of Curators needs diversity," *The Maneater*, 17 February 2016, 10.

66. Kyra Haas, "Diversity officer selection is around the corner," *The Maneater*, 17 February 2016, 7.

67. Joel J. Gold, "1955 Maneater policy," *The Maneater*, 18 February 1955, accessed May 2016, http://www.themaneater.com/stories/1955/2/18/1955-maneater-policy/.

68. Ibid.

69. Becky Diehl, adviser, email interview by author, 20 July 2016.

70. "About the Missourian," *The Columbia Missourian*, accessed May 2016, http://www.columbiamissourian. com/about/.

71. Knott interview.

72. Loutfi interview.

73. Kate Talerico, "When student activists refuse to talk to campus newspapers," *The Atlantic*, 30 June 2016, accessed May 2016, http://www.theatlantic.com/education/archive/2016/06/when-student-activists-refuse-to-talk-to-campus-newspapers/486326/.

74. Knott interview.

75. Knott interview.

76. Benjamin Mullin, "For Mizzou's student-run newspaper, university tumult helps shake off weekly print mentality," Poynter Institute, 16 November 2015, accessed May 2016, http://www.poynter.org/2015/for-mizzous-student-run-newspaper-university-tumult-helps-shake-off-weekly-print-mentality/384593/.

77. Taylor Blatchford, telephone interview by author 20 June 2016; Knott interview.

78. Blatchford interview.

79. See http://www.nytimes.com/2015/11/10/us/university-of-missouri-system-president-resigns.html

80. See https://www.washingtonpost.com/news/post-nation/wp/2015/11/09/justice-is-worth-fighting-for-a-qa-with-the-graduate-student-whose-hunger-strike-has-upended-the-university-of-missouri/?utm_term=.29a33b78dce7

81. Loutfi interview.

82. Knott interview.

83. Retrieved from University of Missouri-Columbia Institutional Research office at http://ir.missouri.edu/DiversityData.html.

84. University of Missouri-Columbia Division of Enrollment Management, "Fall 2015 Enrollment Summary," 33.

85. Loutfi interview.

86. Knott interview.

87. Kennedy Jones, telephone interview by author, 31 May 2016.

88. Jones interview.

89. Jones interview.

90. Jack Herrick, telephone interview by author, 13 June 2016.

91. Kennedy Jones, "The Kaleidoscope View: Beyonce is back and black," *The Maneater*, 24 February 2016, 10.

92. Kennedy Jones, "The Kaleidoscope View: Is your definition of diversity even feasible?" *The Maneater*, 16 September 2015, 11.

93. Kennedy Jones, "The Kaleidoscope View: Is anyone allowed to say 'nigga'?" *The Maneater*, 28 October 2015, 16.

94. Kennedy Jones, "The Kaleidoscope View: Racism lives here, Chancellor Loftin," *The Maneater*, 30 September 2015, 10.

95. Kennedy Jones, "The Kaleidoscope View: What the black community needs to do to progress as a race," *The Maneater*, 3 February 2016, 8.

96. Emily Gallion and Thomas Oide, "Protest reminds students, faculty that 'Racism Lives Here'," *The Maneater*, 25 September 2015, accessed May 2016, http://www.themaneater.com/stories/2015/9/25/protest-reminds-students-faculty-racism-lives-here/.

97. Thomas Oide, "Social Justice: Reuben Faloughi looks to change race culture at MU," *The Maneater*, 7 October 2015, 3,8.

98. Thomas Oide, "Social Justice: CS1950 continues awareness efforts," *The Maneater*, 9 December 2015, 1,8–9.

99. Thomas Oide, telephone interview by author, 6 June 2016.

100. Knott interview.

101. Oide interview.

102. Herrick interview.

103. Kennedy interview.

104. Alec Lewis, telephone interview by author, 30 June 2016.

105. Knott interview.

106. George Roberson, telephone interview by author, 24 June 2016.

107. Knott interview.

108. Blatchford interview.

109. Knott interview.

110. Blatchford interview.

111. Katherine Knott, follow-up telephone interview by author, 12 August 2016.

112. Knott follow-up interview.

113. Knott follow-up interview.

114. Knott follow-up interview.

115. Knott follow-up interview.

116. Loutfi interview.

117. Quinn Malloy answered one telephone call and agreed to an interview at a later date. However, multiple attempts to reach him by telephone for that interview were unsuccessful. He did not respond to several voicemails or texts.

118. Thomas Oide and Katherine Knott, "Student's hunger strike aims to take Wolfe down," *The Maneater*, 4 November 2015, 1.

119. Blatchford interview.

120. Knott interview.

121. Blatchford interview.

122. Loutfi interview.

123. Knott interview.

124. Knott interview.

125. Lewis interview.

126. Lewis interview.

127. Bruno Vernaschi, Alec Lewis and Will Jarvis, "In light of Wolfe's resignation, Missouri football team 'closer and tighter'," *The Maneater*, 10 November 2015, special E-edition.

128. Lewis interview.

129. Blatchford interview.

130. Knott interview.

131. Hailey Stolze, Nancy Coleman, Taylor Blatchford and Waverly Colville, "UM President Wolfe resigns amid growing racial tensions," *The Maneater*, 10 November 2015, 1–2; Taylor Blatchford and Quinn Malloy, "Loftin announces resignation as chancellor effective Jan. 1," *The Maneater*, 10 November 2015, 1–2.

132. Nancy Coleman, "Board of Curators announces new diversity initiatives following Loftin's resignation," *The Maneater*, 10 November 2015, 2.

133. George Roberson, "Concerned Student 1950 reacts to Wolfe's resignation," *The Maneater*, 10 November 2015, 3.

134. Bruno Vernaschi, Alec Lewis and Will Jarvis, "In light of Wolfe's resignation, Missouri football team 'closer and tighter'," *The Maneater*, 10 November 2015, 4.

135. Knott interview.

136. Quinn Malloy and Thomas Oide, "Hank Foley to take over as interim chancellor Jan. 1," *The Maneater*, 11 November 2015, 9.

137. Alycia Washington and Lauren Wortman, "Grad students stage walk out amid protests," *The Maneater*, 11 November 2015, 10.

138. Neeti Butala, Jennifer Prohov, Emily Gallion, Claire Mitzel, Allyson Vasilopulos, David Soler Crespo, "Get to know the 2015 MSA candidates," *The Maneater*, 11 November 2015, 11.

139. Hailey Stolze, "Campus Safety: Students fear for safety after Yik Yak threats," *The Maneater*, 11 November 2015, 3, 8.

140. Katherine Knott, email interview by author,10 June 2016.

141. Knott interview.

142. Knott interview.

143. Knott interview.

144. Roberson interview.

145. Blatchford interview.

146. Roberson interview.

147. Roberson interview.

148. "Graduate student unity is crucial to progress," *The Maneater*, 26 August 2015, 8.

149. "Schaefer should focus on more pressing issues," *The Maneater*, 2 September 2015, 8.

150. "DACA students deserve a fair shot at an affordable education, *The Maneater*, 30 September 2015, 9.

151. "MSA president's post is not surprising, and that's a problem," *The Maneater*, 16 September 2015, 10.

152. "We must come to terms with racist past," *The Maneater* 7 October 2015, 9.

153. "From the editors," *The Maneater*, 11 November 2016, 17.

154. Herrick interview.

155. Knott interview.

156. Blatchford interview.

157. Loutfi interview.

158. Jones interview.

159. Knott interview.

160. Herrick interview.

161. Loutfi interview.

162. Loutfi interview.

163. Knott interview.

164. Knott interview.

165. Lewis interview.

166. Loutfi interview.

167. Knott interview.
168. Oide interview.
169. Blatchford interview.

*Chapter Seven*

# Telling Their Own Stories

Students working on *The Daily Tar Heel* in 1993 celebrated the 100th anniversary of the newspaper with a special edition. Centennial Edition editor Jen Pilla Taylor included an essay she wrote about the enduring student newspaper at the University of North Carolina-Chapel Hill:

> After weathering a century of change, the DTH is not the graying, battered lady one might expect. For she is reborn each year, with the coming of a fresh crop of new writers and editors. With them comes a renewed sense of enthusiasm, a fresh set of ideas and a vibrant hope for the future.
>
> Writers still "misspell words, omit commas and employ hackneyed phrases" that reveal them as inexperienced journalists.
>
> But the eternal youth of *The Tar Heel* nevertheless, is considered a blessing because it is youth that keeps it, like a typical adolescent, defiant in the face of authority, eager for growth, and protective of its freedoms. [1]

Taylor's words would still ring true today on college campuses throughout the country and indeed for almost every year for the last 200 years as student journalists created what *Newsweek* publisher Philip Graham called "a first rough draft of history."[2] Most student journalists do not realize that's what they are doing. Certainly the reporters and editors in the 1960s who were interviewed for this book didn't realize they were making history though their counterparts in 2015 recognized they were a part of something historic; mostly they were all just trying to be good journalists doing the best jobs they could. They showed the kind of dedication that student journalists have displayed since the first student publications began to appear in the early 1800s, a dedication that continues to keep student newspapers alive.

Some significant themes emerged in this study of student newspapers and the student journalists during the protest years. First, student journalists considered themselves as professionals, worked diligently to be objective and accurate reporters and editors, and truly dedicated themselves to the job, even without monetary remuneration for their efforts in some cases. Many of these same students, working tirelessly on their college newspapers, began honing the writing and editing skills they would use to excel first in their professional journalism careers and then later in other careers. They also gained other skills in leadership, time management, and interpersonal communication that they found invaluable in any of their careers.

For student journalists during the 1960s' protest era, the demand for change translated into regular breaking campus news that the student newspaper reporters and editors would do their best to cover. Mark Morrison's summation of his time as editor of *The Daily Texan* at the University of Texas-Austin in 1970 could apply to hundreds of other student journalists from that time as well as in 2015: "I just remember it being a sort of wonderful period to be a journalist. We always had something to write about, and it was exciting."[3]

The protests discussed in this project have provided a basis for not only telling the story of how student journalists reported and wrote stories of protests on their campuses, but also telling the individual stories of these reporters and editors as budding journalists. It examined some of the issues that student journalists faced then and actually continue to grapple with today. The key issues include maintaining freedom of the press, understanding the role of the student newspaper, defining one's personal position as a journalist, and developing journalistic skills. Each chapter has focused on one particular journalistic issue, but elements of most of these issues can be seen throughout almost all the student newspapers studied here.

## FREEDOM OF THE PRESS

Freedom of the press without interference from government (in the form of administrators employed by the state government to manage the college or university) often is a top priority for student journalists. The nature of the student newspaper actually opens it up to the possibility of censorship, certainly more than professional newspapers. Oftentimes the student newspaper on any college campus has strong ties to the administration or student body government simply because the newspaper gets some if not most of its funding through them. On many campuses, this funding often comes in the form of fees that students pay each term, which are administered by student government leaders. Sometimes the funds come directly from the university coffers to the student newspaper. In either case, the administration or student leaders may then believe they should have some kind power over the student newspaper, and they may attempt to have influence and outright control over what the newspaper prints. In the professional world, the publisher, who controls the newspaper's funding, often also wields editorial control. The administrators and student leaders, who sometimes consider themselves to be the publishers of the student newspaper, at times feel justified in their attempt to control content in the same way. This is not just a problem with which students journalists contended during the protest years, but one that continues as an issue today. The Student Press Law Center reported in 2010 that about a third of the calls they receive from high school and college student journalists involve concerns about censorship, and usually that censorship is coming from administrators.[4] In 2017, many of the high school students still call the center about censorship whereas college students call more about issues related to access to records.[5]

All of the editors and reporters interviewed about the 1960s' protests believed their particular student newspaper was much freer from administration and student government influence than they thought other student newspapers were at the time. To varying degrees, many administrations at the time still tightly controlled student behavior of all kinds, not just on the newspaper. Such a practice, known by the Latin term in loco parentis (literally, in place of the parent), still existed at the time on various college campuses across the country, both public and private, even on some of the campuses featured in this book.

Under this system, college administrators did not treat students as responsible young adults but as children requiring parental supervision, a concept colleges and universities had practiced probably since the first educational institutions were established in this country. The practice was only beginning to wane as the 1960s' protest years began.[6] As part of that parental duty, administrators deemed it their responsibility to make sure that students were behaving as a parent would expect and then taking action, when necessary, to punish or correct students who failed to meet those expectations, on- or off-campus. For instance, female students at many campuses had to abide by curfew hours at their dorms and sorority houses or face disciplinary action.[7]

Brigham Young University, the largest church-owned university in the country, provides another example of tight administration control. In an address at the beginning of each school year during the protest years, the university president warned students against joining their fellow students nationwide in staging protests of any kind.[8] After the shootings at Kent State, the BYU student newspaper reported that whereas other campuses were rocked by protest, Brigham Young University was peaceful and quiet.[9] It should also be noted that for at least the last forty-five years of its existence, the BYU student newspaper, *The Universe,* has operated under strict adviser review of all student work prior to publication, further substantiating the notion that some student newspapers still deal with censorship issues even in the twenty-first century.[10]

Of course, without a massive survey of student staffs from the 1960s, it is impossible to generalize beyond the newspapers studied here to determine how much administrative control existed nationwide. However, it is likely that campuses with varying degrees of administrative control of the student newspaper could be found throughout the country.

At least one editor in the 1960s faced what could be another form of censorship—threat of removal from her position. Though a newspaper board of some kind appointed most of the editors interviewed here, the student body at Ole Miss still elected the newspaper editor during the 1960s. That editor was Sidna Brower in 1962–1963. Student government officials at Ole Miss believed they had the responsibility to ensure that elected representatives were appropriately reflecting the desires of the students who elected them. When the student government members became unhappy with the content of the newspaper, they felt justified in calling Brower before them and eventually levying a reprimand. Bowers said the action did not affect how she continued to do her job at the newspaper, but it did affect her personally—the combined incidents of that school year left her with nightmares for some time. Other editors throughout the protest years who were interviewed here reported difficult telephone calls from administration and even state government officials complaining about the student newspaper. None believe such calls affected their work substantially, but all found such actions added to the pressure of the job they were trying to do.

One might be tempted to assume the student reporters and editors completely supported whatever goals their fellow student protesters had at the time, but that would not be true. In fact, though many student newspapers supported the proposed outcome for the major protests (namely, end the war, give students more power, improve conditions for black students), all the student newspapers from the 1960s and 1970s studied here called for civility among the protesters and did not condone the use of violence and property damage as a method to reach the goals.

Indeed, nonviolent work for change was a prevailing idea throughout the general population of America during the 1960s and could be seen in such Civil Rights-oriented organizations as the NAACP (National Association for the Advancement of Colored People) and SNCC (Student Nonviolent Coordination Committee), both of which espoused working peacefully for social change. Also, the student protesters on any campus for any cause, including the protest at Mizzou in 2015, only represented a minority of the students enrolled there though the general public throughout the country may have had the notion that all college students were demonstrating.

Still, calling for civility of action was not always a popular position for the student newspapers to take. The vocal protesters often wanted the newspaper to join them in their cause and assumed that if the newspaper took a more neutral position, it was against the cause. Such was the case at Ole Miss in 1962 where protesters interpreted *The Mississippian's* support for civil discourse as tacit approval of integration even though the newspaper ultimately never took a position on the issue. *The Daily Utah Chronicle* felt the same pressure in 1970 from protesters who tried to take over the newspaper because it did not throw its full support behind a proposed student strike demanding an end to the Vietnam War. Because a majority of students did not support a strike, the newspaper editor would not agree to do so either.[11] *The Maneater* editors made a conscious choice not to editorialize about the 2015 protest.

Despite the belief that they were completely free to report any way they wished, all of the student journalists studied here certainly faced several issues that influenced their work. Access to information, which is a problem all journalists encounter, played a role at every student newspaper. Some newspapers throughout the 1960s did not subscribe to wire services, which limited what they could use outside their own reporting. Such was the case in Mississippi in 1970 after the shootings at Kent State and Jackson State. Because they did not have this access, the student newspaper rarely carried reports of breaking news such as the shootings. Only one Mississippi student newspaper actually reported either shooting—a short notice about the Jackson State event in the Ole Miss newspaper.

The university administration often was a key local source for any campus protest. Administrators at Ole Miss, who were just such a primary source for *The Mississippian* in 1962, could exercise some control over the newspaper by simply not sharing information with the editors and reporters (editors did not think administers did so, however). Administrators at such schools as Berkeley in 1964 and Columbia in 1968 were often reluctant to talk to student reporters, especially about their plans to deal with the building occupations at each school. It was apparently an effort to keep information from the student protesters that might help them cause more problems or thwart the university's attempts to take control of the situation.

Sometimes, as in the cases of Howard and Columbia universities in 1968, the president basically disappeared and thus was unavailable to any student reporters throughout the crisis. Some reporters and editors found specific administrators would be helpful in explaining issues, acting as sounding boards, and providing information.

However, many of the student reporters and editors noted that at times, both before and after the protests, the newspaper staffs had strained relationships with administrators that affected how much information the students could obtain about any issues. Sometimes the protesters themselves did not want to talk to the newspaper staff either. Reporters at Columbia in 1968 found it difficult to write about what was happening inside Hamilton Hall, one of the occupied buildings, because the black students barricaded inside refused to allow in any white students, including reporters from the all-white staff of the *Spectator*. Other newspaper staff members throughout the period also reported problems getting information from the protest leaders. Students at Mizzou also had a hard time getting protest leaders to talk in 2015. The boycotting football players also refused to talk to reporters.

## ROLE OF THE STUDENT NEWSPAPER

Most of the student newspaper editors and reporters saw their role during whatever conflict was occurring at the time as that of objective observer only. They also believed their reporting and editorials were not responsible in any way for the events that happened. Opinions were supposed to appear only on the editorial page or with a headline or note identifying it as an editorial if it appeared elsewhere. Objective news accounts would fill the remainder of the paper. Of course, to paraphrase an old adage, it is all in the eye of the beholder. Readers and protesters would not always agree that the newspapers followed this guideline. For instance, students protesting a business near Berkeley in 1964 accused *The Daily Californian* of having two editorial pages—both the front page and the editorial page. The reporter who wrote the news story they questioned said he believed the protesters were just unhappy that the article had pointed out vandalism that protesters committed during the demonstration, which made them and their cause look bad even without editorializing about it. [12]

The editor of the Berkeley newspaper during the first semester of the Free Speech Movement in 1964 recognized that the newspaper also had the role of being the campus conscience. In filling such a role, the newspaper has an obligation to present various viewpoints and explore ideas that might not be popular with the administration, the protesters, or even the rest of the student body. At Berkeley, neither the administration nor the protesters were always completely happy that the newspaper insisted on discussing all kinds of alternatives rather than just supporting one side or the other. *The Mississippian's* call for peace in 1962 instead of continued protest—another example of pricking the campus conscience—angered many who wanted the student press to follow the majority of newspapers in the state and support continued segregation. The editors believe their continued neutrality on the issue probably aided in maintaining order on the campus.

## BECOMING JOURNALISTS

All of the students—those in the 1960s and 1970s as well as 2015—faced the crucial problem of time constraints. Even though they were supposed to be students first, all found that working for the student newspaper was the most important thing in their lives at the time. Most reported that their grades suffered dramatically during this time because they were spending more time at the newspaper than a full-time job would have required. For students, like the all-volunteer staff at Columbia's *Spectator*, it was more than just a job—they received no financial remuneration for their efforts, so the personal satisfaction they felt had to be enough. Many felt they had a responsibility to the student body, and perhaps the public at large, in their work for the newspaper. "I think we had a sense of enormous responsibility that there were momentous events going on around us," Lee Stephenson explained about his time at *The BG News* at Bowling Green University. "A lot of students were really grappling in a serious way with these things, and we had an obligation to try to keep up with reporting events that were occurring, trying to bring some additional perspective to the issues."[13]

The student newspaper became a starting point for many of the future reporters and editors who participated in interviews for this project. Student journalists interviewed from Mizzou were, at the time of this writing, still deciding where their careers would go. Indeed, many famous journalists and writers, some of which were mentioned in the introduction, spent time working for their college publications as well.

Berkeley students interviewed for this project who went on to careers in journalism all highly praised the experience at *The Daily Californian* as being more beneficial than any other experience during their college time. John Oppedahl's comment of the value of his experience could be mirrored by many other student journalists throughout the protest period: "I probably learned more as a reporter [at the student newspaper, *The Daily Californian*] than I learned in my career later."[14] The student newspaper experience even helped the editors and reporters if they did not make journalism their careers. Former editors and reporters at the *Spectator* said they learned valuable skills that they used in their other professions. One who became an attorney said the investigative skills gleaned throughout his time working on the protest stories and the book that followed have served him well as he researches legal cases.[15] Another attorney noted that successfully learning to write up against a newspaper deadline has made him better at doing the same thing for court deadlines.[16]

The student newspaper experience was also a part of the process that developed the student editors and reporters into the kind of journalists they would become. All tried to be as professional as possible in their reporting even though they were just students. *The Maneater* editors and reporters felt additional pressure to be professional as they tried to live down a bad reputation from previous staffs. The *Spectator* staff particularly held themselves up against *The New York Times* as they reviewed their work, always working to meet a similar standard in quality. Yet, they were critical of the professional press for treating the building occupations at Columbia University in 1968 as a police story that did not warrant any deeper understanding of the issues. It was then that the student press outshone the pros. Student editors at Ole Miss felt much the same way about how the Jackson metro papers wrote about the protest there in 1962, noting the errors and misinterpretations, not only about the protest but about the student newspaper and its staff as well.

One would expect students to have a different point of view about the protest events because they were so close to what was happening, both physically and psychologically. They also had sources that the professional journalists did not, and in some cases, as during the building occupations at Columbia in 1968, the professionals relied heavily on the student reporters to help them gather information because the student protesters would not talk to them. Though this work has not attempted to compare student and professional newspapers, one can generalize with very little research that the focus generally differed between the two. The student press concentrated on protest coverage, which was the biggest news on campus, unlike the professional papers that covered all kinds of local, national, and international news. Coverage of student protests did not necessarily dominate the professional press.

Some of the students' desire for professionalism also included trying to be objective. Most student journalists reported this as their general goal for the newspaper, one they were even more diligent about during the protests. Objectivity in journalism was a well-established principle by the time of the 1960s' student protests, so it would be expected that most student journalists would be taught about it and be expected to work toward it. Adrienne Mann at Howard University was the lone student journalist in this study with another goal for her life—she wanted to be a crusading journalist who effected change through her newspaper work.[17] Most of the writing of other students in *The Hilltop* student newspaper at Howard University also reflected similar feelings. The university had no journalism program, and the student newspaper was staffed by students from various majors and interests. The writers had a position on just about everything and made that position abundantly clear in what they wrote for the student newspaper, whether editorials or news stories. Of the 1960s protests studied for this project, the Howard University building occupation in 1968 was the only one during which any of the newspaper staff members were active protesters. A columnist for *The Maneater* in 2015 said she participated in the protests when she could, but as a columnist she was not listed as a staff member.

None of the other editors at other universities reported any staffers involved with the protests though some might have done so without the editor's permission or knowledge. Mann herself was one of three demonstration leaders and at least one of her reporters was a participant. In the end, Mann was never able to fulfill her crusading journalist dreams, and she left journalism behind for a career in higher education. She is representative of the difficulty of succeeding in advocacy journalism, which certainly was the less traditional path.

Working for a student newspaper teaches future journalists important lessons about more than just writing and editing stories. The editor of the *Illini* in 1970 noted that he had learned the important lesson of working hard for complete coverage of an event in the first news cycle when black students were angered about the initial coverage of the Jackson State shootings.[18] The editor of the *Texan* learned a hard lesson about conflict of interest when he accepted a gift that the donor expected should be repaid with positive newspaper stories. He said the experience made him doubly cautious as a professional journalist to make sure no conflicts ever occurred again.[19]

Learning the fundamentals of being a journalist during crisis situations also had a profound, life-changing effect on many of those interviewed for this study. "It was the highlight of my college experience, no question," said Stephenson of his time at *The BG News* in 1970. "The involvement with the newspaper really made my education. They were very exciting and challenging times that I just thrived on. I'm enormously thankful I had the opportunity and the experience for a period of enormous personal growth."[20]

## CONCLUSION

Though none of the former student editors or reporters in the 1960s and 1970s recounted stories of censorship, they all faced pressures at times from administrators or others who voiced concerns about the newspaper's role at the time. Of particular interest is the fact that all of these former students thought their own student newspaper remained free from control and censorship while they believed other student newspapers around the country did not. All of the newspapers from the 1960s and 1970s studied here published on the campuses where some of the major demonstrations occurred during the protest era. Further study might show a link between the amount of free press students enjoyed and the intensity of the protests that occurred on campus during this time.

The newspapers studied here, 1962–1970 and 2015, also provide excellent examples of how student journalists begin to shape their own ideas about the role of the press and the kind of journalists they would become. Most relied heavily on their former knowledge of the professional press and often aspired to emulate the kind of journalism they read in professional papers. Almost always that emulation meant practicing objective journalism instead of advocacy journalism. Sometimes, the students' work outshone the professionals covering the same protests, particularly when it came to understanding the student point of view and the underlying causes of the protests.

# NOTES

1. Jen Pilla Taylor, "100th Anniversary: The Ground Just Covered," *The Daily Tar Heel*, February, 23, 1993, 1.

2. Andrew Romano, "'The First Rough Draft of History," *The Daily Beast*, accessed May 22, 2013 at http://www.thedailybeast.com/newsweek/2012/12/23/an-oral-history-of-news-week-magazine.html.

3. Mark Morrison, telephone interview by author, December 7, 2012.

4. Frank LoMonte, telephone interview with the author, April 15, 2010.

5. Frank LoMonte, email interview with the author, May 30, 2017.

6. Joseph Storch, "In Loco Parentis, Post-Juicy Campus," *Inside Higher Ed*, September 17, 2009, accessed April 26, 2013, http://www.insidehighered.com/views/2009/09/17/storch.

7. Remembrances of Sidna Brower Mitchell and Jan Humber Robertson, interviews by author.

8. Ernest L. Wilkinson and Cleon W. Skousen, *Brigham Young University: A School of Destiny* (Provo, UT: Brigham Young University Press, 1976), 616.

9. "After Kent State Incident, Nation's Campuses Erupt," *The Daily Universe* (Provo, UT), May 6, 1970, 1.

10. Author was an undergraduate student editor at *The Daily Universe* under this system, 1974–1976, and served as the supervising adviser for six years, 2002–2008. In 2012, the newspaper reverted to a previous name, *The Universe*, and now publishes weekly, with daily updates online.

11. Angelyn Nelson, telephone interview by author, November 27, 2012.

12. James Willwerth, telephone interview by author, April 3, 2012.

13. Lee Stephenson, telephone interview by author, December 27, 2012.

14. John F. Oppedahl, telephone interview by author, May 9, 2012.

15. Robert Stulberg, telephone interview by author, September 27 and October 7, 2012.

16. Oren Root, telephone interview by author, August 28, 2012.

17. Adrienne Manns, telephone interview by author, August 11, 2012.

18. Carl Schwartz, telephone interview by author, December 5, 2012.

19. Morrison interview.

20. Stephenson interview.

# References

## STUDENT NEWSPAPERS

### Chapter 1: 1800–1960

*Argo,* Williams College, Williamstown, Massachusetts
*Columbia Spectator,* Columbia University, New York, New York
*Dartmouth,* Dartmouth College, Hanover, New Hampshire
*Harvard Crimson,* Harvard University, Cambridge, Massachusetts
*Harvard Register,* Harvard University, Cambridge, Massachusetts
*Lafayette,* Lafayette College, Easton, Pennsylvania
*Lehigh Burr,* Lehigh University, Bethlehem, Pennsylvania
*Literary Focus* , Miami University, Oxford, Ohio
*Literary Register,* Miami University, Oxford, Ohio
*Magenta,* Harvard University, Cambridge, Massachusetts
*Miami Student* , Miami University, Oxford, Ohio
*Michigan Argonaut,* Ann Arbor, Michigan,
*Oracle,* University of Michigan, Ann Arbor, Michigan
*Purdue Exponent,* Purdue University, West LaFayette, Indiana
*Students' Herald, Kansas Aggie, Kansas State Collegian,* Kansas State University, Manhattan, Kansas
*Tech,* Massachusetts Institute of Technology, Boston, Massachusetts
*University Chronicle,* University of Michigan, Ann Arbor, Michigan
*Vassar Miscellany,* Vassar College, Poughkeepsie, New York
*Yale News,* Yale University, New Haven, Connecticut

### Chapters 2–5: 1962–1970

*Alcorn Herald,* Alcorn Agriculture and Mechanical College, Alcorn, Mississippi
*BG News,* Bowling Green University, Bowling Green, Ohio
*Blue and White Flash,* Jackson State College, Jackson, Mississippi
*Columbia Spectator,* Columbia University, New York City, New York
*Daily Californian,* University of California-Berkeley, Berkeley, California
*Daily Illini,* University of Illinois at Urbana-Champaigne, Urbana, Illinois
*Daily Kent Stater,* Kent State University, Kent, Ohio

193

*Daily Texan* , University of Texas at Austin, Austin, Texas
*Daily Universe* , Brigham Young University, Provo, Utah
*Daily Utah Chronicle*, University of Utah, Salt Lake City, Utah
*Hilltop*, Howard University, Washington, D.C.
*Lantern*, Ohio State University, Columbus, Ohio
*Miss Delta,* Delta State College, Cleveland, Mississippi
*Mississippian*, University of Mississippi, Oxford, Mississippi
*Post*, Ohio University, Athens, Ohio
*Reflector*, Mississippi State University, Starksville, Mississippi
*Student Printz*, University of Southern Mississippi, Hattiesburg, Mississippi

## Chapter 6: 2015

*The Maneater*, University of Missouri-Columbia, Columbia, Missouri

## STUDENT NEWSPAPER HISTORIES

*125 Years of The Daily Pennsylvanian.* Philadelphia, Pa: The Daily Pennsylvanian, Inc., 2009.

Alison, Charles Yancey. "*The Arkansas Traveler:* The First Seventy-Five Years of a Student Newspaper." Master's thesis, University of Arkansas, 2004.

Anderson, Vera K.S. "A History of the *Daily O'Collegian*, Student Newspaper of Oklahoma A&M College, 1924—1934." Master's thesis, Oklahoma State University, 1975

Barrell, Jennifer, and Christopher Fusco, *Through the Eyes of The Argus*. Bloomington, Ill: Illinois Wesleyan University Press, 1994.

Basolo, Kathy. "The History of Student Journalism at Northern Michigan University, 1919—2002."Master's thesis, Northern Michigan University, 2008.

Collins, Allyson ,Ashleigh Graf, and Courtney Rile, eds. *100 Years of* The Daily Orange's *Best Stories (1903—2003).* Syracuse, NY: The Daily Orange Corporation, 2003.

Copp, Tara, and Robert L. Rogers, *The Daily Texan: The First Hundred Years*. Austin, TX: Eakins Press, 1999.

Dellaporta, Angela, and Joann Steck, *The Daily Californian's Best of Berkeley 1960—1980.* Oakland, CA: Abbey Press Inc., 1980.

Di Meglio, Francesca, Margaret Magee, and Joshua Prezant, eds. *The GW Hatchet: A Century in Focus 1904—2004.* Washington, D.C.: Hatchet Publications, 2004.

Ebert, Roger, ed. *An Illini Century: One Hundred Years of Campus Life.* Chicago: University of Illinois Press, 1967.

Fenyo, Ken, ed. *The Stanford Daily: 100 Years of Headlines — Stanford University 1892—2003 as Presented in The Stanford Daily.* Portola Valley, CA: Ladera Publishing, 2003.

Hantschel, Allison *It Doesn't End With Us: The Story of The Daily Cardinal.* Westminster, MD: Heritage Books, 2007.

Holtzer, Susan, ed. *Special to The Daily: One Hundred Years of Editorial Freedom at The Michigan Daily.* Ann Arbor, Mich.: Caddo Gap Press, 1990.

Jenkins, Norma J. "A History of a University Student Newspaper." Master's thesis. Ohio University, 1960.

Kelley, Dayton. "A History of Journalism & Journalists at Mary Hardin-Baylor College." Master's thesis, U. of Texas, 1959.

Kessel, Geraldine. "History of the *Daily Athenaeum*." Master's thesis, West Virginia University, 1963.

Kiser, James M. "*The Sunflower*: A History of the Student Newspaper at Wichita State University." Master's thesis. West Virginia University, 1971.

Lawless, Greg, ed. *The Harvard Crimson Anthology: 100 Years at Harvard.* Boston: Houghton Mifflin Co., 1980.

Marks, Larry. *"Daily Cal —* Part II: The Strike of 1960," in Michael Rossman and Lynne Hollander, *Administrative Pressures and Student Political Activity at the University of California: A Preliminary Report.* University of California, 1964. http://www.cdlib.org.

Myers, Gail E. "A Narrative History of the *Daily Iowan* (1901—1949)."Master's thesis, State University of Iowa, 1949.

Spencer, Karen. *"Daily Cal —* Part 1, 1947—1060," in Michael Rossman and Lynne Hollander, *Administrative Pressures and Student Political Activity at the University of California: A Preliminary Report.* University of California, 1964. http://www.cdlib.org

Whitt, Kenneth L. *"The Shorthorn* 1919—1969: A History of a Student Newspaper." Master's thesis, East Texas State University, 1970.

## SELECTED REFERENCES

*American Newspaper Directory.* New York: Geo. P. Rowell & Co., 1882.

Anderson, Terry H. *The Movement and the Sixties.* New York: Oxford University Press, 1995.

Avorn, Jerry, et. al., *Up Against the Ivy Wall.* New York: Atheneum, 1968.

Barrett, Russell H. *Integration at Ole Miss.* Chicago: Quadrangle Books, 1965.

Boren, Mark Edelman . *Student Resistance: A History of the Unruly Subject,* Routledge: New York, 2001.

Chatfield, Charles, and Robert Kleidman. *The American Peace Movement: Ideals and Activism.* New York: Twayne Publishers, 1992.

Cohodas, Nadine .*The Band Played Dixie: Race and the Liberal Conscience at Ole Miss.* New York: Free Press, 1997.

Columbia Spectator. Crisis at Columbia. New York: Columbia Spectator, 1968. http://www.columbia.edu/cu/lweb/digital/collections/cul/texts/ldpd_8603880_000

Eagles, Charles W. *The Price of Defiance: James Meredith and the Integration of Ole Miss.* Chapel Hill: University of North Carolina Press, 2009.

Gallagher, Henry T. *James Meredith and the Ole Miss Riot: A Soldier's Story.* Jackson: University Press of Mississippi, 2012.

Gitlin, Todd. *The Sixties: Years of Hope, Days of Rage.* New York: Bantam Books, 1987.

Goines, David Lance. *The Free Speech Movement: Coming of Age in the 1960s.* Berkeley, CA: Ten Speed Press, 1993.

"The Grievances of the Students," in Michael Rossman and Lynne Hollander, *Administrative Pressures and Student Political Activity at the University of California: A Preliminary Report* Berkeley: University of California, 1964. http://www.cdlib.org

Havighurst, Walter .*The Miami Years 1809-1984.* New York: G.P. Putnam's Sons, 1984.

Hieneman, Kenneth J. *Campus Wars: The Peace Movement at American State Universities in the Vietnam Era.* New York: New York University Press, 1993.

Hudson, Frederic .*Journalism in the United States, from 1690 to 1872.* New York: Harper & Brothers, 1873.

Junen, James Simon .*The Strawberry Statement: Notes of a College Revolutionary.* New York: Avon, 1970.

Kurlansky,Mark.*1968: The year that rocked the world.* New York: Ballantine Books, 2004.

Lambert, Frank .*The Battle of Ole Miss: Civil Rights v. States' Rights.* New York: Oxford University Press, 2010.

Lord, Walter. *The Past That Would Not Die.* New York: Harper and Row, 1965.

Margolis, Jon. *The Last Innocent Year: America in 1964: The beginning of the "sixties."* New York: William Morrow and Co., 1999.

McDowell, Sophia F. , Gilbert A. Lowe Jr., and Doris A Dockett, "Howard University's Student Protest Movement," *Public Opinion Quarterly* 34, no. 3: 383–388.

Mott, Frank Luther .*American Journalism: A History of Newspapers in the United States Through 260 years: 1690—1950, Revised Edition.* New York: The MacMillan Company, 1950.

Myles, Tom. *Centennial Plus 1: A Photographic and Narrative Account of the Black Student Revolution: Howard University 1965—1968.* Washington, DC: Black-Light Graphics, 1969.

Peterson, R. E., and J. A. Bilorusky. *May 1970: The Campus Aftermath of Cambodia and Kent State.* Berkley, CA: The Carnegie Commission on Higher Education, 1971.

Peterson, Richard E. *Scope of Organized Student Protest in 1967–68.* Princeton, NJ: Educational Testing Service, 1968.

*President's Commission on Campus Unrest* . Washington, DC: United States Government, 1970

Rorabaugh, W. J. *Berkeley at War: The 1960s.* New York: Oxford University Press, 1989.

Sansing, David G. *The University of Mississippi: A Sesquicentennial History.* Jackson: University Press of Mississippi, 1999.

Schudson, Michael .*Discovering the News: A Social History of American Newspapers.* New York: Basic Books, 1978.

Searle, John R. *The Campus War: A Sympathetic Look at the University in Agony.* New York: The World Publishing Company, 1971.

Silver, James W. *Mississippi: The Closed Society.* New York: Harcourt, Brace & World, 1963.

———. "Mississippi: The Closed Society," *The Journal of Southern History* 30, no. 1 (February 1964).

Smith, Baxter Perry .*The History of Dartmouth College.* Boston: Houghton, Osgood and Company, 1878.

Spofford, Tim. *Lynch Street: The May 1970 Slayings at Jackson State.* Kent, OH: Kent State University Press, 1988.

*The Student Newspaper: Report of the Special Commission on the Student Press to the President of the University of California.* Washington, DC: American Council on Education, 1970.

Unger, Irwin, and Debi Unger. *Turning Point, 1968.* New York: Scribner, 1988.

Van Tubergen, G. Norman. "The Student Press and Campus Unrest," *Journalism Quarterly* 47 (Summer 1970).

Vorst, Milton, ed. *Fire in the Streets: America in the 1960s.* New York: Simon and Schuster, 1979.

Westby, David L. *The Clouded Vision: The student movement in the United States in the 1960s.* Lewisburg, PA: Bucknell University Press, 1976.

Zaroulis, Nancy, and Gerald Sullivan. *Who Spoke Up? American Protest Against the War in Vietnam 1963–1975.* Garden City, NY: Doubleday, 1984.

# Index

# About the Author

**Dr. Kaylene Dial Armstrong** spent about twenty years as a reporter and editor for professional daily newspapers before going into higher education. She has taught journalism at six universities and one college as well as advised four student newspapers. She currently teaches at Northwestern Oklahoma State University in Alva, Oklahoma, where she advises the *Northwestern News*, a weekly student newspaper.

Lightning Source UK Ltd.
Milton Keynes UK
UKOW04n1432231117
313231UK00001B/25/P